New Casebooks

D0153446

POETRY

WILLIAM BLAKE Edited by David Punter
CHAUCER Edited by Valerie Allen and Aries Axiotis
COLERIDGE, KEATS AND SHELLEY Edited by Peter J. Kitson
JOHN DONNE Edited by Andrew Mousley
SEAMUS HEANEY Edited by Michael Allen
PHILIP LARKIN Edited by Stephen Regan
DYLAN THOMAS Edited by John Goodby and Chris Wigginton
VICTORIAN WOMEN POETS Edited by Joseph Bristow
WORDSWORTH Edited by John Williams
PARADISE LOST Edited by William Zunder

NOVELS AND PROSE

AUSTEN: *Emma* Edited by David Monaghan
AUSTEN: *Mansfield Park* and *Persuasion* Edited by Judy Simons
AUSTEN: *Sense and Sensibility* and *Pride and Prejudice* Edited by Robert Clark
CHARLOTTE BRONTË: *Jane Eyre* Edited by Heather Glen
CHARLOTTE BRONTË: *Villette* Edited by Pauline Nestor
EMILY BRONTË: *Wuthering Heights* Edited by Patsy Stoneman
ANGELA CARTER Edited by Alison Easton
WILKIE COLLINS Edited by Lyn Pykett
JOSEPH CONRAD Edited by Elaine Jordan
DICKENS: *Bleak House* Edited by Jeremy Tambling
DICKENS: *David Copperfield* and *Hard Times* Edited by John Peck
DICKENS: *Great Expectations* Edited by Roger Sell
ELIOT: *The Mill on the Floss* and *Silas Marner* Edited by Nahem Yousaf and
    Andrew Maunder
ELIOT: *Middlemarch* Edited by John Peck
E.M. FORSTER Edited by Jeremy Tambling
HARDY: *Jude the Obscure* Edited by Penny Boumelha
HARDY: *The Mayor of Casterbridge* Edited by Julian Wolfreys
HARDY: *Tess of the D'Urbervilles* Edited by Peter Widdowson
JAMES: *Turn of the Screw* and *What Maisie Knew* Edited by Neil Cornwell and
    Maggie Malone
LAWRENCE: *Sons and Lovers* Edited by Rick Rylance
TONI MORRISON Edited by Linden Peach
GEORGE ORWELL Edited by Byran Loughrey
SHELLEY: *Frankenstein* Edited by Fred Botting
STOKER: *Dracula* Edited by Glennis Byron
WOOLF: *Mrs Dalloway* and *To the Lighthouse* Edited by Su Reid

(continued overleaf)

DRAMA

BECKETT: *Waiting for Godot and Endgame* Edited by Steven Connor
APHRA BEHN Edited by Janet Todd
REVENGE TRAGEDY Edited by Stevie Simkin
SHAKESPEARE: *Antony and Cleopatra* Edited by John Drakakis
SHAKESPEARE: *Hamlet* Edited by Martin Coyle
SHAKESPEARE: *Julius Caesar* Edited by Richard Wilson
SHAKESPEARE: *King Lear* Edited by Kiernan Ryan
SHAKESPEARE: *Macbeth* Edited by Alan Sinfield
SHAKESPEARE: *The Merchant of Venice* Edited by Martin Coyle
SHAKESPEARE: *A Midsummer Night's Dream* Edited by Richard Dutton
SHAKESPEARE: *Much Ado About Nothing* and *The Taming of the Shrew*
    Edited by Marion Wynne-Davies
SHAKESPEARE: *Romeo and Juliet* Edited by R. S. White
SHAKESPEARE: *The Tempest* Edited by R. S. White
SHAKESPEARE: *Twelfth Night* Edited by R. S. White
SHAKESPEARE ON FILM Edited by Robert Shaughnessy
SHAKESPEARE IN PERFORMANCE Edited by Robert Shaughnessy
SHAKESPEARE'S HISTORY PLAYS Edited by Graham Holderness
SHAKESPEARE'S ROMANCES Edited by Alison Thorne
SHAKESPEARE'S TRAGEDIES Edited by Susan Zimmerman
JOHN WEBSTER: *The Duchess of Malfi* Edited by Dympna Callaghan

GENERAL THEMES

FEMINIST THEATRE AND THEORY Edited by Helene Keyssar
POSTCOLONIAL LITERATURES Edited by Michael Parker and Roger Starkey

New Casebooks Series
Series Standing Order
ISBN 0–333–71702–3 hardcover
ISBN 0–333–69345–0 paperback
(*outside North America only*)

You can receive future titles in this series as they are published by placing a standing order.
Please contact your bookseller or, in case of difficulty, write to us at the address below with your
name and address, the title of the series and the ISBN quoted above.

Customer Services Department, Macmillan Distribution Ltd
Houndmills, Basingstoke, Hampshire RG21 6XS, England

New Casebooks

SHAKESPEARE'S ROMANCES

EDITED BY ALISON THORNE

palgrave
macmillan

First published 2003 by
PALGRAVE MACMILLAN
Houndmills, Basingstoke, Hampshire RG21 6XS and
175 Fifth Avenue, New York, N. Y. 10010
Companies and representatives throughout the world

PALGRAVE MACMILLAN is the global academic imprint of the Palgrave Macmillan division of St. Martin's press, LLC and of Palgrave Macmillan Ltd. Macmillan[pr] is a registered trademark in the United States, United Kingdom and other countries. Palgrave is a registered trademark in the European Union and other countries.

ISBN 0–333–67974–1 hardback
ISBN 0–333–67975–X paperback

This book is printed on paper suitable for recycling and made from fully managed and sustained forest sources.

A catalogue record for this book is available from the British Library.

Library of Congress Cataloging-in-Publication Data

Shakespeare's romances/edited by Alison Thorne.
    p. cm. – (New casebooks)
    Includes bibliographical references and index.
    ISBN 0–333–67974–1 – ISBN 0–333–67975–X (pbk.)
    1. Shakespeare, William, 1564–1616 – Tragicomedies. 2. Tragicomedy.
I. Thorne, Alison, 1959– II. New casebooks (Palgrave Macmillan (Firm))

PR2981.5 .S488 2002
822.3'3–dc21

                                                    2002030377

10 9 8 7 6 5 4 3 2 1
12 11 10 09 08 07 06 05 04 03

Printed and bound in Great Britain by
Creative Print and Design (Wales), Ebbw Vale

For George and Perdita

Contents

Acknowledgements

Thanks to John Drakakis, Helen Hackett, Robert Maslen and Jennifer Richards for their helpful comments on an earlier draft of the introduction, to James Knowles for sharing his knowledge of Jacobean stage practices with me, and, above all, to Martin Coyle whose unfailing patience and encouragement ensured the completion of this volume.

The editor and publisher wish to thank the following for permission to use copyright material:

Janet Adelman, for material from *Suffocating Mothers: Fantasies of Maternal Origin in Shakespeare's Plays, 'Hamlet' to 'The Tempest'* by Janet Adelman (1992), pp. 193–235, by permission of Routledge, Inc, part of the Taylor & Francis Group; James Ellison, for '*The Winter's Tale* and the Religious Politics of Europe', previously unpublished, by permission of the author; Margaret Healy, for '*Pericles* and the Pox' from Jennifer Richards and James Knowles (eds), *Shakespeare's Late Plays: New Readings*, Edinburgh University Press (1999), pp. 92–107, by permission of the author; David Scott Kastan, for material from *Shakespeare After Theory* by David Scott Kastan (1999), pp. 183–97, by permission of Routledge, Inc, part of the Taylor & Francis Group; Jodi Mikalachki, for 'The Masculine Romance of Roman Britain: *Cymbeline* and Early Modern English Nationalism', *Shakespeare Quarterly*, 46:3 (1995), 301–22, by permission of the Johns Hopkins University Press; Ruth Nevo, for material from *Shakespeare's Other Language* by Ruth Nevo, Routledge (1987), pp. 62–94, by permission of Routledge, Inc, part of the Taylor & Francis Group; Constance C. Relihan, for 'Liminal Geography: *Pericles* and the Politics of Place', *Philological Quarterly*, 71

(1992), 281–94, by permission of the author; Kiernan Ryan, for material from *Shakespeare* by Kiernan Ryan, third edition (2001), pp. 106–35, by permission of Palgrave Macmillan; Jyotsna G. Singh, for 'Caliban Versus Miranda: Race and Gender Conflicts in Postcolonial Rewritings of *The Tempest*', from Valerie Traub, M. Lindsay Kaplan and Dympna Callaghan (eds), *Feminist Readings of Early Modern Culture, Emerging Subjects* (1996), pp. 191–207, by permission of Cambridge University Press.

Every effort has been made to trace the copyright holders but if any have been inadvertently overlooked the publishers will be pleased to make the necessary arrangement at the first opportunity.

General Editors' Preface

The purpose of this series of New Casebooks is to reveal some of the ways in which contemporary criticism has changed our understanding of commonly studied texts and writers and, indeed, of the nature of criticism itself. Central to the series is a concern with modern critical theory and its effect on current approaches to the study of literature. Each New Casebook editor has been asked to select a sequence of essays which will introduce the reader to the new critical approaches to the text or texts being discussed in the volume and also illuminate the rich interchange between critical theory and critical practice that characterises so much current writing about literature.

In this focus on modern critical thinking and practice New Casebooks aim not only to inform but also to stimulate, with volumes seeking to reflect both the controversy and the excitement of current criticism. Because much of this criticism is difficult and often employs an unfamiliar critical language, editors have been asked to give the reader as much help as they feel is appropriate, but without simplifying the essays or the issues they raise. Again, editors have been asked to supply a list of further reading which will enable readers to follow up issues raised by the essays in the volume.

The project of New Casebooks, then, is to bring together in an illuminating way those critics who best illustrate the ways in which contemporary criticism has established new methods of anlaysing texts and who have reinvigorated the important debate about how we 'read' literature. The hope is, of course, that New Casebooks will not only open up this debate to a wider audience, but will also encourage students to extend their own ideas, and think afresh about their responses to the texts they are studying.

John Peck and Martin Coyle
University of Wales, Cardiff

Introduction

ALISON THORNE

The group of four plays written towards the end of Shakespeare's career and commonly known as the 'romances' presents us with something of a conundrum.[1] On the one hand, *Pericles* (1607–8), *Cymbeline* (1609–10), *The Winter's Tale* (1610–11) and *The Tempest* (1611) display a striking family resemblance owing to their mutual reliance on a set of readily identifiable thematic motifs and structural devices: the loss and recovery of royal children; flawed rulers who, after enduring many years of hardship, find redemption through the restitution of their families; miraculous twists of fate, reunions and resurrections of characters presumed dead engineered by some divine agency, providential force or mage-like figure.[2] Such obvious commonalities make the basic format of these plays deceptively easy to define. On the other hand, the action of these same plays is replete with incidents so bizarre, fantastical and uncanny as to evade rational exegesis, while their dramatic language is 'such / As sense [alone] cannot untie' (*Cymbeline*, V.iii.241). Their endings, too, are charged with a powerful aura of suggestiveness, tantalising us with intimations of some larger significance (whether experiential, religious or political) that refuses to be pinned down. All these features mark the plays out as among the most enigmatic, if also most beguiling, productions in the Shakespeare canon.

The problem of genre

The elusiveness of the 'romances' is exacerbated by problems of nomenclature and classification. To begin with, there is the vexed question of their relationship to the three plays Shakespeare co-authored with John Fletcher (*Henry VIII* [1612–13], *The Two Noble Kinsmen* [1613] and the lost *Cardenio* [1612–13]) which came after them, and with which they undeniably have certain affinities in outlook and shared preoccupations. In restricting itself to the four 'romances' this anthology sustains the traditional consensus that they form a distinct grouping, though quite a few of the general observations made below might also apply (with some reservations) to the three later collaborative plays. Then there is the difficulty of establishing to which genre they belong. 'Romance' and 'tragicomedy', the labels preferred by the majority of modern editors and critics, are both anachronistic terms imposed retrospectively on the plays; the first coined by Coleridge in his 'notes on *The Tempest*', the second (though not unknown in the early Jacobean era) only achieving currency as a dramatic category after Shakespeare's death. Neither tallies with the generic rubrics under which the plays appeared in their earliest printed versions. In the First Folio, the first collected edition of Shakespeare's works published in 1623, *The Tempest* and *The Winter's Tale* are placed among the comedies, while *Cymbeline* brings up the rear of the tragedies. *Pericles*, which was excluded from the Folio perhaps on the grounds of its mixed authorship, is referred to simply as a 'play' on the title page of the 1609 Quarto edition.

As the seemingly arbitrary decision to categorise *Cymbeline* (a play with no recognisable tragic protagonists, and deaths that are represented in a comically grotesque vein) as a tragedy suggests, generic classification was, and still is, far from an exact science. This is not to say that the Renaissance lacked a highly evolved awareness of, and interest in, genre; indeed, from the early sixteenth century neo-Aristotelian critics on the Continent had been busily codifying the rules governing the literary 'kinds' in accordance with the principle of decorum which specified the style and subject matter appropriate to each and outlawed their intermixture. But, in actuality, generic practice was always more fluid, inclusive and experimental than theoretical prescription allowed.[3] Nowhere was this more evident than in the context of the popular commercial theatre for which these plays were written. Assigning generic labels was bound to be a haphazard business here, partly because the available set of dramatic categories was always in danger of being destabilised and superseded by the frenetic pace of innovation on the stage, but also because hybridised forms had become the *de facto* norm – much to the chagrin of a classically trained observer such as Philip Sidney, who deplored the popular appetite for 'mongrel tragi-comedy' which flouted the dramatic 'unities' and promiscuously 'mingl[ed] kings and clowns', 'hornpipes and funerals'.[4] Shakespeare himself showed notoriously little regard for the purity of the various genres he worked in and whose boundaries he continually extended and redefined. Moreover, throughout his career, as Lawrence Danson notes, he made a habit of revisiting and reworking his earlier experiments with generic form, so that his plays 'refer back and forth among themselves, endlessly invoking and endlessly complicating the genres they simultaneously inherit and make'.[5] The 'romances' represent the culmination of this revisionary process, inasmuch as they appear to recapitulate, subsume and thereby transcend all his previous forays into the comic, tragic and historical modes. It is as though Shakespeare were searching for a syncretic framework that would enable him to project the most comprehensive, wide-angled vision of life, as free as possible from the cognitive limitations imposed by our inherited system of generic divisions. If Rosalie Colie's proposition that different genres offer 'different "frames" or "fixes" on the world' is accepted, the mingling of dramatic modes in plays like *The Winter's Tale* or *Cymbeline* may be seen as crucial to the realisation of such a project. Indeed, the 'romances' as a group would seem to support Colie's conclusion that the mixed genres favoured by Renaissance writers were an attempt to represent a 'larger collective vision' that encompasses multiple ways of knowing and mapping their social habitat.[6]

For many critics, identifying the generic matrix from which Shakespeare's 'romances' evolved has seemed to hold the key to their meaning. Following the lead given by E. C. Pettet and John Danby, Frank Kermode's acclaimed 1953 edition of *The Tempest* and J. M. Nosworthy's edition of *Cymbeline,* two years later, explored the relationship of these texts to pastoral tragicomedy and native romance traditions respectively. Interest in this line of inquiry was also spurred by the intervention of Philip Edwards who, in an important essay published in 1958 reviewing twentieth-century criticism of the four plays to date, opined that investigating the 'formal requirements of romance' offered the best hope yet of finding a suitable critical language in which to address them.[7] The trend peaked in the 1970s and 80s with an outpouring of scholarly monographs devoted to the task of explicating the peculiarities of the 'romances' by reference to the generic conventions they deploy.[8] Many of these studies might be accused of overstating the explanatory power of such an approach, besides taking too little account of the provisionality of generic nomenclatures and the evidence that the literary conventions attached to the 'kinds' tended to be regarded (by the more talented writers at least) not as a binding set of rules, but, at most, as a starting-point for individual experimentation. Handled cautiously with such provisos in mind, however, generic definitions can be a valuable analytical tool. They provide an indispensable frame of reference that allows us to trace how received forms are being invoked and manipulated in the 'romances'. With their assistance we can begin to reconstruct the 'horizon of expectations' brought to bear on these plays by their original audiences, intensifying our awareness of how such normative expectations would have been variously satisfied, adjusted or subverted by what they saw.

'Romance' and 'tragicomedy'

'Romance' and 'tragicomedy' are both useful descriptive terms, despite (or perhaps because of) their problematic breadth of meaning. Throughout the Elizabethan and Jacobean period the romance tradition flourished in a kaleidoscopic variety of forms: in drama, prose narrative and courtly spectacle, in amatory, chivalric or parodic vein, in aristocratic and more plebeian versions. Although romance motifs crop up everywhere in Shakespeare's oeuvre (from the early *Comedy of Errors* and mature comedies like *Twelfth Night* to tragedies such as *King Lear* or *Antony and Cleopatra*), the specific applicability of this label to the four late plays is authorised by their open indebtedness to the Greek 'romances' of the first to third century AD, and the hugely popular Elizabethan prose fictions of Sidney, Lodge, Greene and others derived from them. Apart from supplying the main literary source for *Pericles* (based on a fifteenth-century retelling of a lost classical romance, *Apollonius of Tyre*) and *The Winter's Tale* (based on Greene's *Pandosto*), this corpus of ancient Greek and Renaissance 'romances' bequeathed to the late plays their sprawling narrative structure and familiar repertoire of plot devices: journeys to far-away places, abandoned offspring, shipwrecks, oracles, pirates, astonishing reversals of fortune and elaborate recognition scenes.[9]

Significantly, the plays themselves frequently call attention to their dependence on the 'thrice-told tales' and antiquated conventions of romance, but in ways that simultaneously point up their temporal and critical distance from the naïve or 'primitive' consciousness associated with this type of fiction. Thus *Pericles* resurrects the medieval poet, 'ancient Gower', so that he might, in the guise of Chorus, present a 'song that old was sung' for the nostalgic gratification of an audience 'born in these latter times / When wit's more ripe' (I.0.1–12). The very title of *The Winter's Tale* announces its kinship with old wives' tales ('like an old tale still') and the fantastic inventions of Autolycus's ballads, which 'will have matter to rehearse, though credit be asleep and not an ear open' (V.ii.62–3), even as the play's impossible denouement demands of its audience a more reflective, yet not dissimilar, act of 'faith'. But, as Howard Felperin has shown, Shakespeare also engages in a more thoroughgoing revaluation of his inherited romance models by 'testing [them] against a reality [they] cannot cope with'.[10] *The Tempest*, in particular, can be read as a sustained critique of the more simplistic utopian impulses at work in the genre.

If the word 'romance' evokes an archaic pedigree, 'tragicomedy' acknowledges the possible influence of a more recently imported and self-consciously stylish model: Italian pastoral tragicomedy. Here, too, we encounter problems of definition. Students of the genre have stressed the need to distinguish the use of the term 'tragicomedy' to denote a 'third dramatic kind', which combines those elements of comedy and tragedy 'that with most verisimilitude can stand together' to create a new type of play in the style of Guarini's *Il Pastor Fido* (1590), from other less formal generic mixtures, the sort of 'hodge-podge' or 'mongrel tragi-comedy' that had long been part of the English dramatic tradition.[11] How far Shakespeare – or, for that matter, Beaumont and Fletcher, his fellow dramatists at the King's Men who are generally credited with introducing the form to the Jacobean stage – consciously set out to imitate the Guarinian scheme remains a point of controversy. All that may safely be affirmed is that there are suggestive parallels between Shakespeare's late plays and the poetics of tragicomedy, as expounded in Guarini's *Compendio della Poesia Tragicomica* (1601). In each we find the same interweaving of grave and humorous incidents, plots that are 'tragic in potentiality, but not in action', and the reversal of the threatened catastrophe, by means of a 'credible miracle', into the mandatory happy ending.[12] Perhaps the most resonant aspect of Guarini's theory is the emphasis it places on the affective dimensions of tragicomedy; the dramatist is advised to control the effects created on his audience through a careful modulation of tone which must steer a middle course between 'tragic melancholy' and 'comic relaxation'.[13] Although Shakespeare generally prefers to intensify, rather than temper, contrasting emotional extremes (especially in his recognition scenes where 'joy wades in tears'), his 'romances' display similar skill in manoeuvring the spectators, through the production of pathos, delight and wonder, into a complex affective response, one poised as finely between imaginative involvement and detachment as between serious and light-hearted moods. Given the large degree of overlap between their narrative vocabularies, 'romance' and 'tragicomedy' are probably best treated as complementary 'frames' through which to view the late plays. What these genres pre-eminently share with the latter are the use of non-realistic modes of representation and a capaciousness that allows them not only to accommodate seemingly divergent generic perspectives, but to explore a wide range of emotional registers and speak to both aristocratic and popular interests in ways that can make their political ideology hard to locate.

To the extent that the four late plays in question are rooted in (though by no means reducible to) romance typology, however, they have always been vulnerable to the sort of critical disparagement routinely directed at this mode of writing. By common consent, romance is the 'nearest of all literary forms to the wish-fulfilment dream', its characteristic movement towards reunion and regeneration driven more by the dictates of desire than by adhesion to any reality principle.[14] To those reluctant to surrender themselves to its imaginative premises, romantic fiction, in any shape or form, is therefore liable to seem suspect: a naïve, escapist and self-indulgent fantasy with nothing useful to teach us about 'real life'. Neoclassical critics, committed to an opposing set of artistic principles, understandably found the 'romances' hard to stomach. Ben Jonson clearly had plays like *Pericles* and *The Tempest* in his sights when he gibed at dramatists who pander to vulgar taste by recycling 'mouldy tales' and whose overactive imagination gives birth to '*Tales, Tempests*, and such like *Drolleries*'.[15] It was their casual violation of the realist creed of probability, verisimilitude and decorum which most scandalised him and subsequent generations of like-minded commentators. Instead of 'imitating to the life', Shakespeare's 'romances' choose to 'runne away from Nature' by creating overtly imaginary settings and events 'monstrous to our human reason' (*Winter's Tale*, V.i.41). Instead of keeping decently to one register, they repeatedly confound the distinction between the fantastic and the everyday, the 'high' and the 'low' (the barely human Caliban, for example, is given eloquent verse to speak). With the partial exception of *The Tempest*, they flout the 'unities' of time and space, expanding to take in far-flung locations and the growing up to adulthood of a new generation of royal children. Worse still, they may inhabit more than one geographical and temporal frame simultaneously: *Cymbeline* conflates ancient Rome with Renaissance Italy, while the proliferating layers of allusion in *The Tempest* locate its action within both a Virgilian old world and a contemporary new world context. Even that relatively broad-minded neoclassicist, Dr Johnson, drew the line at *Cymbeline*, dismissing the 'folly of the fiction, the absurdity of the conduct, the confusion of the names and manners of different times and the impossibility of the events in any system of life' as beneath serious critical consideration.[16]

But as defenders of romance, past and present, have pointed out, a writer's refusal to defer to the constraints of everyday life need not serve frivolous ends. By revoking the laws of causation and probability which obtain in the here-and-now, romantic fictions may provide an intuition of other levels of existence – be they mythical, supernatural or unconscious – to which neither realism nor rational thought can give us access. Equally, as Kiernan Ryan argues in this volume (essay 1), they may enable us to imagine alternative or more desirable forms of society inconceivable within the terms of the existing status quo, and thereby sharpen our sense of the deficiencies of current social arrangements. Far from withdrawing us from 'history' and 'reality', then, that imaginative licence which is the special prerogative of romance can create the conditions for a renewed, and more searching, engagement with both these areas of experience. The fact that historical and supernatural agencies, utopian longings and social criticism, can and do coexist so easily in Shakespeare's 'romances' is therefore not as aberrant as it has sometimes seemed even to modern eyes. These plays continually invite us to revise our most basic assumptions, challenging us to take a more flexible view of what constitutes decorum, truth-to-nature and even 'real life'. For while (as we noted earlier) the plays quite happily confess the monstrous implausibility of their plots, they also, paradoxically, require us to accept that, in another sense, the very 'strangeness of this business' (*Tempest*, V.i.247) confirms their truth.

Early twentieth-century criticism

A dismissive attitude to the achievement of the 'romances' lingered on into the twentieth century, despite the robust defence mounted by Romantic critics against the objections of neoclassical pedantry. Traces of this negative reception are not hard to detect, beneath an overlay of Romantic bardolatry, in Edward Dowden's enormously influential late-Victorian reading of these plays as the final chapter in Shakespeare's emotional autobiography. For Dowden and his many disciples, the benign parables of forgiveness and reconcilia- tion they saw in the 'romances' testified to a new-found mood of 'serene optimism', a spirit of 'all-embracing tolerance and kind- liness', in the author after the nihilistic despair expressed by the preceding tragedies. To explain this change of direction they were obliged to postulate a severe spiritual crisis (coterminous with the writing of the tragedies) from which Shakespeare had emerged with his faith in humanity restored and 'well disposed to spend the afternoon of life in unexacting and agreeable dreams'.[17] But there was a sting in the tail of this particular biographical myth which assumed that the spiritual elevation of the late plays, their Prospero-like aloofness from human suffering, was achieved at the cost of a loss of intensity and technical control. Evidence of this putative slackening of the playwright's creative powers was found in his reversion to what appeared to be less sophisticated drama- turgical techniques, to 'loose and rambling' plots and 'crude' effects, in the twilight of his career. In 1904 Lytton Strachey famously launched a full-frontal assault on this sentimental vision of the Bard's declining years, arguing that the 'romances' reveal not a mind at peace with itself, basking in the wisdom of maturity, but a man 'grown bored with people, bored with real life, bored, in fact, with everything except poetry and poetical dreams'.[18] Strachey's provocative rewriting of the myth did nothing, however, to dislodge the trivialising assumptions which had dogged these plays from the outset; indeed, its notoriety only served to reinforce the widely held belief that Shakespeare's 'romances' are the product of an impulse to retreat from the bruising facts of 'real life' into pleasing fairy tales or daydreams, sublimely beautiful and morally uplifting perhaps but rather 'facile' nonetheless, and that they lack what Jonson called 'art'. Despite later attempts to show that the apparent artlessness of these plays is actually a self- consciously contrived and dramatically appropriate effect, a *faux-*

naïveté, such preconceptions have proved difficult to uproot. As Margaret Healy notes (essay 2), their invidious legacy still colours our response to *Pericles*, and the same holds true, to a lesser degree, of the other plays.

In fact, it is not a huge over-simplification to argue that the critical history of the 'romances' from the early twentieth century down to the present has, in a fundamental sense, been formed in opposition to such a view, as successive commentators have sought by various methods to prove these 'idle fables' worthy of serious analysis. Since several excellent surveys covering the earlier part of the century are available, I propose to focus instead on the critical interventions of the last two decades.[19] In order to understand the positions taken by recent critics, however, we need to have some idea of how they relate to prior trends. During the first half of the twentieth century critical work on these plays was dominated by allegorical readings of varying hues, some more esoteric or overtly Christian than others and many still inflected by the biographical concerns of the post-Romantic era, but all bent on deciphering the symbolic meanings believed to be cryptically encoded in the dramatic narratives of the 'romances'. Perhaps because it has a fair claim to being Shakespeare's most enigmatic play, *The Tempest* has always acted as a magnet for the allegorising urge. As one editor notes, the dog-eared theory that it represents Shakespeare's valediction to his art is only one symptom of

> a persistent tendency to regard the play as allegorical, to feel that the heart of its mystery can be plucked out by means of some superimposed system of ideas. Whole books have been written to prove that *The Tempest* is really an account of the purification and redemption of the soul as conceived of by Christian mystics, or in the mystery cults of the pagan world … At various times the play has been said to be about almost everything: from the nature of the poetic imagination to the three-part division of the soul, the wonders of Renaissance science to man's colonial responsibilities.[20]

Other late plays also came in for their share of this type of treatment. S. L. Bethell, for instance, maintained that *The Winter's Tale* re-enacts the Christian story of sin, atonement and regeneration, culminating in the coming to life of Hermione's statue which he took to be a 'carefully prepared symbol of spiritual and actual redemption', pointing to 'fulfilment beyond this life'.[21] Why is it, we may wonder, that the 'romances' as a group have attracted more allegorical interest than any other part of the canon? In part this can be seen as a natural response to the archetypal resonances and power of suggestion vested in these plays. Moreover, the frequently elliptical quality of their dialogue and dramatic organisation, their many gaps, lacunae and 'fierce abridgements', issue an open invitation to the reader's speculative ingenuity. So, too, does their chronological position as the last of Shakespeare's single-authored plays (though this is as likely to be the result of accident as design), which has tended to give a strong teleological bias to interpretation, tempting critics to discover in these plays in general, and in *The Tempest* especially, a summation of the playwright's artistic development or his final vision of life. But, of course, the greater the provocation, the greater the danger of the plays themselves being lost from view beneath a tidal wave of mostly extraneous and unverifiable conjecture.

The semi-mystical language and frank abstraction from both the text itself and its historical conditions of production typical of such readings reached their apogee in the work of the two greatest practitioners of the allegorical or 'symbolic' approach: G. Wilson Knight and Northrop Frye. In *The Crown of Life* (1947) Wilson Knight resolves not to be deflected by the 'side issues of Elizabethan and Jacobean manners, politics, patronage, audiences, revolutions and explorations', or by the 'poetic forms' which are also 'things of time and history', but to fix his attention solely on 'the spirit which burns through them and is eternal in its rhythm of pain, endurance, and joy'. All the late plays, he contends, should be read as 'myths of immortality' on a par with Dante's *Divina Commedia*; each goes beyond 'objective imitation' in order to project the dramatist's 'transcendental apprehension' of a 'life that conquers death'.[22] Frye's study of Shakespearean comedy and romance, *A Natural Perspective* (1965), owes more to structural anthropology than to Christian or Platonic doctrine – a fact that may account for its relative sobriety of tone. But it, too, holds the later plays to be a displaced expression of the central myths of Western culture. According to Frye, the natural cycle which destroys and recreates constitutes the 'mythical backbone of all literature', and romance (the 'mythos' to which these plays belong) is 'based on the second half of [that] great cycle, moving from death to rebirth, decadence to renewal, winter to spring, darkness to a new dawn'.[23] Shakespeare's 'romances' are seen as standing in closer proximity to this archetypal narrative than his comedies; hence the clarity with which the imagery of a play such as *The Winter's Tale* replicates its cyclical logic, and hence also the 'archaising tendencies' evinced by this group of plays. It is nature's 'miraculous … reviving power', he argues, which finally lifts the action of the 'romances' onto a higher plane, affording us glimpses of a paradisal reality we are striving to regain.[24] What has rightly been deplored as Frye's withdrawal from history into 'an insulated and synchronic world of myth', also, by the same token, cuts him off from the textual nuances of these plays, so that, like Wilson Knight, he remains oblivious to the manifold ways in which they qualify and complicate the redemptive paradigms they invoke.[25]

The once hallowed view of Shakespeare as the purveyor of universal and immutable truths, uncontaminated by the local circumstances in which he wrote, has, of course, been thoroughly demolished by the 'return to history' which literary criticism has witnessed in recent years. Consequently, Wilson Knight, Frye and their fellow-travellers have weathered this 'sea-change' in critical fashions much worse than various historicising lines of inquiry that were being pursued around the same time. Of these none would have a more lasting impact than a ground-breaking essay by the theatre historian, G. E. Bentley, published in 1948, which contended that the late plays were the product not of Shakespeare's personal odyssey or visionary powers, but of his response, as a professional playwright, to the new theatrical opportunities generated by his company's take-over of the 'private' Blackfriars theatre in 1608.[26] Acquiring this more up-market indoor venue meant that the King's Men had to cater for a new clientele composed chiefly of the gentry and professional classes, and it was this practical consideration, according to Bentley, which dictated Shakespeare's turn towards the fashionable 'courtly' genre of romantic tragicomedy in the final years of his career.

Despite vigorous opposition from some quarters, the hypothesis that the late plays were tailored to the tastes of a coterie audience gained wide acceptance.[27] In fact, as we shall see, it remains an article of faith for many contemporary critics. A spate of topical readings produced in the 1960s and 70s reaffirmed the courtly leanings of the 'romances', finding in them veiled compliments to the reigning monarch and his family. Glynne Wickham, in particular, devoted a sequence of articles to elaborating the thesis that Shakespeare's shift from revenge tragedy to tragicomedy around 1607 was directly occasioned by the new climate of political optimism created by the accession of James VI and I in 1603.[28] Wickham's argument rested on a shaky network of suppositions: that Shakespeare, as a loyal servant of the crown, wished to pay homage in the 'romances', albeit obliquely, to the pacific policies James pursued at home, through the union of the crowns, and abroad, by means of dynastic alliances for his children; that these plays were meant to be construed as theatrical equivalents of the *roman-à-clef*, with leading characters 'standing in' for individual members of the royal family; and that some of the plays (notably *The Winter's Tale*, allegedly written for the investiture of the Prince of Wales in 1610) must have been commissioned for a specific court occasion. Although purportedly arising out of, and authorised by, historical fact, topical readings of this type often turn out to be no less prone to unbridled speculation and driven by the need to impose a preconceived scheme of ideas on the plays than their transcendental relatives.[29]

More recent historicist readings

Over the past two decades the impact of literary theory has transformed many aspects of the critical landscape and, with it, our ways of thinking and talking about Shakespeare. Yet it is easy to overstate the magnitude of this revolution. Certainly as far as the 'romances' are concerned, obvious differences in critical jargon and a more self-consciously politicised stance cannot entirely mask the underlying continuities with older pre-theoretical methodologies. As Simon Palfrey notes, 'the critical approach to these plays in recent years has remained basically allegorical, only now with the ambition of discovering specific, local, topical sources'.[30] Once seen as timeless fables of human experience, the late plays are now found to encode the workings of Jacobean royal absolutism. Predictably, *The Tempest* offers the most blatant example of the persistence of this tropological tendency, the belief that the play is a parable of the soul's redemptive journey having been supplanted by a virtual consensus that it presents an allegory of British colonialist ventures in America and Ireland.[31] In their choice of historical focus recent topical readings have also, for the most part, been content to plough the same narrow field as their predecessors. For critics such as David Bergeron, Donna Hamilton, Stuart Kurland, Constance Jordan and Leah Marcus, the question of what may legitimately be taken to constitute the relevant historical context of these plays continues to be artificially circumscribed by a familiar set of royal issues: the proposed English-Scottish union, constitutional debate over the monarch's prerogative, James's conjugal version of foreign policy and concern over dynastic succession.[32]

Moreover, despite showing greater theoretical alertness to the pitfalls of topical interpretation than their precursors, contemporary critics have not always managed to resist the pull towards reductive schematism it exerts. Bergeron, for example, deliberately eschews the one-to-one identification and direct referentiality favoured by Wickham in arguing that the Stuart royal family constituted a 'text' which Shakespeare appropriated and transformed alongside other sources. Yet he discerns a similar deferential impulse at work, suggesting that the late plays construct 'a mythos, an idealisation of the [royal] family'.[33] Marcus also takes her cue from the previous generation of historicist critics when she undertakes to explicate *Cymbeline* as an elaborate allegorical commentary on James's pet project of forging a united 'empire' of great Britain and the problems which beset this, symbolised (she argues) by the 'ruptured then revitalised marriage of Imogen and Posthumus' and the final resolution of the Rome–Britain conflict in a spirit of international accord. What sets her essay apart is a willingness to recognise the play's resistance to being translated into this kind of state 'authorised' propaganda. Hence she concedes that, through a 'subtle critique' of hermeneutic procedures and ideas of royal authorship, the play 'work[s] against the communication of its Stuart message', and that its political significance may have fluctuated, depending on where and before whom it was staged.[34] Unfortunately, this insight is largely nullified by the in-built limitations of Marcus's methodology which requires that such textual obstacles be overridden in the interests of extrapolating a clear-cut set of meanings from the play.

Underpinning many of these recent historical readings is the still prevalent – and still largely unexamined – assumption that the aesthetic and political affiliations of the 'romances' are predominantly courtly or aristocratic. Undue weight continues to be placed on the significance of Shakespeare's becoming a member of the King's household as a consequence of the royal patronage bestowed on his company in 1603, the implication being that his elevation to this largely honorary position would have compelled him thereafter to toe the 'Jacobean line'.[35] The fact that three of the 'romances' are known to have been staged at court during the early to mid-Stuart period (first performed before the King in October 1611, *The Winter's Tale* was revived with *The Tempest* in 1612–13 as part of the festivities celebrating the marriage of Princess Elizabeth to the Elector Palatine, and again with *Cymbeline* in 1634) has been adduced as further proof of their royalist sympathies. It is worth reminding ourselves, though, that no firm evidence has been found to corroborate claims that these plays were either written or revised for the court milieu. On the contrary, the extant records suggest that the Revels Office selected for the court's entertainment a wide and eclectic range of plays drawn from the existing repertoires of both the public and 'private' theatres, few of which obviously pandered to the monarchy's interests.[36]

Many critics who reject the proposition that Shakespeare's 'romances' originated in the requirements of James I's court nevertheless continue to accept that these plays (with the possible exception of *Pericles*) were aimed primarily at the sophisticated playgoers at Blackfriars and are thus steeped in the fashionable aesthetic culture, based on continental models and emanating from the court, which left its imprint on the 'private' theatres. Courtly influences have been detected not only in the verse style and themes of these plays, but in the prominent place they give to music, dance and spectacle, most conspicuously in their extensive use of masque forms (evident, for instance, in Jupiter's spectacular descent astride an eagle in *Cymbeline*, V.iii; the dance of satyrs in *The Winter's Tale*, IV.i, and the betrothal masque in *The Tempest*, IV.i). These quotations from the court masque, the definitive artistic statement of Jacobean absolutism, have done more than anything perhaps to skew our view of the late plays, licensing some critics to see them as colluding in the deification of monarchy and actively propagating an 'iconography of state'. Gary Schmidgall, one of the more extreme proponents of this view, finds *The Tempest* barely distinguishable from the Whitehall masques in terms of its medium and ideological content; either type of artefact, he reasons, may serve conveniently to illustrate the effects of the 'new Jacobean royalism in the arts' in that both present 'orthodox political assumptions' wrapped up in an avant-garde aesthetic form.[37]

However, this line of argument will not withstand much scrutiny. For a start, there is the awkward fact that *Pericles* predates the move to Blackfriars (owing to an outbreak of the plague Shakespeare's company was unable to take up occupancy of its new theatre until late 1609 or early 1610), thereby jeopardising

Bentley's entire theory. Moreover, the Globe remained the King's Men's 'usual house' even after this date. Simon Forman saw a performance of *The Winter's Tale* at the Globe in May 1611 and also of *Cymbeline* (probably at the same playhouse) sometime that year. Although no record survives of *The Tempest* being staged at the Globe, it is highly likely that all three plays were put on at both the King's Men's regular venues in keeping with the company's practice of alternating seasonally between them. While it is quite possible that ambitious musical and spectacular effects were built into these plays to exploit the superior technology available at the indoor playhouses, their staging requirements, as far as we can ascertain, did not include anything beyond the resources of the Globe.[38] It may reasonably be concluded, then, that rather than marking a rejection of popular taste, Shakespeare's 'romances' were addressed and designed to appeal (in rather different ways perhaps) both to the ordinary citizens at the Globe *and* to the more affluent patrons of Blackfriars. A less partial encounter with these plays is also likely to find few textual traces that might indicate a curtailment, due to the pressures of royal patronage or coterie expectation, of the considerable degree of creative autonomy (within the clearly defined limits set by the censorship laws) that Shakespeare enjoyed as a leading commercial playwright. Far from holding a flattering mirror up to royalty, the late plays would appear in many respects to be intensely critical of rulers like Pericles, Cymbeline and Leontes (as the essays by Healy [2], Relihan [3], Ellison [7] and Adelman [6] in this volume suggest), and are arguably no less bent on demystifying the 'great image of authority' (*King Lear*, IV.vi.156) than the preceding tragedies. To be sure, these rulers are not so severely punished for their misdemeanours and errors of judgement as their tragic forbears, but it is in the nature of romance to grant second chances. Other recent commentators, including David Norbook, Graham Holderness and Simon Palfrey, have also taken steps to correct the lopsided elitist version of the late plays with salutary reminders of their indebtedness, via their romance sources, to popular tradition and the frequency with which they give voice to anti-authoritarian or anti-court sentiments. As Norbrook wryly observes, 'there is no need for twentieth-century readings to be more royalist than the King's Men'.[39]

This charge may also be laid at the door of the 'new historicism', which since its emergence in the late 1970s has installed itself as the most powerful of the new theoretical paradigms currently reorganising our understanding of Renaissance literature. Refusing to segregate literary texts from other kinds of cultural practice, new historicists see these texts as participating in the production of social meanings and identities and in the symbolic mediation of power relations. This insistence on the 'social embedment of all modes of writing' (to borrow a phrase from Louis A. Montrose) has undoubtedly had beneficial repercussions for our reading of the late plays, helping lay to rest the fallacy that their preference for remote or make-believe settings signals a retreat from social reality and the pressing concerns of the day. More specifically, the trade-mark new historicist focus on the self-legitimating operations of state power has served to highlight Shakespeare's continuing engagement with political issues more often associated with his history plays and tragedies, issues such as colonial expansion, the need for strong government and a clear succession, and the destabilising effects of tyranny, treachery and usurpation on such goals. Conversely, this same narrowness of focus has proved to be something of an Achilles heel for the new historicist movement, laying it open to attack. Two recurrent complaints are especially germane to work on the 'romances' produced during the first wave of new historicist criticism.[40] The first is that the interests of the monarchy and the court are privileged to the exclusion of other voices and forms of cultural expression, as though their authority 'suffuse[d] everything' and was 'virtually synonymous with the reality of seventeenth-century life'.[41] Secondly, it is objected that the new historicism promotes a monolithic view of power which, in emphasising the capacity of the dominant order to absorb or 'contain' whatever might threaten to 'subvert' its hegemony, forecloses the possibility of effective resistance by individual or collective agencies.[42] Admittedly, several of the movement's leading practitioners have latterly called for a more complex, supple and dynamic model of culture, one that makes greater provision for 'negotiation', 'appropriation' and dialogic exchange between competing ideological positions.[43] Yet it is still necessary for historical criticism to be on guard against the totalising tendencies identified (fairly or not) with this mode of analysis. In this volume, for example, James Ellison (essay 7) argues that religion, regarded by Stephen Greenblatt and other new historicists as a 'mechanism of state repression', was 'far from being the monolithic force this might imply: on the contrary it was a hotly contested site, inseparable from politics and marked by continuing negotiations and rapid change'. Similarly, Ellison rejects the catch-all new historicist term, 'subversion', as inadequate to express the varying shades of dissenting (but non-revolutionary) opinion he finds inscribed in *The Winter's Tale*.

It is partly in reaction to such appropriations of Shakespeare's work as a conservative, pro-monarchical political force – which seem to allow no space for contestation and change, nor for alternative, non-elitist perspectives – that another group of critics has sought to retrieve the radical possibilities latent within his oeuvre. To some the world of the late plays appears particularly rich in such possibilities. As we noted earlier, it can be argued that their removal from the everyday does not merely create scope for a stringent critique of the structures governing our actual social existence; it also allows us to imagine redemption in the shape of less divisive forms of community. Thus both Annabel Patterson and David Norbrook, from rather different standpoints, have traced in *The Tempest* a 'possible republican sub-text' that taps into the language of radical utopianism along with an age-old tradition of popular protest – such as speaks through the Boatswain's mockery of established hierarchies in the play's opening scene.[44] This type of reading owes much to Marxist reappraisals of the ideology of romance. For revisionist Marxist critics such as Fredric Jameson and Walter Cohen, this genre, precisely because of its freedom from the reality principle and ability to accommodate multiple temporalities and viewpoints, 'seems to offer the possibility of sensing other historical rhythms' than those sanctioned by the present. Notwithstanding its aristocratic bias, it may evoke a 'genuinely utopian' resolution of social conflict, providing an intimation 'not of the prehistory lived in class society, but of that authentic history that might someday succeed it'.[45] Kiernan Ryan's account of the 'romances' (essay 1) clearly locates itself within the same critical tradition. Like the earlier comedies, he suggests, these plays throw off the shackles of realism in order to project a world where 'the art of the possible triumphs over the intransigence of the actual'. By telescoping historical process, their 'precursive imagination' is empowered to anticipate a time when the 'bitter reality of "being to the world and awkward casualties / Bound in servitude" (*Pericles*, V.i.94–5) might be surmounted and converted into co-operative harmony and mutual delight', and thereby whet our appetite for change. Ryan is careful to acknowledge that none of the later plays, least of all *The Tempest*, evokes the prospect of a 'brave new world' without strong qualification.

More controversially, the Marxist teleology which underwrites his reading creates a presupposition that the plays' final beneficent transformations, however insistently they may allude to their status as a fiction, a wishful fantasy, nevertheless augur future realities.

Psychoanalytic and feminist readings

Psychoanalytic critics have also been drawn to the elements of wish-fulfilment in the 'romances'. Rather than regarding the dream-like aspect of these plays and their other 'primitive' features as confirmation of Shakespeare's failing artistry or truancy from the serious business of life, they find clues therein to the plays' buried meanings. In her study of the psychological dynamic of the 'romances' Ruth Nevo takes the plays' 'defiance of commonsense', their lively commerce with the improbable and irrational, the strange and uncanny, as her starting-point, with the aim of showing that what fails to make sense from a realist standpoint becomes intelligible, indeed profoundly resonant, when viewed in the light of a Lacanian 'hermeneutic of dream analysis'.[46] Unravelling their lexicon of ambiguities, parapraxes, puns, obsessive reiterations and figurations, doubling and splitting of characters, she contends, can give us access to the plays' 'textual unconscious': the repressed primary processes and unspeakable desires which such formal oddities at once conceal and reveal. Nevo's chapter on *Cymbeline*, reprinted here (essay 4), explores the subterranean 'psychomachia' which comes close to destroying all sexual and familial relation-ships between the characters. In this respect it is indicative of the general orientation of post-Freudian criticism of the late plays which has set about excavating the dark subtext that lurks within their versions of the Shakespearean family romance. Significantly, several essays in a landmark collection of psychoanalytic criticism published in 1980 focus on the imaginative energy invested by the 'romances' in negotiating a range of psychic threats to the family's survival, the greatest of these being the spectre of incest first confronted by Pericles in the illicit union of Antiochus and his daughter, but also including various pre-Oedipal attachments, generational conflicts and sibling rivalries.[47] Fractured and dysfunc-tional, the familial history uncovered by psychoanalytic critics reveals a disturbing flipside to the idealisation of the royal family which historicists, old and new, impute to the 'romances'. If this institution is reinstated as a bastion of redemptive values and political stability by the time we reach the denouement, they remind us that it is only with difficulty and at the cost of great suffering.

Nobody reading or watching a performance of the 'romances' could fail to notice the conspicuous role that sexual difference plays in their domestic *agon*, giving the emotional conflicts re-enacted there a crucial gender dimension which invites the combined feminist and psychoanalytic approach deployed by several critics in this volume (in particular, the essays by Adelman [6], Mikalachki [5] and Singh [8]). As Helen Hackett has shown, our modern perception of romance as a specifically feminine genre was already well established in the sixteenth century; male authors regularly addressed their romance fictions to an imagined female readership.[48] Shakespeare's late plays comply with this generic convention in so far as they accord special significance to mothers and daughters: dramatically, as figures whose recovery by a paternal ruler makes them the agents of his redemption, but also symbolically, through their figurative construction as emblems of chaste fertility and nature's restorative powers. This valorising of women's creative potential would appear to mark a decisive turning away from the demonisation of female sexuality which was so fundamental to the imaginative economy of tragedies like *Hamlet* and *King Lear*. In privileging the reparative relationship between fathers and daughters (based on the Lear–Cordelia model), Cyrus Hoy argued in 1978,

> the dramatist is engaged in a quest to free the imagination from all the shrill mistress–wife–mother figures who have inhabited the late tragedies, and to create in their place an ideal of femininity on whom the imagination can bestow its tenderest sentiments, without the distractions of sexual desire.[49]

The belief that the heroines of the 'romances' are represented simply as radiant paragons of womanly virtue and objects of paternalistic worship held sway throughout the nineteenth and much of the twentieth centuries. It was only with the appearance in 1980 of the first anthology of feminist Shakespeare criticism, *The Woman's Part* (see 'Further Reading'), that the sentimental idealism on which this view is predicated really began to be challenged. Since then revisionist interpretations of the 'romances' by feminist critics have tended to emphasise their continuities with the more blatantly misogynistic tragedies. Besides making the obvious point that such icons of female monstrosity as Dionyzia, Sycorax and Cymbeline's evil queen are recognisably products of the same paranoid masculine imagination which gave birth to Regan, Goneril and Lady Macbeth, they note that even the treatment meted out to their virtuous counterparts continues to be dictated to a large extent by deep-seated anxieties over women's maternal functions, sexuality and autonomy.

Janet Adelman (essay 6), for example, argues that what drives the tragic action of the first half of *The Winter's Tale* is Leontes's frantic efforts to deny his dependency on the sexualised maternal body (graphically displayed in Hermione's 'goodly bulk') which he fears will undo his adult masculine identity. And according to Jodi Mikalachki (essay 5), similar imperatives shape *Cymbeline*'s historical plot, which contrives to expunge the powerful female leaders (Cymbeline's queen and her historical precursor, Boadicea) whose militancy is seen as an obstacle to the acquisition of civility and a respectable all-male version of nationalism. Other feminist critics have highlighted the plays' tendency to invert the consolatory theoretical maxim that what is socially peripheral may yet be symbolically central.[50] Thus despite carrying a heavy freight of figurative meaning, female characters suffer various forms of marginalisation in the 'romances'. They may be relegated to a footnote in history or traded as pawns between fathers and potential sons-in-law in the dynastic marriage market (cf. Marina, Imogen, Miranda); their celebrated generative powers may be metaphorically appropriated by men (cf. *Pericles*, V.i.105; *Cymbeline*, V.v.369–71; *The Tempest*, I.ii.153–8), or their presence banished from the stage for the whole or most of the duration of the play. The many rewritings of *The Tempest* as an anti-colonial manifesto produced by Latin-American and Caribbean authors since the 1950s have gone furthest in realising the play's potentially subversive applications. Yet ironically, as Jyotsna Singh shows (essay 8), these writers perpetuate the process of female erasure in Shakespeare's text, colluding with the repressive gender ideologies which sustain Prospero's authority through their inability to conceive of Miranda having any role other than as the colonisers' sexual property or to imagine a native mate for Caliban.

The reassessment of attitudes to female agency and sexuality in the 'romances' undertaken by feminist, psychoanalytic and post-colonial critics raises some important questions. If these plays can indeed be understood, on a certain level, to follow the same unconscious laws as do dreams or waking fantasies, must we see them as the emanations of a decidedly patriarchal psyche? Do the female characters exist solely as the projection of the male protagonists' (or their creator's) primal wishes and fears? Or are they given scope to inscribe their own subjectivity and alternative feminine values, however tentatively, outside the confines of the diseased masculine imagination – as Adelman argues is the case with Hermione's return at the end of *The Winter's Tale*?[51]

Future critical directions

How far the essays collected in this volume have succeeded in cracking the problem of the 'romances' must be for individual readers to determine. What is clear, I think, is that, taken as a representative snapshot of the critical orientation of Shakespeare studies on the brink of the twenty-first century, they build upon but also move on from the work done in the 1980s in significant ways. The first thing that is likely to strike the reader is how few of the pieces reprinted here lend themselves to being pigeonholed in terms of particular 'isms'. Although clearly informed by developments in the field of poststructuralist theory and fully alert to the ideological functions of the Shakespearean text, they tend not to be tied to so narrow and explicit a theoretical or political agenda as was much of the criticism produced a decade or more ago. Unwilling to limit their attention to the dynamics of state power or court culture after the fashion of earlier historicist readings, many of the essays seek to locate the 'romances' within a broader discursive terrain which encompasses such historically important but hitherto neglected topics as nationalism (Mikalachki), topography (Relihan, Ellison), 'medico-moral' polemics (Healy), the religious politics of seven- teenth-century Europe (Ellison, Kastan) and its representation of non-Christian cultures (Relihan). A growing sense that this group of plays calls for a more flexible, eclectic and wide-ranging critical discourse is also apparent in the ease with which some of the contrib- utors slip between, or attempt to combine, theoretical approaches generally regarded as divergent, even incompatible. Mikalachki, for example, shows how effectively feminist, new historicist and psycho- analytic perspectives can be synthesised in the interests of capturing the shifting registers of the strangest hybrid among all Shakespeare's mongrel tragicomedies, *Cymbeline*. Other essays take issue directly with what might be called the new critical orthodoxy. Both

Constance Relihan (essay 3) and Margaret Healy (essay 2) chip away at the received 'King James version' of *Pericles*, while David Scott Kastan (essay 9) interrogates the now all-but axiomatic belief that English colonial history supplies the definitive context for interpreting *The Tempest* by reminding us just how much of the play this framework occludes. Collectively, the essays assembled here illustrate how much we stand to gain from such an enlargement of the parameters of critical discussion in attempting to get to grips with these remarkably elusive and multi-faceted plays.

Notes

1. The term 'romances' is used in inverted commas here, as a way of signalling the imprecision of this nevertheless critically useful label – a point discussed further below.

2. I follow the dates given in *The Riverside Shakespeare* (2nd edn, 1997). However, some uncertainty remains over the dating and order of composition of the 'romances', and the general editors of the Oxford edition offer a slightly different chronology: *Pericles* (1607), *The Winter's Tale* (1609), *Cymbeline* (1610), *The Tempest* (1611) (Stanley Wells and Gary Taylor [eds], *William Shakespeare: A Textual Companion* [Oxford, 1987], pp. 130–2).

3. See, e.g., Rosalie Colie, *The Resources of Kind: Genre Theory in the Renaissance*, ed. Barbara K. Lewalski (Berkeley, CA, 1973). For a useful discussion of generic hybridity and instability on the Elizabethan/Jacobean stage, see Jean Howard, 'Shakespeare and Genre', in David Scott Kastan (ed.), *A Companion to Shakespeare* (Oxford, 1999), pp. 297–310.

4. Philip Sidney, *An Apology for Poetry*, ed. Geoffrey Shepherd (Manchester, 1965), pp. 135-6. Elsewhere Sidney condones mixed genres (p. 116).

5. Lawrence Danson, *Shakespeare's Dramatic Genres* (Oxford, 2000), p. 7.

6. Colie, *Resources of Kind*, pp. 8, 21, 27–9. For further discussion of this point, see Jennifer Richards and James Knowles's introduction to *Shakespeare's Late Plays* (Edinburgh, 1999), pp. 8–9.

7. Philip Edwards, 'Shakespeare's Romances: 1900–57', *Shakespeare Survey*, 11 (1958), 18.

8. See, e.g., Joan Hartwig, *Shakespeare's Tragicomic Vision* (Baton Rouge, LA, 1972); Howard Felperin, *Shakespearean Romance* (Princeton, NJ, 1972); Barbara Mowat, *The Dramaturgy of*

Shakespeare's Romances (Athens, GA, 1976); R. W. Uphaus, *Beyond Tragedy: Structure and Experiment in Shakespeare's Romances* (Lexington, KY, 1970); and R. S. White, *'Let Wonder Seem Familiar': Endings in Shakespeare's Romance Vision* (London, 1985).

9. On Shakespeare's use of romance motifs, see esp. Carol Gesner, *Shakespeare and the Greek Romance* (Lexington, KY, 1970), and Stanley Wells, 'Shakespeare and Romance', in John Russell Brown and Bernard Harris (eds), *Later Shakespeare* (London, 1966), pp. 48–79.

10. Felperin, *Shakespearean Romance*, p. 54.

11. See Barbara Mowat, 'Shakespearean Tragicomedy', in Nancy Klein Maguire (ed.), *Renaissance Tragicomedy: Explorations in Genre and Politics* (New York, 1987), pp. 81–3, and Gordon McMullan and Jonathan Hope (eds), *The Politics of Tragicomedy: Shakespeare and After* (London, 1992), pp. 1–7.

12. Citations of the *Compendio* are taken from Mowat, 'Shakespearean Tragicomedy', and Madeleine Doran, *Endeavours of Art* (Madison, WI, 1964), pp. 203–8. The fullest English translation of this text is in Allan H. Gilbert, *Literary Criticism: Plato to Dryden* (New York, 1940), pp. 504–33.

13. For a useful discussion of this aspect of Guarinian tragicomedy in relation to the dramaturgy of the 'romances', see Robert Henke, *Pastoral Transformations: Italian Tragicomedy and Shakespeare's Late Plays* (Delaware, 1997), ch. 6.

14. Northrop Frye, *Anatomy of Criticism* (Princeton, NJ, 1957), p. 186.

15. Citations are taken from 'Ode to Himself' and the Induction to *Bartholomew Fair*. See *Ben Jonson*, ed. C. H. Herford and P. Simpson, 11 vols (Oxford, 1925–52), VI: 16, 492.

16. H. R. Woudhuysen (ed.), *Samuel Johnson on Shakespeare* (London, 1989), p. 235.

17. See Walter Raleigh, *Shakespeare* (1907; repr. London, 1928), p. 209, and E. K. Chambers, *Shakespeare: A Survey* (London, 1925), pp. 286, 292. Cf. Edward Dowden, *Shakespeare: A Critical Study of His Mind and Art* (Edinburgh, 1874).

18. Lytton Strachey, 'Shakespeare's Final Period', repr. in *Books and Characters* (London, 1922), p. 60.

19. See, esp., Edwards, 'Shakespeare's Romances: 1900–57', and Kiernan Ryan's introduction to *Shakespeare: The Last Plays* (London and New York, 1999), pp. 4–12.

20. See Anne Barton's introduction to the New Penguin edition (1968), p. 21.

21. S. L. Bethell, *The Winter's Tale: A Study* (London, 1947), pp. 103–4.

22. All citations are from G. Wilson Knight's introductory essay, 'Myth and Miracle' (1929), reprinted in *The Crown of Life* (1948; repr. London, 1969), pp. 9, 16–17, 30–1.

23. Northrop Frye, *A Natural Perspective: The Development of Shakespearean Comedy and Romance* (New York, 1965), pp. 119–21.

24. Ibid., pp. 135–59.

25. Felperin, *Shakespearean Romance*, p. 316.

26. See G. E. Bentley, 'Shakespeare and the Blackfriars Theatre', *Shakespeare Survey*, 1 (1948), 38–50.

27. See, for example, Alfred Harbage's counter-argument in *Shakespeare and the Rival Traditions* (New York, 1952).

28. See Glynne Wickham, 'Shakespeare's Investiture Play: The Occasion and Subject of *The Winter's Tale*', *TLS*, 18 December 1969; 'From Tragedy to Tragi-Comedy: *King Lear* as Prologue', *Shakespeare Survey*, 26 (1973), 33–48; 'Masque and Anti-masque in *The Tempest*', *Essays and Studies* 28 (1975), 1–14; 'Riddle and Emblem: A Study in the Dramatic Structure of *Cymbeline*', in John Carey (ed.), *English Renaissance Studies Presented to Dame Helen Gardner in Honour of Her Seventieth Birthday* (Oxford, 1980), pp. 94–113.

29. Perhaps the most extreme instance of this tendency is to be found in Frances Yates, *Shakespeare's Last Plays: A New Approach* (London, 1975).

30. Simon Palfrey, *Late Shakespeare: A New World of Words* (Oxford, 1997), p. 5.

31. Admittedly, not all colonial readings are allegorical. Some are more interested in the structural and discursive aspects of the play's imbrication in the colonialist project, e.g., Francis Barker and Peter Hulme, '"Nymphs and Reapers Heavily Vanish": The Discursive Contexts of *The Tempest*', in John Drakakis (ed.), *Alternative Shakespeares* (London and New York, 1985), pp. 191–205.

32. See, e.g., David Bergeron, *Shakespeare's Romances and the Royal Family* (Lawrence, KS, 1985); Donna Hamilton, *Virgil and The Tempest: The Politics of Imitation* (Columbus, OH, 1990); Stuart Kurland, '"We Need No More of Your Advice": Political Realism in *The Winter's Tale*', *Studies in English Literature*, 31 (1991), 365–79; Constance Jordan, *Shakespeare's Monarchies: Ruler and Subject in the Romances* (Ithaca, NY and London, 1997); and Leah Marcus, '*Cymbeline* and the Unease of Topicality', in her *Puzzling Shakespeare: Local Reading and Its Discontents* (Berkeley, CA, 1988), pp. 116–48.

33. Bergeron, *Shakespeare's Romances*, pp. 19–22, 114.

34. Marcus, '*Cymbeline*', pp. 117, 139–44. Marcus acknowledges her debt to both Wickham and Emrys Jones's 'Stuart Cymbeline', *Essays in Criticism*, 11 (1961), 84–99.

35. On the 'purely ceremonial' status of this position, see Graham Holderness et al., *Shakespeare Out of Court: Dramatizations of Court Society* (London, 1990), pp. 132–5.

36. For the early Jacobean period (1603–13), see E. K. Chambers, *The Elizabethan Stage* (London, 1923), IV: 115–30, 168–83.

37. See Gary Schmidgall, *Shakespeare and the Courtly Aesthetic* (Berkeley, CA, 1981).

38. Andrew Gurr concludes that, like the two earlier 'romances', '*The Winter's Tale* has nothing that could not have been staged as easily at the Globe as at Blackfriars', and even the special musical effects of *The Tempest* might have been recreated by the famed Blackfriars musicians at the Globe ('*The Tempest*'s Tempest at Blackfriars', *Shakespeare Survey*, 41 [1988], pp.92–3). As Stephen Orgel and Roger Warren also point out in their Oxford editions of *The Tempest* (p. 2) and *Cymbeline* (pp. 2–3) respectively, the flight machinery employed in these plays derives from the public theatres.

39. David Norbrook, '"What Cares These Roarers for the Name of King": Language and Utopia in *The Tempest*', in McMullan and Hope (eds), *The Politics of Tragicomedy*, p. 24.

40. See, e.g., Paul Brown, '"This thing of darkness I acknowledge mine": *The Tempest* and the discourse of colonialism', in Jonathan Dollimore and Alan Sinfield (eds), *Political Shakespeare: New Essays in Cultural Materialism* (Manchester, 1985), pp. 48–71; Leonard Tennenhouse, *Power on Display: The Politics of Shakespeare's Genres* (New York and London, 1986), pp. 171–86; and Stephen Greenblatt, 'Martial Law in the Land of Cockaigne', in his *Shakespearean Negotiations: The Circulation of Social Energy in Renaissance England* (Oxford, 1988), pp. 129–63. Curiously, new historicists have written little specifically on the 'romances' since this first wave.

41. See Albert Tricomi, *Reading Tudor-Stuart Texts Through Cultural Historicism* (Gainseville, FL, 1996), p. 10.

42. This point has been made too often to enumerate, but see, e.g., Frank Lentricchia, 'Foucault's Legacy – A New Historicism?', in H. Aram Veeser (ed.), *The New Historicism* (London, 1989), pp. 231–42.

43. See, e.g., Louis A. Montrose, 'The Poetics and Politics of Culture', in Veeser (ed.), *New Historicism*, pp. 20–3, and Steven Mullaney, 'After the new historicism', in Terence Hawkes (ed.), *Alternative Shakespeares 2* (London, 1996), pp. 17–37.

44. See Annabel Patterson, '"Thought is Free": *The Tempest*', in her *Shakespeare and the Popular Voice* (Oxford, 1989), pp. 154–62, and Norbrook, '"What Cares These Roarers"'.

45. See, respectively, Fredric Jameson, *The Political Unconscious: Narrative as a Socially Symbolic Act* (revised edn, London, 1983), pp. 103–5; and Walter Cohen, *Drama of a Nation: Public Theater in Renaissance England and Spain* (Ithaca, NY, 1985), pp. 390–1.

46. See Ruth Nevo, *Shakespeare's Other Language* (London, 1987).

47. See, esp., the contributions of David Sundelson, Meredith Skura and Coppélia Kahn to Murray Schwartz and Coppélia Kahn (eds), *Representing Shakespeare: New Psychoanalytic Essays* (Baltimore, MD, 1980). Hovering behind these and most other psychoanalytic readings of the 'romances' is C. L. Barber's seminal essay, '"Thou that beget'st him that did thee beget": Transformation in *Pericles* and *The Winter's Tale*', *Shakespeare Survey*, 22 (1969), 59–67.

48. See Helen Hackett, *Women and Romance Fiction in the English Renaissance* (Cambridge, 2000).

49. Cyrus Hoy, 'Fathers and Daughters in Shakespeare's Romances', in Carol McGinnis Kay and Henry Jacobs (eds), *Shakespeare's Romances Reconsidered* (Lincoln, NE, 1978), p. 84.

50. See, e.g., Ann Thompson, '"Miranda, Where's Your Sister?": Reading Shakespeare's *The Tempest*' (1991), reprinted in R. S. White (ed.) *The Tempest*, New Casebook series (Basingstoke, 1999), pp. 155–66.

51. For a taste of the radically opposed positions feminist critics take on these issues in relation to *The Winter's Tale*, see Carol Thomas Neely, *Broken Nuptials in Shakespeare's Plays* (New Haven, CT, 1985), pp. 166–209, and Valerie Traub, *Desire and Anxiety: Circulations of Sexuality in Shakespearean Drama* (London, 1992), pp. 42–9.

1

Shakespearean Comedy and Romance: the Utopian Imagination

KIERNAN RYAN

'Let wonder seem familiar'

If Shakespeare's tragedies give us the measure of what it means to sink beneath the burden of history, crushed by 'The weight of this sad time' (*King Lear*, V.iii.324), his comedies and romances create opportunities to explore the way the world might look and feel with the dead weight of prevalence and probability lifted from its shoulders. The tragedies are preoccupied with the destruction of the potential by the actual, of the more desirable forms living might take by the forces currently conspiring to obstruct their realisation. But in his Elizabethan romantic comedies and in the haunting last plays of his Jacobean period, Shakespeare's gaze is levelled at the remote horizon of what could be, rather than absorbed in the immediate tyranny of what is. The primary concern of these plays is to dramatise the surrender of the prevailing to the possible, the triumph of benevolent human desires over the harsh constraints of historical actuality. The wishful projection of this metamorphosis is always qualified, however, by a realistic registration of the fact that humanity remains in thrall so far to the callous sway of the here and now. Reassessed from this point of view, Shakespearean comedy and romance could be argued to be no less powerful and valuable than the tragedies. For they can be seen as pursuing an equally uncompromising assault on the existing terms of life, through their overt education of our imagination in utopian norms and expectations.

Needless to say, this is not how plays such as *As You Like It* or *The Winter's Tale* are regarded in the standard accounts. Consider, for example, C. L. Barber's immensely influential study, *Shakespeare's Festive Comedy*. The many virtues of this book are ultimately yoked to a reading of the comedies as cathartic parables of orthodoxy preserved. In these plays, Barber contends, the usual order of things is suspended for a licensed period of therapeutic inversion and release, in order to discharge the subversive steam built up by the repression of unruly appetites. Having given vent to these dangerous drives and turbulent desires, society is able to rein-stall its normal form all the more securely, once the midsummer madness, the unbridled misrule of Twelfth Night, or the levelling liberty of Arden is over. If Shakespearean comedy exploits the special freedom of carnival to turn the Elizabethan world upside down, it does so only to reinforce the rationale for keeping it the right way up: 'Just as a saturnalian reversal of social roles need not threaten the social structure, but can serve instead to consolidate it, so a temporary, playful reversal of sexual roles can renew the meaning of the normal relation.'[1]

Still dominating the reading-lists alongside Barber is Northrop Frye's study of Shakespearean comedy and romance, *A Natural Perspective*. At first glance, Frye appears to offer a more promising view of these plays as enacting a desirable transformation rather than a purified restoration of the status quo. At the start of them, he suggests at one point, 'the irrational society represents social reality, the obstacles to our desires that we recognise in the world around us, whereas the society of the conclusion is the realising of what we want but seldom expect to see'. But on closer inspection it becomes evident that the longed-for new society forged at the conclusion is nothing more than 'the old reformed'. For, according to Frye, 'The mythical backbone of all literature is the cycle of nature, which rolls from birth to death and back again to rebirth'; and the structure of comedy and romance 'is based on the second half of the great cycle, moving from death to rebirth, decadence to renewal, winter to spring, darkness to a new dawn'. The 'new reality' in which *Cymbeline* or *Much Ado* culminates is a rejuve-nated, idealised instance of a society whose rank-ridden constitution Frye endows with the evergreen authority of natural law. Frye's observation that at the close of these plays 'Kings remain kings, and clowns clowns',[2] that the structure of society is left unchanged by the comic action, can scarcely be faulted as far as it goes. But it fails to see that what *is* dramatically altered by Shakespearean comedy is our perception of that stratified structure. Far from boosting their power to point us beyond the established order, Frye's 'natural perspective' reduces these plays to a servile means of conserving that order, as surely as Barber's conception of them as 'a civilised equivalent for exorcism'.[3]

Elliot Krieger's *A Marxist Study of Shakespeare's Comedies* proceeds on the same basic assumption as the orthodox critics it might otherwise seem to contest. For Krieger too the comedies seek to idealise and stabilise Elizabethan society, but they do so by disguising the hegemony of the aristocracy and blurring the actual class-divisions. This is achieved mainly through the creation of a parallel 'second world' within the plays, such as the forest of Arden in *As You Like It*:

> The clarified image that the second world reveals serves the interests of the ruling class protagonists ... by creating the illusion that ruling class interests do not exist – more specifically, that the protagonists seek only harmony and concord, universal good. Harmony and concord, however, originate not as universal truths but as aspects of aristocratic needs and fantasies. When seen in terms of aristocratic needs, the abstractions harmony and concord become rephrased and translated into social policy: hierarchy and stability.[4]

In a new-historicist variation on this manoeuvre, Leonard Tennenhouse argues that Shakespeare's comedies exercise 'the power of theatre to create the illusion of a totalising community out of the contradictory bodies of power':

> The multiple marriages at a comedy's conclusion make it seem as if desire had brought about a politically homogeneous community. At the same time, desire also preserves the sexual hierarchy, for the subordination of wife to husband invariably invokes that of subject to king.

For all their revelling in inversion and disguising, 'the romantic comedies demonstrate that festival breaks down the hierarchical distinctions organising Elizabethan society only – in the end – to be taken within the social order where it authorises a new form of political authority'. The argument transparently recycles Barber's contention that the comedies introduce disorder as a means of fixing the established order more firmly in place. And for Tennenhouse 'the strategy at work in all the romances' is an equally 'perfect collaboration of art and ideology', accomplished this time through the disruption and reunification of the family: 'the unfolding of disorder within the domestic unit operates to reinscribe this unit within a hierarchy governed by the metaphysics of blood.' *Pericles, Cymbeline, The Winter's Tale* and *The Tempest* are exposed as reactionary fables, whose distinction is 'their use of the family to dramatise the need for a patriarchal figure who can reform corrupt social practices, supervise the exchange of women and ensure the proper distribution of power'.[5] In the name of progressive criticism the comedies and romances are divorced from us and cased up in a cynical misconstruction of their past significance, which renders them impotent to assume the militant new meanings they are disposed to deliver to the present.[6]

Too many conventional and radical readings are crippled by their supposition that the imaginative energy of these plays must be invested in perpetuating the current social formation.[7] An excellent point from which to launch a refutation of this tenacious misconception is supplied, somewhat surprisingly, by a passage in H. B. Charlton's *Shakespearian Comedy*, which does much to redeem the same author's ploddingly predictable ideas on Shakespearean tragedy:

> Classical comedy is conservative. It implies a world which has reached stability sufficient for itself. Its members are assumed to be fully aware of the habits and the morals which preserve an already attained state of general well being. The main interest is the exposure of offenders against common practice and against unquestioned propriety in the established fitness of things. Hence its manner is satire, and its standpoint is public common sense. But Shakespearian comedy is a more venturesome and a more imaginative undertaking. It does not assume that the conditions and the requisites of man's welfare have been certainly established, and are therefore a sanctity only to be safeguarded. It speculates imaginatively on modes, not of preserving a good already reached, but of enlarging and extending the possibilities of this and other kinds of good. Its heroes (or heroines, to give them the dues of their sex) are voyagers in pursuit of a happiness not yet attained, a brave new world wherein man's life may be fuller, his sensations more exquisite and his joys more widespread, more lasting, and so more humane.[8]

This seems to me a fundamentally accurate formulation of the rationale and dynamic of Shakespearean comedy. These plays are indeed not concerned with 'preserving a good already reached' under existing social conditions. They are powered by their commitment to unfolding forms of life liberated from whatever forbids the free play and shared satisfaction of justified desires.

Walter Cohen is equally helpful in steering our perception of Shakespeare's last plays in the same direction. As he rightly observes, although tragedy has seemed until now to speak more compellingly than romance to audiences and critics alike,

> this difference has nothing to do with any timeless, intrinsically greater truth content of tragedy. Indeed, Marxism has always wagered that in the long run human history would have, or at least could have, the structure of romance. Precisely in its utopianism, then, romance may offer a legitimate vision not of the prehistory lived in class society, but of that authentic history that may someday succeed it.[9]

The radical possibilities of romance possess another persuasive advocate in Tom Moylan, who defines this form of literature at its most effective as

> a process of wish-fulfilment or utopian fantasy, that aims at *a displacement and transfiguration* of the given historical world in such a way as to revive the conditions of a lost paradise or to anticipate a future kingdom in which suffering and limitations have been effaced.[10]

The utopian romance dislocates and reshapes the present moment of history, and so 'serves to stimulate in its readers a desire for a better life and to motivate that desire toward action by conveying a sense that the world is not fixed once and for all'.[11] Romances invite us to recognise and play experimentally with imaginable alternatives, which strengthen our conviction that a different kind of world could actually be realised.[12]

Both the major romantic comedies and the late romances of Shakespeare are engaged, I would suggest, in the dramatisation of just such a vision. These plays exploit the powers of compression conserved in their fairy-tale formula to encapsulate the benign course of collective development which they anticipate. The coded projection of this speculative evolution demands a far higher level of abstraction from social reality than that on which the English or

Roman history plays, or even the great tragedies, are obliged to operate. It is worth recalling in this connection Northrop Frye's shrewd observation that 'princes and princesses may be wish-fulfilment dreams as well as social facts'.[13] These plays have no intention of satisfying our appetite for convincing characterisation and narrative. So much may be inferred at once from their notorious generic clichés: the gratuitous, incredible predicaments; the outrageous coincidences; the oversimplified extremes of innocence and malevolence; the abrupt, psychologically unaccountable transfigurations of character and plot; and the shamelessly contrived conclusions, especially those effected by the arbitrary intervention of fairies or gods. Such features signal from the start that literal-minded attempts to square a play like *Twelfth Night* or *Pericles* with the verifiable routines of familiar experience are doomed to founder and should be abandoned as irrelevant. This undisguised surrender of the laws of likelihood to the rule of the miraculous, to eventualities 'monstrous to our human reason' (*The Winter's Tale*, V.i.41), frees Shakespeare's imagination to forsake the plausible logic of past or probable events, and follow instead the implausible logic of the *as yet* improbable wherever it may lead.

[...]

The comedies and the romances project, through symbolically condensed dramatic parables, foreshortened accounts of our voyage to the land where 'wishes fall out as they're will'd' (*Pericles*, V.ii.16). They provide us with a means of grasping the future concretely in the guise of the present, of experiencing the possible as if it were already actual. Or as *A Midsummer Night's Dream* puts it:

> as imagination bodies forth
> The forms of things unknown, the poet's pen
> Turns them to shapes, and gives to aery nothing
> A local habitation and a name.
> Such tricks hath strong imagination
> That if it would but apprehend some joy,
> It comprehends some bringer of that joy;
>   (V.i.14–20)

The 'strong imagination' of Shakespearean comedy and romance telescopes the process by which the bitter reality of being 'to the world and awkward casualties / Bound ... in servitude' (*Pericles*, V.i.94–5) might be surmounted and converted into co-operative harmony and mutual delight.

The otherwise inconceivable means and tracts of time required to effect this transition – the 'circumstantial branches, which / Distinction should be rich in' (*Cymbeline*, V.v.383–4) – are imaginatively contracted and accelerated by the plays. They are subjected to a 'fierce abridgment' (*Cymbeline*, V.v.382), which advances the arrival of the utopian resolution summoned by the anguish of the present. In the comedies the compression is achieved mainly by displacing the action from the customary reality depicted or posited by the play into an exceptional, permissive environment: the unpredictable pastoral world of Arden; the delirious nightwood invisibly ruled by Oberon and Puck; the festive post-war pause for courtship and regeneration in *Much Ado*; or the brief reign of absurdity and bewilderment in Illyria. Prospero's enchanted island serves a similar purpose in *The Tempest*: it speeds up history in order to bring within the compass of the present a premonition of the future's power to grant it absolution.

In *Pericles* the narratorial interventions of Gower achieve the abbreviated convergence of desire and reality by enlisting the audience's collaboration at every stage:

> Thus time we waste, and long leagues make short;
> Sail seas in cockles, have and wish but for't,
>   (IV.iv.1–2)

> That he can hither come so soon
> Is by your fancies' thankful doom.
>   (V.ii.19–20)

The deliberately naïve, archaic doggerel that distinguishes the choric couplets of 'ancient Gower' (I.Chorus.2) distances the brazenly concocted universe of *Pericles* still further. His outmoded idiom sharpens the audience's sense of the contrasting modernity, and hence the historicity, of the world in which they themselves, 'born in these latter times' (1.Chorus.11), watch the play. All these effects are explicitly advertised in the amazing speech by Time, 'that makes and unfolds error' (IV.i.2), in *The Winter's Tale*. As he steps onto the threshold of Act IV to conjure a bridge across the void dividing 'things dying' from 'things new born' (III.iii.114), he accosts the audience directly with this plea:

> Impute it not a crime
> To me, or my swift passage, that I slide
> O'er sixteen years and leave the growth untried

> Of that wide gap, since it is in my pow'r
> To o'erthrow law, and in one self-born hour
> To plant and o'erwhelm custom. Let me pass
> The same I am, ere ancient'st order was,
> Or what is now receiv'd. I witness to
> The times that brought them in; so shall I do
> To th'freshest things now reigning, and make stale
> The glistering of this present, as my tale
> Now seems to it.
>
> (IV.i.4–15)

Time's speech lays bare the creative methods at work throughout the romantic comedies and the last plays: the revolutionary quickening of historical change; the unmasking of 'what is now receiv'd' as simply 'custom'; the humbling of whatever 'glistering present' the spectators inhabit; and the emphasis on the play as a theatrical manipulation of fabricated events in which the audience must conspire.

These techniques of relativisation and estrangement radicalise our perception of the conventional categories with which the plays undeniably operate. Their impact is amplified by the intrinsic polyphony of Shakespeare's drama. A *Midsummer Night's Dream* embraces not only the views and values of the Athenian ruling class (Theseus, Hippolyta, the lovers), but those of the fairies (Oberon, Titania, Puck) and those of the 'Hardhanded men that work in Athens here' (V.i.72) – Bottom, Flute, Snout and the rest of the 'hempen home-spuns' (III.i.77); and divergent attitudes to love and life thrive within these groups as well, especially between the sexes. *Twelfth Night* juxtaposes and confuses the romantic 'upstairs' agonising of Orsino, Olivia and Viola with the intoxicated 'downstairs' misrule of Sir Toby, Feste, Sir Andrew and Maria, and these in turn with the puritanical authoritarianism of Malvolio. And *The Tempest* intertwines the incongruous outlooks expressed or embodied by the world-weary wizard Prospero, the wide-eyed innocent Miranda, the drunken buffoons Stephano and Trinculo, the mercurial, lyrical spirit Ariel and the sullen, vengeful slave Caliban, the 'freckled whelp, hag born' (I.ii.283).

By extending our sympathies, and diverting our attention, across a range of conflicting selves and standpoints, the plays strive to free us from the reductive grip of a single attitude or interest. Their covert mission is to release all the positions they dramatise into dialogic solution, and thus divest them of the authority each might exercise alone over our conception of the world. The experience of assimilating a discordant plurality of theatrical voices fosters a levelling mode of perception. Shakespeare's multivocal comedy cuts across the lived divisions of class and gender, breaking down the barriers of language and ideology which protract their dominion. This submerged vision sometimes surfaces as an explicit formulation, as when the disguised Imogen replies to Arviragus's question, 'Are we not brothers?':

> So man and man should be,
> But clay and clay differs in dignity,
> Whose dust is both alike.
> (*Cymbeline*, IV.ii.3–5)

The same wish is memorably echoed in the Jailer's words towards the end of the same play: 'I would we were all of one mind, and one mind good' (V.iv.203–5). Such quotations afford only the most patent confirmation of the consistent, deep pressure exerted by these plays to transport us to a realm liberated from the dictatorship of divisive ways of seeing.

[...]

By turning themselves into minefields of quibbles and semantic quicksands, these scripts resist invasion by essentialist notions of language and meaning that plague us still. But that is not their only line of defence against these insidious preconceptions. Equally vital is the way the multiple voices of a play flourish their fabrication from a shifting spectrum of literary and theatrical discourses. *The Winter's Tale*, for example, shuffles together the formal and more idiomatic modes of blank verse and prose in the court scenes, the colloquial prose and naturalistic phrasing of the shepherds and the wily Autolycus, and the distinctive registers and styles of the pastoral lyric, the popular ballad and the masque. Indeed, lest the fact of their play's verbal artifice escape us, the characters themselves have a habit of tilting it towards our attention: 'Nay then God buy you,' exclaims a disgusted Jaques to Orlando, 'and you talk in blank verse' (*As You Like It*, IV.i.31–2); while an exasperated Posthumus upbraids an incredulous Lord with 'You have put me into rhyme' (*Cymbeline*, V.iii.63). Spectator and reader are repeatedly reminded of the linguistic loom on which the illusions and illuminations of the play have been woven. The language of works like *The Winter's Tale* or *Twelfth Night* forbids discursive unity and transparency, which could imply a consistent experience and agreed perception of reality. It insists instead on the diversity of the text's discourses, whose conflicting values disclose the plural, contested character of the real society transfigured by the play.[14]

The verbal self-consciousness of the comedies and romances is reinforced by their keenness to cite their own status as a staged event, as a scripted and performed fiction reflecting, yet not to be conflated with, the realities lived beyond the charmed circumference of the Globe. This feature is most obvious in the mounting of an actual or virtual play, complete with audience, within the play proper, as in the masque of the Muscovites and the disastrous Pageant of the Nine Worthies in *Love's Labour's Lost*. The same comedy contrives a still more complex situation, in which the audience finds itself watching Berowne eavesdropping on the King spying on Longaville, who is covertly observing Dumaine: '"All hid, all hid", an old infant play' (IV.iii.76), as Berowne points out in one of the scene's many staggered asides to the audience. In *A Midsummer Night's Dream* we are treated to the mechanicals' unwittingly hilarious, parodic demolition of the tragic course the main plot might have followed; but that plot itself, including its happy resolution, is framed as a production stage-managed by its internal authors and audience, Oberon and Puck, who leaps through the layers of illusion at the very end to address us directly, as actor to audience, about the performance we have witnessed.

The characters periodically jolt us into consciousness of our relationship with the play through overtly self-mirroring remarks. 'I see the play so lies,' muses Perdita, 'That I must bear a part' (*The Winter's Tale*, IV.iv.655–6). And the same work's closing review of its fantastic events is admitted to be 'Like an old tale still, which will have matter to rehearse, though credit be asleep and not an ear open' (V.ii.63). In *Pericles*, as we have already noted, Gower persistently appeals to the spectators to collude in creating the necessary illusion:

> In your imagination hold
> This stage the ship, upon whose deck
> The seas-toss'd Pericles appears to speak.
> (III.Chorus.58–60)

The most glaring instance occurs, however, in *Twelfth Night* when, after watching a play within a play, into whose leading role Malvolio has unwittingly stepped, Fabian exclaims, 'If this were play'd upon a stage now, I could condemn it as an improbable fiction' (III.iv.127–8).

The effect of these elaborate strategies is not, however, to leave the mind lost in a maze of visual and verbal deception, in which the border between representation and reality has been abolished. They stimulate in the spectator an awareness that both the stage world and the lived world it transposes are provisional versions of experience which invite revision, not inviolable instances or definitive editions of what life is or might be like. The audience is obliged to assess the validity of the theatrical representation in the light of the actualities with which it begs comparison; but they must also reappraise the rationale of the real production in which they have been cast by history in the light of the play's fresh account of it. As with all the defamiliarising devices embedded in Shakespeare's drama, the aim is to charge the ways of life transformed upon the stage with historicity, and so sharpen our sense of their transience and susceptibility to change.

We can now turn to the decisive task of disputing the conservative reading to which the endings of the comedies and romances are tirelessly subjected. In the first place, these plays frankly confess that their resolutions cannot be achieved *within* the normal social framework they present or presuppose. The dire predicament confounding the characters can be surmounted and turned to delight only by removing them from their regular roles and familiar circumstances. The protagonists' problems are solved by releasing events to evolve in a privileged realm or parenthetical state in which the grim imperatives responsible for their plight have been suspended. This can be an imaginary location like Arden or Illyria, or it can be a more diffuse condition, like the phase of aimless exile and disguised wandering which Pericles and Imogen must endure before coming home at last to reunion. Those who would construe the ends of the plays as surrenders to conformity must face the fact that the adequacy of those endings is undermined by the richer definitions of identity and possibility adumbrated in the previous acts. In the wake of this widening of horizons and raising of expectations, the final return to the old regime, as kingdoms, ranks, families and gender roles are restored, exposes the shrunken poverty of what custom and habit decree.

But this is not the only reason why a diagnosis of the endings as ideologically enslaved cannot be sustained. The culminating moments of concord, 'When earthly things made even / Atone together' (*As You Like It,* V.iv.109–10), also bristle with estrangement-effects. These demand that the denouement be grasped as a symbolic fiction,

whose mood is subjunctive rather than indicative, and whose satis-
factions therefore lie beyond the reach of contemporary society.

Hence the blatantly contrived resolution of *Twelfth Night*,
centred on the ritual recognition-scene between the identical twins,
Viola and Sebastian: 'One face, one voice, one habit, and two
persons' (V.i.216). In the same way *As You Like It* ruptures any
surviving illusions of verisimilitude by introducing Hymen, the god
of marriage, who materialises from nowhere to conduct a mass
wedding of all the 'country copulatives' (V.iv.556). The romances
proclaim their shameless resorts to the incredible no less boldly.
The revelations and reunions of *Pericles* are triggered by a dream-
vision, in which the hero receives the vital instructions direct from
'celestial Dian' (V.i.250). In a still more spectacular dream-
sequence, it takes nothing less than the descent of Jupiter astride an
eagle, in answer to the prayers of the ghosts of Posthumus's
parents, to set the winding-up of *Cymbeline* in motion. And at the
marvellous, moving close of *The Winter's Tale* we find ourselves
being gently 'mock'd with art' (V.iii.68), when we are required by
Paulina to 'awake [our] faith' (V.iii.95) that a statue of one thought
dead might 'be stone no more' (V.iii.99) and breathe again; that the
open wound of 'this wide gap of time, since first / We were
dissever'd' (V.iii.154–5) might be healed by a magical 'art / Lawful
as eating' (V.iii.110–11). As Paulina readily concedes:

> That she is living,
> Were it but told you, should be hooted at
> Like an old tale; but it appears she lives,
> (V.iii.115–17)

That tentative 'appears' highlights the proliferation of circum-
spect verbs and conjunctions at the climactic moments of recognition and reconciliation. Consider, for example, the phrasing of
Rosalind's formal, stylised pledge: 'I'll have no father, if you be not
he; / I'll have no husband, if you be not he;' (*As You Like It*,
V.iv.122–3). Or take the reservation attached to Hymen's summons
to collective wedlock: 'Here's eight that must take hands / To join
in Hymen's bands, / If truth holds true contents' (*As You Like It*,
V.iv.128–30). The same formula inflects Orsino's response to the
clarification of identities in *Twelfth Night*: 'If this be so, as yet the
glass seems true, / I shall have share in this most happy wrack'
(V.i.265–6). 'If you have told Diana's altar true,' Pericles is informed in the temple, 'This is your wife' (V.iii.17–18). The close of

The Tempest, too, is riddled with expressions of uncertainty, such as Alonso's 'This must crave / (And if this be at all) a most strange story' (V.i.116–17), or Gonzalo's 'whether this be, / Or be not, I'll not swear' (V.i.22–3). The presence and the object of this strategy are brought explicitly into focus by the fool: 'Your If is the only peacemaker; much virtue in If' (*As You Like It*, V.iv.102–3). The profusion of conditional locutions places the close of the play in brackets, suspends it between quotation marks. We are being urged to regard the denouement as a frankly imaginary resolution of conflicts which remain unresolved outside the theatre, and which are not even contained by the devices of fiction within the pale of the play.

[...]

Uncomfortable insinuations infect the ending of *The Winter's Tale* too, as when Leontes observes of the supposed statue, 'But yet, Paulina, / Hermione was not so much wrinkled, nothing / So aged as this seems' (V.iii.27–9). The unwittingly cruel remark recalls the callous facts of time, loss and physical decay, which the enchantment of the scene strives to hold at bay. A different kind of sceptical unease is prompted at the end of *Cymbeline*. Whether 'The harmony of this peace' (V.v.467) has indeed been attained hangs on a soothsayer's strained reading of Jupiter's cryptic prophecy, which would seem to have been fulfilled by recent events. The echoes of unvoiced incredulity reverberate long after the proclamations of lasting concord and prosperity have died away.

The utopian closure of Shakespearean comedy and romance is qualified by the intrusion of these harsher, unredeemed realities and disquieting intimations which it cannot repress, and which stress the fragile fictionality and incompleteness of its state of concord. By casting their comedic resolutions of the tragedy of history in contemporary social terms, these plays reveal the text of the future stored inside the narrative of the present. Obstructive actualities are made to serve as the symbolic guarantee of their own ultimate transformation. Through their infiltration and subversion of conventional plots and conclusions the comedies and romances dramatise the utopian within the historical. They excite our hope that these dreams of release from history's coercions might one day be realised, by giving us provisional images, lodged in recognisable and thus more persuasive forms, of what such a realisation might look and feel like. But our sense of the real world's intransigence is never allowed to dissolve into an escapist delusion of fantasies vicariously fulfilled. On the contrary, as these plays take pains to caution us, the bridges between the lives we tolerate and a truly happy ending of historical struggle in genuine community have yet to be completed. In the meantime, the precursive imagination of Shakespearean comedy and romance inspires us to dream ahead and 'let wonder seem familiar' (*Much Ado About Nothing*, V.iv.70). It accustoms us to the inconceivable and paves the way for the impossible, granting us a foretaste of the future through its estranged vision of our past.

The Tempest: the complicities of art

The Tempest is remarkable for the tenacity and complexity with which it probes the darker implications of making the improbable plausible, of dramatising the eventual as a dimension of the given. In this play Shakespeare stretches the powers of romance to breaking-point, broaching a searching process of reflection on the rationale and function of his dramatic art. I want, therefore, to conclude this book by considering Shakespeare's last masterpiece in more detail.

As one might expect, the available criticism on *The Tempest* proves largely unhelpful in guiding us towards a satisfactory account of the play. 'Historically', as Stephen Orgel points out, 'there has been a consistent tendency to ignore its ambivalences, sweeten and sentimentalise it, render it altogether neater and more comfortable than the text that has come down to us.'[15] Thus the Arden editor believes that in *The Tempest* 'Shakespeare offers an exposition of the themes of Fall and Redemption by means of analogous narrative'.[16] This allegorising, idealist approach to *The Tempest* derives unsurprisingly from Wilson Knight's reading in *The Crown of Life*, which maintains that 'A reader sensitive to poetic atmosphere must necessarily feel the awakening light of some religious or metaphysical truth symbolised in the plot and attendant machinery'.[17] The continuing prevalence of this view of the play is reflected in the principal British casebook on *The Tempest*, where both the Arden introduction and Wilson Knight's account are still firmly ensconced, several decades after their first publication, as exemplary interpretations.[18]

It is a welcome contrast, therefore, to witness recent radical criticism sweeping this approach aside with illuminating reassessments of *The Tempest* as a play which cannot suppress 'a fundamental disquiet concerning its own functions within the projects of colonialist discourse',[19] and which can thus be repunctuated so that it may 'speak something of the ideological contradictions of its political unconscious'.[20] But the problem with this contribution to our grasp of the play's modern significance is that it excludes the subversive utopian possibilities of *The Tempest* as completely as do the mystifications perpetrated by the work's conservative critics.[21]

The grounds for construing the play as a radical romance are established in the opening storm scene. They crystallise in the exchange between the boatswain, labouring desperately with his crew to save the ship and the lives of everyone it holds, and their noble passengers, who are good for nothing but impeding the sailors' work with pointless questions and reproofs:

> **Gonzalo**   Nay, good, be patient.
> **Boatswain**   When the sea is. Hence! What cares these roarers for the name of king? To cabin! silence! trouble us not.
> **Gonzalo**   Good, yet remember whom thou hast aboard.
> **Boatswain**   None that I more love than myself. You are a councillor; if you can command these elements to silence, and work the peace of the present, we will not hand a rope more. Use your authority.
>
> (I.i.15–22)

The raging elements display a scandalous indifference to 'the name of king' and the 'authority' of his lords. The boatswain's riposte betrays in this moment of crisis the secret that everyone knows: the hierarchy that splits people into masters and servants, and normally keeps the latter in subjection to the former, is a transparent charade, which has no natural foundation or inherent validity. The prospect of the imminent demise of rulers and ruled incites an assertion of equality confirmed by their common mortality, which makes nonsense of rank and the distribution of power and prestige that attends it. The opening scene questions the basis of the roles and relationships of everyone in *The Tempest* from the levelling standpoint of the play's utopian logic.

Looked at from this standpoint, the plot may be summarised thus: Prospero abducts three treacherous voyagers from the heartland of contemporary history in order to bring them to trial at the court of their victim; there he forgoes the exaction of an eye for an eye, treating his prisoners instead to a humane, enlightened judgement, authorised by the island's freedom from the culture that bred the original crime. The confrontation of the all-powerful Prospero with his enemies from the past brings the Machiavellian facts of corruption, duplicity and violence face to face with the means of their transfiguration. Prospero personifies the force required to translate such sordid, demeaning realities into a world stirred by other objectives: the renouncing of dominion and aggression in favour of empathy and concession in a civilised community of peace and plenty.

These priorities become increasingly overt as the play proceeds. They plainly govern the love that binds together Miranda and Ferdinand, the children of the two hostile fathers, and lights the way to a future free not only of the guilt and anger which has scarred the older generation, but from all deprivation and distress. The play's ideals are expansively celebrated in the masque of the spirits, who bless the 'contract of true love' (IV.i.4) with 'a most majestic vision' (IV.i.118) of joyful, unending plenitude:

> **Ceres** Earth's increase, foison plenty,
>   Barns and garners never empty;
>   Vines with clust'ring bunches growing,
>   Plants with goodly burthen bowing;
>   Spring come to you at the farthest
>   In the very end of harvest!
>   Scarcity and want shall shun you,
>   Cares' blessing so is on you.
> > (IV.i.110–17)

The climax of this version of the plot is reached when, with his foes of old at his mercy at last, Prospero swallows his urge to retaliate, founding his preference for compassion and appeasement on his ultimate identity with these 'three men of sin ... 'mongst men / Being most unfit to live' (III.iii.53, 57–8):

> **Ariel** ... if you now beheld them, your affections
>   Would become tender.
> **Prospero** Dost thou think so, spirit?
> **Ariel** Mine would, sir, were I human.
> **Prospero** And mine shall.
>   Hast thou, which art but air, a touch, a feeling,
>   Of their afflictions, and shall not myself,
>   One of their kind, that relish all as sharply
>   Passion as they, be kindlier mov'd than thou art?
>   Though with their high wrongs I am strook to th'quick,
>   Yet, with my nobler reason, 'gainst my fury
>   Do I take part. The rarer action is
>   In virtue than in vengeance.
> > (V.i.18–28)

Thereupon he commands the release of, and absolves, not only Alonso, Antonio and Sebastian, but 'the beast Caliban and his confederates' (IV.i.140), despite their 'foul conspiracy' (IV.i.139) to assassinate him and take over the island. Having given Ariel his last orders before he too becomes free, it remains only for Prospero to keep his promise to renounce the sorcerer's arts ('this rough magic / I here abjure' [V.i.50–1]), and quit his enchanted empire to return to his home in history, there to end his days in the dukedom now restored to him. The play's fulfilment of its aims as a proleptic fable, in which the art of the possible triumphs over the intransigence of the actual, causing it to undergo 'a sea change / Into something rich and strange' (I.ii.401–2), is summed up and sealed by Gonzalo:

> Was Milan thrust from Milan, that his issue
> Should become kings of Naples? O, rejoice
> Beyond a common joy, and set it down
> With gold on lasting pillars: in one voyage
> Did Claribel her husband find at Tunis,
> And Ferdinand, her brother, found a wife
> Where he himself was lost; Prospero, his dukedom
> In a poor isle; and all of us, ourselves,
> When no man was his own.
>
> (V.i.205–13)

But to leave *The Tempest* there would be to withhold the fact that throughout the play, inextricably entwined with its telescoped utopian vision, there is ample evidence of its thraldom to the very forms of oppression it is striving to escape. The creative loyalties of *The Tempest* are divided between a poetic conversion of history to comedy and a sober admission of how tightly our hearts and minds are clutched by inherited perceptions. The utopian impulse gets a rougher ride in *The Tempest* than in the other romances, because the plausibility of that impulse is more severely contested from the start by a less sanguine assessment of its viability.

The double-bind staged and explored by the play is ironically framed in the opening scene of Act II, when Gonzalo's brief flight of utopian fantasy is abruptly grounded by his companions. 'Had I plantation of this isle, my lord,' declares Gonzalo, 'And were the king on't',

> I' th' commonwealth I would, by contraries,
> Execute all things; for no kind of traffic
> Would I admit; no name of magistrate;

> Letters should not be known; riches, poverty,
> And use of service, none; contract, succession,
> Bourn, bound of land, tilth, vineyard, none;
> No use of metal, corn, or wine, or oil
> No occupation, all men idle, all,
> And women too, but innocent and pure;
> No sovereignty –
> **Sebastian**   Yet he would be king on't.
> **Antonio**   The latter end of his commonwealth forgets the beginning.
> (II.i.144, 146, 148–59)

This blank contradiction between hierarchy and community, between authority and liberty, which Sebastian and Antonio expose with such withering sarcasm, is focused throughout *The Tempest* in the figure of Prospero himself. Prospero appears both as the agent of benign transformation, the fount and exemplar of prefigurative values, and as the epitome of the principle obstructing such transformation. He is at once the harbinger of the flourishing state his name invokes and the brooding embodiment of absolute power, who dominates everyone in the play and determines everything that happens to them.

His claim on our sympathy and respect is compromised from the beginning by the irascible, authoritarian attitude he displays towards Miranda ('I, thy schoolmaster' [I.ii.172]). He constantly interrupts his long, expository harangue with bullying commands that she fix her attention on him: 'Obey, and be attentive' (I.ii.38). Prospero contrives and controls his daughter's first encounter with Ferdinand, their courtship and their subsequent betrothal. He supervises their most intimate exchanges like some invisible voyeur, ensuring that every step proceeds according to his plan: '[*Aside*] It goes on, I see, / As my soul prompts it' (I.ii.420–1). Above all, he polices their desire for each other with obsessive, vicious threats:

> If thou dost break her virgin-knot before
> All sanctimonious ceremonies may
> With full and holy rite be minist'red,
> No sweet aspersion shall the heavens let fall
> To make this contract grow; but barren hate,
> Sour-ey'd disdain, and discord shall bestrew
> The union of your bed with weeds so loathly
> That you shall hate it both.
> (IV.i.13–22)[22]

In this respect Prospero answers Ferdinand's judgement of him earlier, when, having been forced to undergo a pointless trial period of menial drudgery, he complains: 'her father's crabbed; / And he's compos'd of harshness' (III.i.8–9). But the external subjection inflicted on the lovers by Prospero is mirrored by their own psychological imprisonment in the language of subjugation. 'The very instant that I saw you,' swears Ferdinand, 'did / My heart fly to your service, there resides, / To make me slave to it' (III.i.64–6). And Miranda protests in turn, 'I'll be your servant, / Whether you will or no' (III.i.84–6). The discourse of conquest, treachery and collusion stains even the brief, showcased exchange between the two, when Prospero reveals them playfully quarrelling over a game of chess:

> **Miranda**   Sweet lord, you play me false.
> **Ferdinand**   No, my dearest love,
>   I would not for the world.
> **Miranda**   Yes, for a score of kingdoms you should wrangle,
>   And I would call it fair play.
>
> (V.i.172–5)

Prospero is the principal link in a chain of domination and subservience which shackles every figure in his programmed universe to him and to each other. The entire cast of Prospero's prescripted play are trapped in narratives of sovereignty and submission, of tyranny and usurpation, which define their actual or imaginary relationships and the way they see themselves. The action of *The Tempest* is dictated from first to last by the original violent seizure of Prospero's dukedom in Milan. Uprooted from history by the storm and tossed onto 'this most desolate isle' (III.iii.80), the perpetrators of that crime import the mentality of their formative millieu intact. Prospero's prompting of Antonio and Sebastian's conspiracy to assassinate Alonso – an action replay of his own former fate – is designed to prove just that. The point is reinforced by the farcical duplication of the conspiracy in the plot of Trinculo, Stephano and Caliban against Prospero himself. Their drunken fantasies and protestations – 'His daughter and I will be king and queen' (III.i.166–7); 'and I, thy Caliban / For aye thy foot licker' (IV.i.218–19) – parody the fictions of subordination ensnaring the minds of their avowed superiors.

It is in Prospero's relationship with Ariel and Caliban that the brutality of his power becomes most graphic. Only if Ariel agrees to endure 'more toil' and 'pains' (I.ii.242) in order to accomplish the plan Prospero could not complete without him, will he be granted the 'liberty' (I.ii.245) he aches for. If he persists in protesting, however:

> I will rend an oak
> And peg thee in his knotty entrails till
> Thou has howl'd away twelve winters.
>   (I.ii.294–6)

The cruelty is even more pronounced in the case of the exploited and tormented creature whom Prospero describes as 'Caliban my slave' (I.ii.308), who 'does make our fire, / Fetch in our wood, and serves in offices / That profit us' (I.ii.311–13). Caliban defiantly refuses to feel grateful or contrite for the consequences of Prospero's attempts to civilise him, which he knows are a cloak for the naked theft of his land and liberty:

> This island's mine by Sycorax my mother,
> Which thou tak'st from me ...
> For I am all the subjects that you have,
> Which first was mine own king;
>   (I.ii.331–2; 341–2)

Dominion demands and creates servitude in order to define and legitimate itself. The injustice of Caliban's being caught in this lethal logic and made 'subject to a tyrant' (III.ii.42), who 'hath cheated [him] of this island' (III.ii.44) and who plagues him with excruciating pains, is never brought home more movingly than when we glimpse the sad, elusive longings concealed in his heart:

> Be not afeard, the isle is full of noises,
> Sounds, and sweet airs, that give delight and hurt not.
> Sometimes a thousand twangling instruments
> Will hum about mine ears; and sometimes voices,
> That if I then had wak'd after long sleep,
> Will make me sleep again, and then in dreaming,
> The clouds methought would open, and show riches
> Ready to drop upon me, that when I wak'd
> I cried to dream again.
>   (III.ii.135–43)

This speech, as much as any in the play, gives us the measure of Prospero's despotism, the price paid in mental and physical suffering for his omnipotence. It discloses the cost of the transfiguring magic that bends the action towards its closure in forgiveness, restitution and renewal.[23]

As both the incarnation of the problem and the source of its solution, Prospero contains the play's discovery that the potential for equality and community cannot be divorced from the structures of domination in which it is rooted. *The Tempest* obliges us to wrestle with the fact that the means of emancipation from our narratives of oppression are contaminated by the forms of power and perception which they are meant to dismantle. In this play Shakespeare acknowledges that the art of the possible is indivisible from the nightmare of history which provokes and constrains its endeavours.

Thus *The Tempest* problematises the nature of its own art and the power of the dramatist himself. It opens up in poetic and theatrical terms issues which had to wait until the present century to be theoretically addressed in this celebrated passage from Walter Benjamin's 'Theses on the Philosophy of History':

> Whoever has emerged victorious participates to this day in the triumphal procession in which the present rulers step over those who are lying prostrate. According to traditional practice, the spoils are carried along in the procession. They are called cultural treasures, and a historical materialist views them with cautious detachment. For without exception the cultural treasures he surveys have an origin which he cannot contemplate without horror. They owe their existence not only to the efforts of the great minds and talents who have created them, but also to the anonymous toil of their contemporaries. There is no document of civilisation which is not at the same time a document of barbarism.[24]

The character of Prospero includes, as is generally accepted, a portrait of the artist as dramatist within the play. Prospero is the omniscient creator of the drama in which he participates, contriving and controlling everything from the tempest of the title to the audience's final response. His most famous speech openly solicits this identification: 'Our revels now are ended. These our actors / (As I foretold you) were all spirits, and / Are melted into air' (IV.i.148–50). At the same time it coaxes the audience yet again to tease out the parallels and contradictions between 'this insubstantial pageant faded' (IV.i.155) and the actualities it mirrors and transmutes. In his metadramatic role as a medium through which the play reflects upon itself, Prospero objectifies the intrinsic complicities of *The Tempest*. He enshrines the play's collusion with the factual oppression which it presupposes, and the authoritarian mentality which it exemplifies. For however complex, self-aware and open-ended the play's vision seeks to be, it cannot avoid inflicting this construction on reality at the expense of all the other versions it excludes.

The Tempest owns up to its involuntary entanglement in barbarity and repression. It knows that every act of representation is also, inescapably, an act of complicity and an act of violence. And with its closing words the play springs on us the awkward question of our own incriminating share in Prospero's creation. In the Epilogue the deviser of the play we have just seen deliberately casts the audience in the role he has relinquished. He bequeaths us the ambivalent authority and magical imaginative power to judge and complete *The Tempest* ourselves:

> Let me not,
> Since I have my dukedom got,
> And pardon'd the deceiver, dwell
> In this bare island by your spell,
> But release me from my bands
> With the help of your good hands.
> Gentle breath of yours my sails
> Must fill, or else my project fails,
> Which was to please. Now I want
> Spirits to enforce, art to enchant,
> And my ending is despair,
> Unless I be reliev'd by prayer,
> Which pierces so, that it assaults
> Mercy itself, and frees all faults.
> As you from crimes would pardon'd be,
> Let your indulgence set me free. [*Exit.*]
>   (Epil.5–20)

Shakespeare's last masterpiece is designed to ensure that we keep the representation and the reality, and the relations between them, under constant surveillance. It urges us to question not only the authority of the author, but also the assumptions that shape our response to his work. *The Tempest* cautions us not to lose sight of the parts played by Shakespeare and ourselves in cultures wedded to violence and exploitation, even as we strive to restore and activate the progressive potential of his drama in our time. It reminds us that the hierarchical principle of social organisation, whose validity Shakespeare's drama so forcefully disputes, remains arrogantly entrenched in our daily lives, and that the task of delivering our kind into an as yet utopian world, undisfigured by class-divisions or by racial and sexual injustice, remains formidable.

From Kiernan Ryan, *Shakespeare*, 3rd edn (London, 2001), pp.106–35.

NOTES

[Kiernan Ryan's Marxist-influenced account of Shakespeare's major comedies and 'romances' attacks both conventional and 'radical' critics for misrepresenting these plays as 'reactionary fables' which, however disruptive of social norms they may seem, always serve to shore up the status quo. His counter-argument contends that the plays exploit the imaginative latitude of their romance origins in order to 'dramatise the surrender of the prevailing to the possible, the triumph of benevolent human desires over the harsh constraints of historical actuality'. Ultimately, Ryan locates the revolutionary potential of these plays in the various 'defamiliarising devices' they use to remind us of the historicity, and hence provisionality, of our current modes of living, and thereby awaken a desire for change. The text that appears here, with the author's permission, represents a shortened version of the original chapter. Ed.]

1. C. L. Barber, *Shakespeare's Festive Comedy* (Princeton, NJ, 1959), p. 245.

2. Northrop Frye, *A Natural Perspective* (New York, 1965), pp. 75, 130, 119, 121, 75, 104.

3. Barber, *Shakespeare's Festive Comedy*, p. 139. Annabel Patterson supplies a salutary antidote to Barber and Frye in her *Shakespeare and the Popular Voice* (Oxford, 1989), ch. 3: 'Bottom's up: festive theory'.

4. Elliot Krieger, *A Marxist Study of Shakespeare's Comedies* (London, 1979), pp. 5–6. *A Midsummer Night's Dream* receives similar treatment from James H. Kavanagh's essay 'Shakespeare in ideology', in *Alternative Shakespeares*, ed. John Drakakis (London and New York, 1985), pp. 152–6.

5. Leonard Tennenhouse, *Power on Display: The Politics of Shakespeare's Genres* (New York and London, 1986), pp. 44, 62, 74, 185, 183, 171.

6. Richard Wilson ploughs the same Foucauldian furrow as Tennenhouse, though with far more elegance and wit, in *Will Power: Essays on Shakespearean Authority* (Hemel Hempstead, 1993), ch. 5: 'The quality of mercy: discipline and punishment in Shakespearean comedy' and ch. 6: 'Observations on English bodies: licensing maternity in Shakespeare's late plays'.

7. For a useful selection of representative recent criticism on the comedies, see Gary Waller (ed.), *Shakespeare's Comedies* (London and New York, 1991).

8. H. B. Charlton, *Shakespearian Comedy* (London, 1938), pp. 277–8.

9. Walter Cohen, *Drama of a Nation: Public Theater in Renaissance England and Spain* (Ithaca, NY, 1985), p. 391.

10. Tom Moylan, *Demand the Impossible* (New York and London, 1986), p. 31 (Moylan's italics).

11. Ibid., p. 35.

12. The contrast between this conception of romance and the religiose assumptions governing more traditional studies of Shakespeare's last plays could scarcely be more pronounced. See especially E. M. W. Tillyard, *Shakespeare's Last Plays* (London, 1938); G. Wilson Knight, *The Crown of Life: Essays in Interpretation of Shakespeare's Final Plays* (London, 1947); and Derek A. Traversi, *Shakespeare: The Last Phase* (London, 1954). The range of conventional criticism on the romances can also be sampled in three collections of essays: John Russell Brown and Bernard Harris (eds), *Later Shakespeare* (London, 1966); Richard Tobias and P. G. Zolbrod (eds), *Shakespeare's Late Plays* (Athens, OH, 1974); and C. M. Kay and H. E. Jacobs (eds), *Shakespeare's Romances Reconsidered* (Lincoln, NE, 1978). Useful surveys of previous criticism on the romances are furnished by Philip Edwards, 'Shakespeare's romances: 1900–1957', *Shakespeare Survey*, 11 (1958), 1–18; F. D. Hoeniger, 'Shakespeare's romances since 1958: a retrospect', *Shakespeare Survey*, 29 (1976), 1–10; and Norman Sanders, 'An overview of critical approaches to the romances', in *Shakespeare's Romances Reconsidered*, ed. Kay and Jacobs, pp. 1–10.

13. Frye, *A Natural Perspective*, p. 146.

14. Different angles on the use of language in Shakespearean comedy and romance can be found in Howard Felperin, ' "Tongue-tied our queen?": the deconstruction of presence in *The Winter's Tale*', in *Shakespeare and the Question of Theory*, ed. Patricia Parker and Geoffrey Hartman (New York and London, 1985), pp. 3–18; Malcolm Evans, 'Deconstructing Shakespeare's comedies', in *Alternative Shakespeares*, ed. Drakakis, pp. 67–94, and *Signifying Nothing: Truth's True Contents in Shakespeare's Text*, 2nd edn (Hemel Hempstead, 1989), pp. 50–68, 145–64; Katharine Eisaman Maus, 'Transfer of title in *Love's Labor's Lost*: language, individualism, gender', in *Shakespeare Left and Right*, ed. Ivo Kamps (New York and London, 1991), pp. 205–23; and Anne Barton, 'Leontes and the spider: language and speaker in Shakespeare's last plays', in her *Essays, Mainly Shakespearean* (Cambridge, 1994), pp. 161–81.

15. Stephen Orgel (ed.), *The Tempest* (Oxford, 1987), p. 10.

16. Frank Kermode (ed.), *The Tempest* (London, 1954), p. lxxxiii.

17. Quoted by Kermode, ibid., p. lxxxiv.

18. D. J. Palmer (ed.), *Shakespeare: The Tempest: A Selection of Critical Essays*, revised edn (London, 1991).

19. Francis Barker and Peter Hulme, 'Nymphs and reapers heavily vanish: the discursive con-texts of *The Tempest*', in *Alternative Shakespeares*, ed. Drakakis, p. 204.

20. Paul Brown, ' "This thing of darkness I acknowledge mine": *The Tempest* and the discourse of colonialism', in *Political Shakespeare: Essays in Cultural Materialism*, ed. Jonathan Dollimore and Alan Sinfield, 2nd edn (Manchester, 1994), pp. 48–71. There is now a formidable body of secondary literature devoted to political readings of the play. See in particular: Terence Hawkes, *That Shakespeherian Rag: Essays on a Critical Process* (London and New York, 1986), pp. 1–26; Thomas Cartelli, 'Prospero in Africa: *The Tempest* as colonialist text and pretext', in *Shakespeare Reproduced*, ed. Howard and O'Connor, pp. 99–115; Stephen Greenblatt, 'Martial law in the land of Cockaigne', in *Shakespearean Negotiations*, pp. 129–63; Annabel Patterson, ' "Thought is free": *The Tempest*', in *Shakespeare and the Popular Voice*, pp. 154–62; Deborah Willis, 'Shakespeare's *Tempest* and the discourse of colonialism', *Studies in English Literature 1500–1900*, 29 (1989), 277–89; Howard Felperin, *The Uses of the Canon: Elizabethan Literature and Contemporary Theory* (Oxford, 1990), ch. 2: 'Romance and romanticism' and ch. 9: '*The Tempest* in our time'; and John Gillies, *Shakespeare and the Geography of Difference* (Cambridge, 1994), pp. 140–55.

21. A recent exception is David Norbrook's fine essay ' "What cares these roarers for the name of king?": language and utopia in *The Tempest*', in *The Politics of Tragicomedy: Shakespeare and After*, ed. Gordon McMullan and Jonathan Hope (London and New York, 1992), pp. 21–54.

22. For a full psychological profile of Prospero as patriarch and discussions of gender and power in the play, see David Sundelson, 'So rare a wonder'd father: Prospero's *Tempest*', in *Representing Shakespeare: New Psychoanalytic Essays*, ed. Murray Schwartz and Coppélia Kahn (Baltimore, MD, 1980), pp. 33–53; Coppélia Kahn, 'The providential tempest and the Shakespearean family', ibid., pp. 217–43; Lorie Jerrell Leininger, 'The Miranda trap: sexism and racism in Shakespeare's *Tempest*', in *The Woman's Part: Feminist Criticism of Shakespeare*, ed. Carolyn Ruth Swift Lenz, Gayle Greene and Carol Thomas Neely (Urbana, IL, and London, 1980), pp. 285–94; and Stephen Orgel, 'Prospero's wife', in *Rewriting the Renaissance: The Discourses of Sexual*

Difference in Early Modern Europe, ed. Margaret W. Ferguson, Maureen Quilligan and Nancy J. Vickers (Chicago and London, 1986), pp. 50–64.

23. For further reflections on Caliban, see Peter Hulme, 'Prospero and Caliban', in his *Colonial Encounters: Europe and the Native Caribbean, 1492–1797* (London and New York, 1986), pp. 89–134; Stephen Orgel, 'Shakespeare and the cannibals', in *Cannibals, Witches and Divorce: Estranging the Renaissance*, ed. Marjorie Garber (London, 1987), pp. 40–66; and Alden T. Vaughan and Virginia Vaughan, *Shakespeare's Caliban: A Cultural History* (Cambridge, 1991).

24. Walter Benjamin, *Illuminations*, trans. Harry Zohn (London, 1970), p. 258.

2

Pericles and the Pox

MARGARET HEALY

Louis MacNeice's poem *Autolycus* (1944–7) gives aptly magical expression to the dominant apprehension of Shakespeare's late plays in our century. *Autolycus* evokes a picture of the Bard at the sunset of his career mysteriously moving away from the 'taut plots and complex characters' of the major tragedies, conjuring instead 'tapestried romances … / With rainbow names and handfuls of sea-spray', and from them turning out 'happy Ever-afters' (ll. 3–6). MacNeice's words capture a certain ambivalence towards this Shakespearean sea change: indeed, the romances, with their emphasis on the production of wonder, their tendency towards straggling plots and emblematic representation, and their preponderance of 'childish horrors' and 'old gags' (*Autolycus* ll. 14, 15), are often experienced as charming but enigmatic and not altogether satisfying puzzles – even as regressive aberrations. The latter is most true of the 'unwanted child' *Pericles*, a play of suspect parentage, excluded from the First Folio, and only available to us through what most editors agree is a particularly bastardised quarto and its numerous offspring (it was printed six times to 1635, including twice in one year, 1609 – an unusual occurrence).[1]

Frequently vilified and rarely performed today, *Pericles* has been the focus of considerable bewilderment: why, critics repeatedly ponder, was this play so acclaimed and popular in the Jacobean age when it has proven so relatively unappealing in ours?[2] The title page of the first quarto of 1609 describes it as 'The Late, and much admired Play … As it hath been divers and sundry times acted by his Majesties Servants, at the Globe'; and contemporary references suggest that it was a huge box-office success in London playhouses, a favourite for private house production, and for court performance, too.³ It was, moreover, one of two Shakespearean plays – the other being *King Lear* – put on by a professional company with recusant sympathies (Sir Richard Cholmeley's Players), which toured Yorkshire in 1609.⁴

When *Pericles* was performed by the RSC in 1990, however, one theatre critic, dismissing the play 'as just a far-fetched fairy tale', could only explain its early seventeenth-century appeal in the following derogatory terms:

> It is fanciful to think that business had been flat at the Globe, and Burbage suggested that something with more sex and violence would pull audiences in. 'Incest and brothels will,' he might have said, 'do the box-office a power of good.'⁵

Steven Mullaney reached much the same conclusion in his important book, *The Place of the Stage*. Contesting the popular thesis that this is an experimental play which evolved to suit the new context of the Blackfriars theatre, Mullaney argues that *Pericles* rather 'represents a radical effort to dissociate the popular stage from its cultural contexts', a shift into 'pure' aestheticism, and that its subsequent literary fortunes testify to 'the limits of any work that seeks to obscure or escape its historical conditions of possibility'.⁶ For Mullaney then, this was an experiment of a different kind which went badly wrong. For him, *Pericles* is unalloyed aestheticism pandering to the tastes of emergent liberal humanism – any quest for dissonant voices will get short shrift here.

Sandra Billington's *Mock Kings in Medieval and Renaissance Drama* obliquely reinforces this perspective. In her view the character of Pericles represents kingly perfection; he is 'an ideal courtly lord and effective prince, whose virtue does not waver despite the effects of the plot on it'. She finds *Pericles* an 'exception' in the world of plays from this period dominated by depictions of dubious and tyrannical monarchs, possibly, she suspects, because 'the devil has the most dramatic plots'.⁷ Frances Yates and Glynne Wickham, and more recently Jonathan Goldberg and David Bergeron, also forestall a more questioning reading of the play when they argue that *Pericles* contains a thinly veiled likeness to James VI and I in the figure of its hero.⁸ Indeed the majority of commentators are admiring of 'patient' king Pericles and if they read James, his family, and the events of his reign into the play, it is almost inevitably viewed as a eulogy to James and a celebration of his rule.[9] Such readings appear to be endorsed by the fact that the text of *Pericles* resonates with James's own aphorisms in his voluminous writings about kingship, a prime example from the beginning of the play being its hero's utterance, 'kings are earth's gods' (i.146) – arguably the monarch's favourite tenet. Thus, once again, Shakespearean drama is construed as shoring up royal absolutism. This play's undisputed 'happy ending' bears witness to this: the royal marriage which allies two kingdoms is understood as a particularly fortuitous and positive outcome, the topical analogy being the projected peaceful Union of England and Scotland through James's mediation. The latter was a highly topical matter in 1607, and one which had achieved extravagant courtly representation in January of that year in *The Lord Hay's Masque* to celebrate the betrothal of a Scottish favourite and the daughter of an English lord. The masque opens with a fulsome address to 'Gracious James, King of Great Britain':

> O then, great Monarch, with how wise a care
> Do you these bloods divided mix in one,
> And with like consanguinities prepare
> The high and everliving Union
>   'Tween Scots and English. Who can wonder then
>   If he that marries kingdoms, marries men.[10]

The 'marriage' of kingdoms was certainly a subject close to the king's heart throughout this decade.

The English–Scottish 'marriage' was not, however, the only one preoccupying James and exercising his patience c.1606–7 when *Pericles* was probably written. The king was simultaneously engaged in plans to ally Britain with Spain, and this projected 'marriage', for the majority of his subjects, was undoubtedly more pressing and more controversial. In fact, 'the Spanish Match' was unlikely to have won widespread public approval: James's repeated attempts to marry his son Henry to the Spanish Infanta and his daughter Elizabeth to the Duke of Savoy would hardly have been construed by the bulk of the populace (for whom Spain was the epitome of the Antichrist) as desirable, or as the stuff of happy endings and fairy-tale romance.[11] Building on this perspective, this chapter will argue that *Pericles'* ending, in particular the betrothal of Marina to Lysimachus, is far from suggestive of uncomplicated 'happy Ever-afters', and that analysis of this play's representations of early modern syphilis (the Pox), and its medico-moral politics, provides new contexts and substantial support for more dissonant readings.

My focus will be on the last two acts of *Pericles*, and in particular on the brothel scenes where discussion of the Pox and its consequences are rife and nauseatingly explicit. I should point out that there are no references to syphilis or its consequences in either of the play's two reputed sources: John Gower's *Confessio Amantis* (Book 8) and Lawrence Twine's *The Patterne of Painfull Adventures* (a translation of the 153rd story of the *Gesta Romanorum*). Interestingly, too, George Wilkins' novel of the play, *The Painfull Adventures of Pericles Prince of Tyre* (1608), erases all references to the Pox, recuperates Lysimachus as a healthful and virtuous governor, and concludes by assuring its readers of the fruitfulness and happiness of this union.[12]

I will begin, though, by reminding you where we are at this stage in the action. The first three Acts of *Pericles* portray its hero being tossed impotently around the exotic world of the eastern Mediterranean, a prey to forces greater than himself, yet – in the manner of romance – managing to fall in love, marry and beget a child, Marina, in the process. Life is cruel but virtue flourishes in hardship: Marina, for all intents and purposes an orphan, grows up to be a paragon princess – beautiful, talented and saintly. Her tragic destiny, however, catches up with her, and her wicked guardian Dionyzia threatens her with murder at the hands of a servant just at the point she is mourning the death of her beloved nurse. Marina's suffering seems unremitting; she escapes murder through being captured by pirates, only to be sold by them to a brothel and to a fate – in her opinion – worse than violent and sudden death ('Alack that Leonine was so slack, so slow. / He should have struck, not spoke' [xvi.61–2]).

Meanwhile the audience is introduced to Pander, Bawd and Bolt bewailing the poor state of their trade, caused not through a lack of customers ('gallants'), but rather through the 'pitifully sodden' condition of their prostitute wares (xvi.18). The comic potential of this scene is undermined by the tragic import of the discussion, which would not have been lost on a Jacobean audience. For early modern playgoers child prostitution and syphilis were very real and allied diseases. The audience learns how the Pox is the inevitable fate of the Bawd's poor 'bastards', but in this subterranean world of inverted moral values the sympathy expressed is solely for an adult lecher (the 'poor Transylvanian' [xvi.20–1]) who has lain with a 'little baggage' – an exhausted commodity grown 'rotten' with 'continual action' (xvi.8–9). Is this to be the Princess Marina's fate?

Installed in the Mytilene brothel Marina bewails her plight, only to be consoled by Bawd with the knowledge that she will 'taste gentlemen of all fashions' – a far from edifying prospect (xvi.75). Whilst Boult, Bawd and Pander banter about the Spaniard's mouth watering at Marina's description, at Monsieur Veroles (the French word for syphilis) cowering 'i' the hams' (xvi.101) – in other words Jacobean society's foppish foreigner stereotypes of the diseased – it is native 'gentlemen' and 'the governor of this country' (xix.58) who actually arrive at the brothel to threaten Marina's well-being. One by one Jacobean society's comforting stereotypes of the disease's victims and polluters are being undermined, 'safe boundaries' for the representation of the Pox are being transgressed: young children and an innocent woman are at risk from 'gentlemen' in this murky play world.[13]

But Marina's eloquent powers of persuasion prove more than a match for Mytilene's lecherous gentlemen, whose wayward morals she reforms in the very brothel.[14] The dramatic climax of the brothel scenes is undoubtedly the arrival and conversion of none other than the 'Lord Lysimachus', governor of Mytilene. Bawd announces that there's no way to be 'rid on't' (Marina's maidenhead) but, as she puts it,

> by the way to the pox.
> *Enter Lysimachus, disguised*
> Here comes the Lord Lysimachus disguised.
> (xix.23–5)

Whilst it is never directly stated or implied by any of the characters that Lysimachus has the Pox, the language of the scene conspires to sow strong seeds of suspicion that he does. The proximity of the words 'pox' to 'it' (Marina's virginity) and the foregrounding of Lysimachus' disguise – disguise being intimately associated in early modern discourse with the Pox, which was also known as the great 'masquerader', the 'secret' disease – begin the process.[15] Lysimachus requests Boult find him some 'wholesome iniquity' (xix.32) with which to do 'the deed of darkness' (xix.37). He hides his dishonourable intentions in a cloak of euphemistic language, but the audience is not to be hoodwinked, for Bawd replies 'Your honour knows what 'tis to say well enough' (xix.39). Furthermore the brothel's mistress is 'bound' (xix.60), as she says, to this governor; by implication Lysimachus is a regular customer, all too familiar with the iniquitous business in hand. This established, Bawd's words serve to highlight Lysimachus' supreme status in Mytilene society; finally she declares 'Come, we will leave his honour and hers together' (xix.69). There is, of course, a pun on 'honour' here. Marina later appropriates Bawd's terms and upbraids Lysimachus with them. She challenges:

> And do you know this house to be a place
> Of such resort and will come into it?
> I hear say you're of honourable blood,
> And are the governor of this whole province.
> (xix.81–4)

Thus Lysimachus' honour is thrown seriously into question, and he increasingly resembles one of the hypocritical types, like Iniquity and Infidelity, who would have been familiar to many amongst the original audiences as stock vices from the morality plays. Tail between legs, the governor leaves the brothel claiming that Marina's speech has altered his 'corrupted mind' (xix.128). Lysimachus' mask may have been temporarily lifted, his vice exposed, but he appears to go quite unpunished for his misdeeds; indeed, he even seems to be rewarded, for Marina's princely father eventually betroths her to this nobleman of dubious honour and health.

But is this not taking the stuff of romance, emerging from a make-believe world, rather too seriously? What may seem just good bawdy and fun to a modern audience, however, is fraught with serious implications for contemporary playgoers familiar with other stage representations of fornication and disease.[16] This play, it has been repeatedly observed, returns to an emblematic form of theatre which invites spectators to search critically for understanding. The audience witnesses a series of emblematic tableaux, is called upon to make sense of the wooing knights' 'devices' on their shields, and listens to riddles, mottoes and endless aphorisms, especially ones about the abusive operations of power and kingship. Frequently there is a disparity between the morals the characters tritely recite and the action the audience observes on the stage. Thus sham morality, hypocrisy, is repeatedly exposed. Through these theatrical structures the audience is encouraged to observe the action with a heightened sceptical consciousness, and to be especially alert to emblematic representations.

Pericles is particularly partial to trotting out mottoes and adages about kingship (much like King James himself), but there is one that he omits which educated Jacobean playgoers may well have been thinking about when witnessing Pericles' rather casual consignment of his daughter to Lysimachus' care. As Gower relates, Lysimachus entertains the king with 'pageantry', 'feats', 'shows', 'minstrelsy and pretty din', which so impresses Pericles that he rewards the governor of Mytilene with a wife – his daughter, the heir to the throne of Tyre (xxii.6–12). It is my contention that many among the original audiences of *Pericles* would have responded with horror to this marriage outcome, to this 'unequal match', because of their familiarity with the horrors of contracting syphilis and the intense and prolonged suffering associated with the most dreaded chronic disease of the Renaissance. Those with at least a grammar-school education would have been familiar, too, with widely disseminated Erasmian views on such hazardous 'matches', and some spectators would undoubtedly have seen a popular emblem which illustrated a 'Nupta contagioso' (see Figure 1).

This emblem first appeared in a collection by Andrea Alciato (*Emblemata*) published in 1550; it was subsequently adapted, translated and distributed widely throughout Europe. It depicts a king on a dais overseeing a man and woman being bound together on the floor with a rope. As the accompanying poem describes, this is a savage deed comparable to that committed by a cruel Etruscan king who was in the habit of punishing his victims by tying them to a corpse. It reveals that for a dowry this king has purchased a son-in-law seared by the Gallic scab, apparent in the dreaded sore on his face: through self-interest he has committed his daughter to a living death, a 'Nupta contagioso'. This horrific emblem about the Pox was undoubtedly influenced by an Erasmian colloquy published in 1529 entitled *The Unequal Match* or *A Marriage in Name Only*, which was among the dramatic dialogues that English pedagogues recommended all boys should read.[17] Erasmus' colloquies were a tool to teach schoolboys colloquial Latin but they were also intended, in Erasmus' own words, to impress on 'young people ... [the] safeguarding of their chastity'.[18]

The two participants in *The Unequal Match*, Gabriel and Petronius, discuss, with horror, how a beautiful, talented girl with winning manners has just been married off by her father to a rotting corpse – unmistakably a chronic syphilitic – because of his title. This wayward nobleman's dicing, drinking, lies and whoring

204   ANDREÆ ALCIATI

Nupta contagioso.

EMBLEMA CXCVII.

Dii *meliora piis, Mezenti, cur age sic me*
  Compellas ? emptus quòd tibi dote gener;
Gallica quem scabies, dira & mentagra perurit:
  Hoc est quidnam aliud, dic mihi saue pater,
Corpora corporibus quàm iungere mortua viuis,
  Efferáqɜ Etrusci facta nouare ducis?

Cupref-

Figure 1   *Nupta contagioso*, from Andrea Alciato's *Emblemata*, 1608.
By courtesy of Edinburgh University Library.

have apparently earned him this 'living death' which will now be inflicted upon his young wife. Gabriel's words are hard-hitting. He exclaims:

> But this outrage – than which you could find nothing more bar- barous, more cruel, more unrighteous – is even a laughing matter with the governing class nowadays, despite the fact that those born to rule ought to have as robust health as possible. And in fact, the condition of the body has its effect on mental power. Undeniably this disease usually depletes whatever brains a man has. So it comes about that rulers of states may be men who are healthy neither in body nor mind. (p. 407)

This colloquy thus functions as a powerful rebuke to parental, and especially princely parental, selfishness, greed and folly.

Pericles, I wish to argue, is a satirical play with the same cau- tionary message as *The Unequal Match*. The potential polluter of a beautiful young woman is a luxurious gentleman who abuses the privileges that his nobility favours him with. Through marriage, an innocent young woman will be placed at his disposal by the very person who should most seek to protect her – her father. Marina's response to the intended match is articulate silence. It is informative to read this outcome in relation to Petronius' condemnation of the 'unequal match' in Erasmus' dialogue: 'Enemies scarcely do this to girls captured in war, pirates to those they kidnap; and yet parents do it to an only daughter, and there's no police official with power to stop them!' (p. 408). Marina has escaped rape and murder at the hands of her enemies, has survived her passage with her pirate- captors intact, and then just when the audience is relaxing, thinking her safely delivered to the protection of her family, her father subjects her to an 'unequal match'. As Gabriel declares in the dialogue, such dubious matches reflect badly on the parents and have important implications for the commonwealth and its govern- ment: '[a]s private individuals, they're disloyal to their family; as citizens, to the state' (p. 408). Irresponsible father-rulers are putting both the health of their offspring and the state in jeopardy through this 'madness'.

The medico-moral politics of *Pericles* depend to some extent on the audience's experience of this tragic and widespread disease of the Renaissance – its unsightly, disfiguring, disabling and painful progress – and on their knowledge of popular humanist texts surrounding it. The Pox was in fact the most widely written-about disease in the Renaissance. These contexts are clearly not readily available to modern audiences and consequently the potential serious import and impact of *Pericles'* late scenes have been considerably watered down, even erased.

However, yet further Renaissance contexts require amplification before modern readers can appreciate the range and density of meanings and resonances circulating, often in partially submerged form, in this richly layered play. Whilst reforming intellectuals like Erasmus worried and wrote about the savage effects of this disease and called for preventive health measures to combat it, they were also not averse to utilising knowledge about its painful and horrific effects for propaganda purposes. Intent on foregrounding what he viewed as the corruption and decay of the Catholic Church, Erasmus began to disperse images of syphilitic priests throughout his writings. His message was that the clergy had grown so corrupt their fornication was spreading the new disease among them, to their innocent victims, and throughout the globe. Lutheran reformers seized upon Erasmus' powerful metaphor of church corruption, and English polemicists like John Bale, John Foxe, Lewis Wager and William Turner quickly appropriated the emblematic syphilitic body for the Protestant cause.

The mid sixteenth-century Edwardian stage displayed spotted, decaying and disabled 'Pocky' bodies lamenting their disease and proclaiming it to be the consequence of fornication encouraged by Catholic vices such as Infidelity and Iniquity, who inevitably disguise their corruption and hypocrisy under their religious vestments. The early Protestant dramatists clearly recognised and exploited the compelling theatrical value, the tantalising erotic and comic possibilities, of sin: 'godly myrth' was extremely bawdy. As John King has argued, in the Protestant interlude fornication tends to become 'a composite symbol for the seven deadly sins'.[19] He cites as the main reason for this John Bale's development and popularisation for the English context of the Lutheran identification of the Whore of Babylon of Revelation with the Church of Rome: dramatic bawdry thus came to symbolise 'the spiritual fornication' of Roman ritualism.

When, therefore, the audience witnessed the seduction and fall of young virgins in the Protestant interludes, they were simultaneously engaging with the plays' allegorical levels of meaning, in which, according to the Protestant reformers' version of history, the True, undefiled Church was sullied and temporarily superseded by the corrupt False Church of Antichrist. Naturally the harlot Church,

like her lascivious priests, had a special imagined affinity with vene-
real disease. In his propaganda pamphlet, provocatively entitled
*A New Booke of Spirituall Physik for Dyverse Diseases of the
Nobilitie and Gentlemen of Englande* (1555), the Marian exile
William Turner reconstrues the origins of the 'pokkes' in a 'noble
hore' of Italy: 'Ther was a certeyne hore in Italy, which had a peril-
lus disease called false religion ... all the kynges and nobilitie of the
earth ... they committed fornication wyth her ... and caught the
Romishe pokkes'.[20]

This symbolism and allegorising surrounding the Pox, fornication
and the Romish church was alive and flourishing in the first decade
of the seventeenth century. Thomas Dekker's play *The Whore of
Babylon*, staged by Prince Henry's Men probably about a year
before the first production of *Pericles*, bears strong witness to this.
Indeed *The Whore of Babylon* provides an important additional
context to illuminate some of the fading emblematic resonances in
Pericles. As the preface to the text explains, *The Whore of Babylon*
is designed to lay bare the 'blody stratagems, of that Purple whore
of Roome' in the reign of Elizabeth I.[21] However, its real thrust was
undoubtedly to persuade Jacobean spectators that the iniquitous
forces of Antichrist continued to pose a substantial threat to
England and the Reformed Church, and to encourage a more militant stance against Rome. It features the lustful harlot the Empresse
of Babylon, alias Rome, strumpet to her slaves, the kings of Spain,
France and the Holy Roman Empire, and her Cardinal entourage.
She is also served by her Bawd, Falsehood, who wears the garb of
Truth (a gown of sanctity) but whose hypocrisy is evidenced by her
red pimples – she, like her mistress, as Plain Dealing informs us,
has a bad case of the Pox. Babylon's design is none other than to
'swallow up the kingdome of Faiery' (IV.iii.37), whose queen is
Titania (Elizabeth I), served by spotless Truth and her fairy lords.

The Empress's first stratagem is to send her kings off to woo
Titania / Elizabeth. When they arrive at her court Titania asks them
if they've come to 'strike off a poore maiden-head' (I.ii.85), that is
to rape her. The sexual manoeuvres and language of this play have
the political meanings common to sixteenth-century Protestant discourse: raping a virgin signified a state adhering to the Reformed,
true faith being engulfed forcibly by a Romish power. Rome is a
rapist as well as a harlot in Protestant polemics. However, the kings
reassure Titania that marriage rather than ravishment is their aim,
but it does not matter which of the three Titania chooses because

their desire is simply to please the Empress by wedding the forces of Babylon to those of Fairyland. Thankfully, Titania is not fooled by this suspect marriage proposal. She declares (and I think these words will throw a very important light on the marriage proposal in *Pericles*):

> When kingdoms marrie, heaven it selfe stands by
> To give the bride: Princes in tying such bands,
> Should use a thousand heads, ten thousand hands:
> For that one Acte gives like an enginous wheele
> Motion to all.
>
> (I.ii.162–6)

The marriage alliance rejected, Babylon and her followers turn grisly: the Spanish Armada is sent into action and a plot is hatched to murder Titania with the aid of recusant spies. At the close of the play the forces of Truth triumph but, importantly, Babylon is not eradicated, just temporarily subdued: the Poxy threat persists.

Many among the original London audiences would probably have shared Dekker's perspective on the threat posed by Popishness and Spanish ambitions; and the Shakespearean play, as represented by the virtually identical 1609 quartos, is undoubtedly engaging in a more subtle way with the same concerns. This is how Pericles addresses Marina in the recognition scene:

> Prithee speak.
> Falseness cannot come from thee, for thou look'st
> Modest as justice, and thou seem'st a palace
> For the crowned truth to dwell in.
>
> (xxi.108–11)

Pericles' words identify his daughter as an embodiment of Truth: Truth which the audience has observed being captured by a pirate with the same name, Valdes, as one of the Spanish Armada captains in *The Whore of Babylon*; whom they have seen threatened with but fending off rape; and who is about to be betrothed to a probably Poxy spouse by her negligent father. Pericles certainly does not use 'a thousand heads' in choosing his son-in-law.

All of this has important negative implications for how we read the character of Pericles in the Jacobean context. Pericles is a prince who is seldom in his own state (Tyre is a troubled kingdom 'without a head' [viii.34]);[22] who flees from danger rather than confronting it; who readily commits his young daughter to the care of

rather dubious others; whose wallowing in self-pity comes danger-
ously close to incurring a charge of effeminacy ('thou art a man,
and I / Have suffered like a girl' [xxi.125–6]); and who, through be-
trothing Marina to a potentially diseased son-in-law, is putting both
her health and his future princely heirs' at stake. He may, unwittingly, through neglect and poor government, be introducing 'corruption' into the virgin body of his daughter and his kingdom.

Indeed, on the latter points King James himself had been nothing
if not voluble in his treatise of advice to his son Henry, *Basilikon
Doron* (1599), which specifically warns about the dangers of bodily
pollution:

> First of all consider, that Mariage is the greatest earthly felicitie or
> miserie ... By your preparation yee must keepe your bodie cleane and
> unpolluted, till yee give it to your wife ... For how can ye justly crave
> to bee joyned with a pure virgine, if your bodie be polluted? Why
> should the one halfe bee cleane, and the other defiled?[23]

The *Basilikon Doron*'s constructions resonate with Erasmian
maxims, and the above illustration suggests that James may well
have been familiar with one of the numerous reproductions of
Alciato's emblem. The treatise proceeds to rail against lust and fornication, reminding the young prince that the right end of sexual
appetite is 'procreation of children', and stressing monarchical duty:
'Especially a King must tymously Marie for the weale of his people
... in a King that were a double fault, as well against his owne
weale, as against the weale of his people [to] ... Marie one of
knowne evill conditions' (p. 35). Crucially, there then follows a
protracted discussion about religion, marriage and monarchy, in
which James advises Henry, 'I would rathest have you to Marie one
that were fully of your owne Religion', and warns about the
hazards of 'disagreement in Religion'. The betrothal of two princely
'members of two opposite Churches' can only 'breed and foster a
dissention among your subjects, taking their example from your
family' (p. 35).

If the neglectful manner of rule of Pericles' royal protagonist bore
resemblances to James VI and I's style of administration *c.*1607–9,
some pointed comments about Jacobean power politics are thinly
concealed in this play. James's management of the country was
being heavily criticised in this period; not least because his instinct
and drive was to make peace with Spain, exercise a policy of le-
niency towards recusants, and seek Catholic Spanish marriages for

his devoutly Protestant children, Henry and Elizabeth. The Venetian ambassador to London confided to the Doge and Senate in 1607, that: 'His majesty ... loves quiet and repose, has no inclination to war ... a fact that little pleases many of his subjects ... The result is he is despised and almost hated.' Furthermore, throughout 1607 the Venetian ambassador (Zorzi Giustinian) sent anxious reports to his masters about the unsettled British populace, who 'would clearly like to, on the excuse of this rumour of a Spanish Armada', disturb 'the calm'. His dispatches repeatedly lamented: 'They [the populace] long for a rupture with Spain.'[24] Meanwhile their monarch was negotiating marital alliances with the enemy, which could well lead to 'dissention' (see above quotation from *Basilikon Doron*) among his subjects. It seems that James, like Pericles, was an expert purveyor of adages about kingship, but for many of his subjects he too seldom put them into action. He would have done well to take note of the emblem and motto of the fifth knight in *Pericles*: 'an hand environèd with clouds, / Holding out gold that's by the touchstone tried' and '*Sic spectanda fides*' (vi.41–3), which might be rendered as, 'the trial of godliness and faith is to be made not of words only, but also by the action and performance of the deeds'.[25]

But all this begs the question of why a Yorkshire company of players with recusant sympathies should choose to stage *Pericles* in 1609. Perhaps it was for counter-propaganda purposes? The very fact that an Erasmian text is glanced at in this play would make it a prime target for appropriation by both sides of the religious divide. The preface to William Burton's translations of seven of the *Colloquies* (1606) is illuminating in this respect, for it reveals a religio-political intent partly motivating his project: readers will readily perceive, he declares in his preface, 'how little cause the Papists have to boast of Erasmus as a man of their side'. Ownership of Erasmus (with all the authority that implied) was hotly contested by English Catholics and Protestants in this period. Furthermore, Cholmeley was accused in 1609 of staging anti-Protestant plays, and the Star Chamber trial documents lend strong support to the view put forward by Sissons in 1942, that the company interpolated and omitted scenes, and improvised, according to 'the religious colour of their audience'.[26] This should perhaps serve as a timely reminder that plays are highly slippery art forms, and that ultimately their meanings reside with their equally unstable audiences. There is no way of knowing, for example, how closely a version of *Pericles* played at the Globe resembled the Yorkshire version(s) or, indeed, a production at Whitehall before distinguished guests: but it is easy to see how with a little fine tuning *Pericles* in performance could be construed as a pro-Jamesian play.

What can be said with certainty is that with its roots deep in the Jacobean cultural context, and engaging critically but obliquely with its power politics, *Pericles* – as represented by the 1609 quartos – has been wrongly consigned to the scrapheap of unalloyed aestheticism and 'happy Ever-afters'. *Pericles* is not a bastion of royal absolutism, though to discern its heterodox perspectives we need to penetrate its mirror-like surface, which appears to be reflecting Jamesian orthodoxy. As *Pericles* reminds its audiences, this was an age in which kings were 'earth's gods' (i.146), one in which saying 'Jove doth ill' (i.147) was fraught with danger. Indeed, as Philip Finkelpearl reminds us in an important essay on stage censorship, 'from 1606 it became a crime to speak against dignitaries even if the libel were true'.[27] Criticism of the reigning monarch was certainly best kept partially occluded, and, in skilful hands, the emblematic characterisation, straggling plots, exotic locations and make-believe worlds of romance were perfect structures for 'artistic cunning' and veiled comment.[28] Pocky bodies, medico-moral politics and dubious marriages were, I have argued, powerful stage vehicles for coded dissent: *c.*1607–9 men could not say the king 'doth ill' but they could seek to reveal it, or at least gesture towards it, through dramatic representation.

From Jennifer Richards and James Knowles (eds), *Shakespeare's Late Plays: New Readings* (Edinburgh, 1999), pp. 92–107.

NOTES

[One of several recent critical interventions aimed at displacing the established view of *Pericles* as a thinly disguised eulogy of James I and 'a bastion of royal absolutism', Margaret Healy's essay argues that investigating 'the play's representations of early modern syphilis [the pox], and its medico-moral politics, provides new contexts and substantial support for more dissonant readings'. In particular, Healy suggests that contemporary playgoers would have been horrified by the supposedly happy ending in which Pericles entrusts his daughter to a suitor who is intimated to be a pox-ridden governor of dubious morals. The 'emblematic resonances' of the play's *nupta contagioso* – which variously recalls the appropriation of poxy bodies by Protestant polemicists as a symbol of the corruption and hypocrisy of the Romish church, and James's highly unpopular policy of seeking Catholic marriages for his offspring – she believes can only have intensified this response.

All quotations of *Pericles* are taken from *William Shakespeare: The Complete Works*, ed. Stanley Wells and Gary Taylor (Oxford, 1988). Ed.]

1. Shakespeare probably collaborated with at least one other playwright in writing *Pericles* – the second writer remains a matter for speculation. I can see no justification for the designation of Q1 as a particularly corrupt, 'bad' quarto.

2. For a taste of this 'vilification' see theatre reviews for April 1990 (Royal Shakespeare Company) and May 1994 (Royal National Theatre) in *London Theatre Record*.

3. F. David Hoeniger, 'Gower and Shakespeare in *Pericles*', *Shakespeare Quarterly*, 33 (1982), 461–79 (p. 461).

4. Charles J. Sisson, 'Shakespeare quartos as prompt-copies', *Review of English Studies*, 18 (1942), 129–43 (pp. 136–7).

5. Milton Shulman, 'Review of *Pericles* (RSC)', *Evening Standard*, 17 April 1990.

6. Steven Mullaney, *The Place of the Stage: Licence, Play, and Power in Renaissance England* (Chicago and London, 1988), pp. 147–51.

7. Sandra Billington, *Mock Kings in Medieval and Renaissance Drama* (Oxford, 1991), p. 238.

8. Glynne Wickham, 'From tragedy to tragi-comedy: *King Lear* as prologue', *Shakespeare Survey*, 26 (1973), 33–48 (p. 44); Jonathan Goldberg, *James I and the Politics of Literature: Jonson, Shakespeare, Donne, and their Contemporaries* (Baltimore and London, 1983); David M. Bergeron, *Shakespeare's Romances and the Royal Family* (Lawrence, KS, 1985), p. 23; see also Leonard Tennenhouse, *Power on Display: The Politics of Shakespeare's Genres* (London, 1986), pp. 182–3.

9. Two notable exceptions are Stephen Dickey, 'Language and role in *Pericles*', *English Literary Renaissance*, 16 (1986), 550–66, and Constance C. Relihan, 'Liminal geography: *Pericles* and the politics of place', *Philological Quarterly*, 71 (1992), 281–99. [Reprinted in this volume – Ed.]

10. Thomas Campion, *The Lord Hay's Masque* (1607), ll.15–20, in David Lindley (ed.), *Court Masques* (Oxford, 1995).

11. See Samuel R. Gardiner, *History of England from the Accession of James I to the Outbreak of Civil War, 1603–42* (London, 1905), vol. I, p. 343; in July 1605 Spain suggested that if Prince Henry

married the eldest daughter of the King of Spain, Spain would surrender to the young couple its claims to a large portion of the Netherlands. Spain later retracted the offer, raising objections to the Infanta marrying a Protestant. Also see Gardiner, *History of England*, vol. II, pp. 22–3; in 1607 the abortive scheme for the marriage was renewed, together with a demand for the conversion of Prince Henry to Catholicism. The offer was refused because of the latter demand. However, in October of the same year James suggested an alternative plan; that his daughter Elizabeth be married to the son of Philip's brother-in-law, the Duke of Savoy. See also *Calendar of State Papers: Venetian, Vol. XI*, 15 August 1607: 'the Ambassadors of Spain are putting it about that by a matrimonial alliance and the death of the Archdukes the States might well come under the dominion of the King of England' (p. 23).

12. Gower's, Twine's and Wilkins' texts are in Geoffrey Bullough (ed.), *Narrative and Dramatic Sources of Shakespeare*, vol. VI (London and Henley, 1957–75).

13. On safe boundaries for the representation of syphilis see Lorraine Helms, 'The saint in the brothel: or, eloquence rewarded', *Shakespeare Quarterly*, 41 (1990), 319–32, and Sander Gilman, *Disease and Representation: Images of Illness from Madness to Aids* (Ithaca and London, 1988).

14. On syphylis and declamation, see Helms, 'The saint in the brothel'.

15. See Richard Davenport-Hines, *Sex, Death and Punishment* (London, 1990).

16. The topic of my forthcoming monograph, 'Fictions of Disease: Bodies, Plagues and Politics in Early Modern Writings'.

17. See Foster Watson, *The English Grammar Schools to 1660* (London, 1968), pp. 328–9, and M. L. Clarke, *Classical Education in Britain, 1500–1900* (Cambridge, 1959), p. 47.

18. Desiderius Ersamus, 'De Utilitate Colloquiorum', in *The Colloquies of Erasmus*, ed. and trans. Craig R. Thompson (Chicago, 1965), p. 629, quoted by Thompson in the same edition, p. 154.

19. John King, *English Reformation Literature: The Tudor Origins of the Protestant Tradition* (Princeton, NJ, 1982), p. 283.

20. William Turner, *A New Booke of Spirituall Physik for Dyverse Diseases of the Nobilitie and Gentlemen of Englande* (n.p., 1555), fol. 74[r].

21. Thomas Dekker, *The Whore of Babylon*, in *The Dramatic Works of Thomas Dekker*, ed. F. Bowers (Cambridge, 1953–61), vol. II (1955), p. 497.

22. On this matter one of Erasmus' adages famously delared; 'Sheep are of no use, if the shepherd is not there ... the common people are useless unless they have the prince's authority to guide them', in Desiderius Erasmus, *Collected Writings of Erasmus: Adages, II.vii.1 to III.iii.100*, trans M. M. Phillips (Buffalo and London, 1982), II.vii.26.

23. James VI and I, *Basilikon Doron*, in *Political Works of James I*, ed. Charles Howard McIlwain (Cambridge, MA, 1918; repr. New York, 1965), p. 34.

24. *Calendar of State Papers: Venetian, Vol. X*, p. 513; and *State Papers: Venetian, Vol. XI*, pp. 17, 27, 39.

25. *Pericles*, ed. F. D. Hoeniger (London, 1963), II.ii.38n. (p. 56), citing Claude Paradin, *Devises Héroiques*, trans. P.S. (London, 1951), sig. O3 (p. 213).

26. See *Star Chamber Proceedings*, PRO, STAC 19 / 10; 12 / 11. Sisson, 'Shakespeare quartos', p. 142.

27. Philip J. Finkelpearl, '"The comedians' liberty": censorship of the Jacobean stage reconsidered', *English Literary Renaissance*, 16 (1986), 123–38 (p. 123). Finkelpearl suggests that 'the employment of arcane codes mastered by the cognoscenti' may have operated in Jacobean England (p. 138). See also Annabel Patterson, *Censorship and Interpretation* (Madison, WI, 1984). Indeed, satire against the king had led to Jonson, Chapman and Marston being imprisoned in 1605 for their parts in *Eastward Ho!*, and in 1606 'sundry were committed to Bridewell' for producing *The Isle of Gulls*.

28. The expression is Finkelpearl's, '"The comedians' liberty"', p. 138.

3

Liminal Geography: *Pericles* and the Politics of Place

CONSTANCE C. RELIHAN

Recent criticism of Shakespeare's romances has begun to examine in fascinating detail representation of James I's court and family within the plays. Studies by David M. Bergeron, Leonard Tennenhouse, and Glynne Wickham, to name only three significant analyses, have explored the various ways social energy circulates throughout and between political and Shakespearean texts. Bergeron's study, for example, has demonstrated possible ways in which James I's family may have provided dramatic source material comparable to Shakespeare's textual sources, as well as possible correspondences between political-familial events in the life of James and his family and specific plays. Additionally, Wickham describes what he finds as dramatic 'traces' of the struggle to unite England and Scotland in the plays. These studies aim to identify the means by which Shakespeare's romances participate in the ability of James I and the aristocracy to represent and authorise their power.[1]

A play such as *Pericles*, however, presents an extremely problematic representation of political power in Jacobean England because unlike the specifically English or European settings of *Cymbeline* and *The Winter's Tale*, or the New World ambience of *The Tempest*,[2] *Pericles* occurs in a series of specifically non-European locations. By dramatising a series of Eastern Mediterranean cultures, Shakespeare amplifies the political implications of his text.[3] I will argue here that in creating a romance so dependent upon locations whose relation to Europe may be considered liminal, and by emphasising the drama's Otherness through the distancing mechanism of Gower's narrative control, Shakespeare undermines interpretations of the play that see it affirming both James I's reign and time's ability to heal and restore.

Certainly, one could dismiss the settings of *Pericles* – Antioch, Tyre, Tharsus, Pentapolis, Ephesus, and Mytilene – as mere abstractions drawn from Shakespeare's sources,[4] or as part of the classical Greek or New Testament worlds with which Jacobean culture would be undoubtedly familiar. Such dismissal, which assumes that the audiences of the play would not imagine the play's geography in relation to their own experience, flattens our analysis by ignoring early seventeenth-century understanding of its contemporary political and religious world. If the play is read in relation to late sixteenth- and early seventeenth-century conceptions of Eastern Mediterranean cultures, it reveals an ambivalence toward the political and familial structures it asks us to accept.

The fundamental impression obtained from contemporary texts about Greek, North African, and Aegean cultures is of their liminality – that is to say, of their function as thresholds connecting the European West and the Asiatic / African East. Anthropologists Victor Turner and Arnold van Gennep identify as liminal rituals that constitute rites of passage, that permit individuals access simultaneously to two modes of existence. Turner further expands notions of liminality to apply to individuals caught in transitional stages, who are 'neither here nor there ... betwixt and between the positions assigned and arrayed by law, custom, convention, and ceremonials'.[5] The cultures of *Pericles*, to extend this metaphor further, similarly represent citeis where concurrent access to two worlds – East and West – is possible, permitting a critique of the Western culture with which both author and audience identify.[6]

Studying *Pericles*'s geographic settings to identify them as either Western or Eastern, as part of European culture *or* as part of the dehumanised and colonised Other (as postcolonial studies would attempt to do[7]), risks creating a too highly dichotomised image of the cultures the play presents.[8] Although Renaissance importation and appropriation of classical texts suggests a strong desire to claim the ancient world as European and Western, a more complex relation exists between sixteenth- and seventeenth-century English and classical Greek cultures, a relation which seems epitomised in

Renaissance perceptions of the connection between Greece and the
infidel Turks. An excerpt from a prayer by John Foxe, reprinted as
late as 1609, demonstrates one set of attitudes towards this relation
and, I would argue, the cultures of *Pericles*:

> First, the Turke w[ith] his sword, what landes, nations, and coun-
> treyes, what empires, kingdomes, and prouinces with Cities innumer-
> able hath he wonne, not from us, but from thee [God]: where thy
> name was wont to be inuocated, thy word preached, thy Sacramentes
> administered, there now reigneth barbarous Mahumet, w[ith] his
> filthy Alcoran. The florishing Churches in Asia, the learned Churches
> of Grecia, the manifold Churches in Africa which were wont to serue
> thee, now are gone from thee ... All the Churches where thy diligent
> Apostle St. Paul, thy Apostle Peter, and John, and other Apostles so
> laboriously trauayled, preachyng [and] writyng to pla[n]t thy
> Gospell, are now gone from thy Gospell. In all the kyngdome of
> Syria, Palestina, Arabia, Persia, in all Armenia, and the Empire of
> Capadocia, through the whole compasse of Asia, with Ægypt, and
> with Africa also (vnles amongest the farre Æthiopians some old
> steppes of Christianitie peraduenture yet do remayne) either els in all
> Asia and Africa, thy Church hath not one foote of free land, but all is
> turned either to infidelitie, or to captiuitie, what soeuer pertaineth to
> thee ... All Thracia with the empire of Constantinople, all Grecia,
> Epyrus, Illyricum, and now of late all the kyngdome almost of
> Hungaria, with much of Austria, with lamentable slaughter of
> Christen bloud is wasted, and all become Turkes.[9]

In 1937, Samuel Chew noted a tendency in early modern England
to blur cultural distinctions between Turks and Moors,[10] and Foxe
clearly exhibits this trait, as we can see in his depiction of Greece:
the military prowess of the Turk has caused barbarous Mahumet to
supplant God in 'the learned churches of Grecia', and all Greece,
among quite a catalogue of cultures, 'is wasted, and all become
Turkes'. Greece, in Foxe's prayer, is aligned with the Turks and
other races which the Renaissance tended to identify not only as
alien and Other, but as versions of Antichrist.[11]

Foxe's prayer is not an isolated example of the multi-dimensional
perceptions of Greek culture which combine classical, contemporary, and early Christian worlds. Early travel and anthropological
literature emphasises its liminal status as well. William Watreman's
The Fardle of Facions (1555), a translation of Johannes Boemus's
widely-read cultural study, *Omnium Gentium Mores* (1520), for
example, describes the geography and cultures of Asia and Africa.[12]
The Fardle of Facions explicitly excludes Greece from the Christian

West by identifying the Christian world as Germany, Italy, France, Spain, England, Scotland, Ireland, Denmark, 'Livon', 'Pruse', 'Pole', Hungary, and 'the Isles of Rhodes, Sicilie, Corsica, Sardinia, with a few other' ('The Preface of the Authour', Avi). In addition, although Boemus discusses Greece while describing Europe, Watreman's translation of his preface, like Foxe's prayer, emphasises that 'the whole cou[n]trie of Grecia' is 'throwyng awaie Christe' to become 'folowers and worshippers of Mahomet and his erroneous doctrine' (Avi). The *Fardle* makes even more explicit the connection between the Greeks and the Turks to which Foxe alludes by explaining that several ethnic groups comprise Turkey: 'All this countrie that now is called Turcquie, is not enhabited by one seuerall nacion, but there be in it Turcques, Grekes, Armenians, Saracenes, Jacobites, Nestorians, Jewes, and christians [sic]' (Piiii). For Boemus, the Greeks are identified as part of the Turkish empire, and Ephesus, one of the major locations of the New Testament's Acts of the Apostles and, in *Pericles*, the city of Thaisa's restoration, is labelled the chief city of the Turkish province called Ionia (Iviii).

Greece's association with the non-Christian and non-classical Ottoman Empire helps to qualify automatic associations between *Pericles*'s cultures and those of the ancient Greek or New Testament worlds. Watreman's explicit naming of Ephesus as a Turkish capital emphasises this point, as do ambiguous references in Samuel Purchas's compendium of travel narratives and reports, *Purchas his Pilgrimes*. Although published in 1625, well after *Pericles* had been written, it presented documents from a wide chronological period and may be said to represent attitudes current during the early seventeenth century.[13] References to the specific cultures of *Pericles* inform us that Tyre was attacked in 1111 as part of the first crusade (7:469), that the Syrians who come from Tyre are the 'greatest sect of Christians in the Orient' (1:351), and that 'Tyrus is destroyed, and no such Citie now standyng, onely the name of the place remayneth, and the place is still knowne where it stood' (8:255). Antioch, which *Pericles*'s Gower calls the 'fairest city in all Syria',[14] is described in terms of its fortifications and spring 'where many were Baptised that became Christians at the Apostles [sic] Preaching' (9:433),[15] and its function as the chief city of the 'Oriens' diocese of the Eastern Church (1:459). Such statements complement the designation of Antioch in Acts of the Apostles as the place where 'the disciples were first called Christians'.[16] Purchas names Ephesus as the major city of the Asian diocese (1:459), an obvious change from *The Fardle of Facions*, but an indication of the complex relationship in which these locations stood to Shakespeare's audience. This complexity is further demonstrated by Purchas's description of four possible 'significations' (11:125) for Tharsus: 'Tarsus, a Citie of Cilicia, Carthage, India, and the Sea' (11:125).[17] This confusion seems at odds with what may be expected as an immediate identification between Tharsus and the home of the apostle Paul: in fact, the 1560 Geneva Bible included a map of the Middle East that clearly identified Tarsus as a city in Asia Minor.[18]

The clear distinction Purchas draws between ancient Greece and its modern descendant further elucidates the complicated relationship between the cultures of *Pericles* and *Purchas his Pilgrimes*. When describing Greek Christian rites, he informs us that they are not conducted in 'the present vulgar [language], but ... the pure and ancient Greeke tongue, whereof ... the common people understand but little' (1:400).[19] This final distinction between pure and vulgar, or vernacular, Greek is crucial for understanding *Pericles*'s relation to its geographic roots. While we may read this comment in relation to the Reformation's elevation of vernacular languages, the simultaneous presence of the Western, classical, 'pure' language and the Eastern, barbarous, 'vulgar' tongue suggests an understanding of Greece and those cities and colonies that participated in its classical tradition as a liminal site: a location that simultaneously permits access to the classical European world and the Eastern cultures that have become linguistically separate from it.

A final example may help solidify our sense of the significance of Renaissance views of the non-European East. In 1581, Barnaby Rich published a collection of narrative fictions, *Riche his Farewell to Militarie Profession*. The conclusion to the work, which stresses the inappropriateness of following courtly fashions in behaviour and dress, contains the story of a devil who, having assumed the shape of a gentleman, marries a London woman obsessed with her appearance. Unable to endure (or finance) her clothing expenditures, the devil flees London and inhabits the body of James VI in Edinburgh. Only when he fears that his wife will be brought to Scotland does he release James's body and return to hell.

As we might expect, James objected to this portrayal. When a fourth edition of the work was published in 1606, after James had ascended the English throne, Rich substituted 'the Turk' and Constantinople for references to James and his court.[20] Such a substitution suggests not only Rich's attitude toward James, but his culture's perceptions of the Ottoman Empire as well. Identifying the Turks with the devil posed no cultural difficulty in 1606 – and Greece's participation in the Turkish empire was clear, if not clearly definable.

These multifarious perceptions about the cultures *Pericles* inhabits complicate the play's relationship to representations of authority in Jacobean England, yet the nature of responses to political power are central to the play. Anthony J. Lewis has observed that *Pericles* 'enacts one theme: the personal, familial, and governmental obligation to nourish self, relations, and citizens'. The interrelation of 'self, relations, and citizens' for the royal protagonist emphasises even further the vast significance of this subject.[21] Moreover, as Stephen Dickey has argued, Pericles repeatedly fails to satisfy his obligations to his state.[22] I would argue that this failure implies the play's response to James I's rule, a response made simultaneously less dangerous for the playwright and more subversive of Jacobean political structures by the play's participation in the liminal cultures of Asia Minor.

Pericles encounters five cultures in addition to his native Tyre, and each of these societies is troubled (in spite of the initial appearance of Pentapolis). Antioch certainly provides the clearest example of a dysfunctional state, as well as family, but it is by no means unique in the play. The incest of Antiochus and his unnamed daughter epitomises the country's condition. Antiochus has perverted his position as father and king, enacting, as Gower tells us, 'a law / To keep her still and men in awe' (l.Chor.35–6), a law which will demand Pericles's death if he fails to solve the painfully obvious riddle. This initial culture provides a powerful but ambiguous force to the play. Instead of arguing that Pericles's awareness of Antiochus's crime indicates an aberration in his own sexual composition,[23] I would emphasise Antioch's position in the play's world as the fairest city in Syria, a designation which connects it to the now destroyed city of Tyre: Gower links Antioch and Syria; Purchas links Syria and Tyre (1:352, 8:255).

Tyre, then, becomes identifiable with Antioch, and its ruler, Pericles, becomes analogous to Antiochus. The King's crime is, geographically speaking, Pericles's as well; consequently, Antiochus's abuses of his political power also implicate Pericles. That Pericles phrases his rejection of Antiochus's daughter in political terms furthers the political / geographic connection between the two rulers: 'For he's no man on whom perfections wait / That knowing sin within, will touch the gate' (I.i.80–1).[24] Pericles seems to recognise a need to reject not just the daughter, but the castle and city to which she would provide political access. The 'gate' that would permit entrance into Antioch's citadel must be actively rejected if Pericles is to sever his geographical link to Antiochus.

Pericles flees Antioch's dysfunctional government and returns to Tyre, and back in his homeland his faulty judgement becomes more apparent. Pericles's desire to seek a bride at the corrupt court of Antiochus suggests a lack of perceptiveness, and his belief that he could solve a riddle which has claimed dozens of 'martyrs' (I.i.39) and escape 'death's net, whom none resist' (I.i.41) may suggest arrogance even as it indicates a concern for a clear line of succession. While Pericles's presence in Antiochus's court constitutes an absence from Tyre the play's initial audience would have understood,[25] it nonetheless marks the first occasion on which we see him abandon active government of Tyre. Pericles's flight from Antioch returns him only momentarily to an active governmental role. Fearing that Antiochus will invade Tyre and 'with th'ostent of war will look so huge, / Amazement shall drive courage from the state / Our men be vanquished ere they do resist / And subjects punished that ne'er thought offence' (I.ii.26–29), Pericles flees Tyre, leaving Helicanus in charge.[26] Certainly, this action informs us that we are not in the military world of *Coriolanus*, or other of the Roman plays, in which corruption must be fought and the honour of a ruler is very closely linked to his military strength. In this romance, and perhaps because of the nature of romance, Pericles does not act to stop the corruption in Antioch, and, rather than have his subjects overcome with fear and awe, he himself runs from his knowledge of the crime.

Tyre, then, becomes a country without its prince, a position it maintains for virtually the entire play. We learn that during Pericles's absence following his flight from Tyre Helicanus must quell an attempted rebellion that would install him as king (II.iv); during his second absence, Pericles shifts his responsibility to 'Old Escanes, whom Helicanus late / Advanced in time to great and high estate' (IV.iv.15–16). Pericles's lack of involvement in Escanes's career significantly reflects his separation from the kingdom as a whole: his initial desire to establish a clear line of succession, which illustrates the unification between familial and political roles, yields to a separation between his personal and political *personae*. Because Pericles does not return to govern Tyre at the play's end, this separation is never fully reconciled.

The remainder of the play takes Pericles to Tharsus, Pentapolis, Ephesus, and Mytilene. Tharsus and Mytilene are, like Antioch, clearly malfunctioning governments in the liminal realm of Asia Minor. Tharsus, that ambiguously imagined location identifiable with the New Testament's Paul of Tarsus,[27] is a famine-stricken country whose crisis is connected to its citizens' pride and degeneracy. Cleon describes it as:

> A city on whom plenty held full hand,
> For riches strew'd herself even in her streets;
> Whose towers bore heads so high they kiss'd the clouds,
> And strangers ne'er beheld but wond'red at;
> Whose men and dames so jetted and adorn'd,
> Like one another's glass to trim them by –
> Their tables were stor'd full, to glad the sight,
> And not so much to feed on as delight:
> All poverty was scorn'd, and pride so great,
> The name of help grew odious to repeat.
>
> (I.iv.22–31)

This pride, which had required perpetual 'inventions to delight the taste' (I.iv.40), has become a society that 'would now be glad of bread, and beg for it' (I.iv.41). Pericles relieves this hunger, in a gesture that has been variously interpreted as an act of generous mercy and as an empty self-serving gesture.[28] It is probably both. Like James, who distributed what may be broadly termed largess in order to confirm his sense of self, Pericles distributes grain to relieve the famine and to permit himself to believe that he deserves the friendship and respect of the citizens of Tharsus.[29]

Pericles's choice of Tharsus as a safe haven from Antiochus's murderers is troubling. The clear and immediate indication of the city's former profligacy coupled with its current military weakness suggest the seriousness of its problems.[30] The murderous actions of Dionyza and Leonine make its political weakness even more explicit. Moreover, Pericles's later willingness to entrust his infant daughter to this realm strengthens a sense of his faulty judgement and his unsuitability as a ruler.[31] It also resonates with James's frequent separations from his own children – and especially from Prince Henry and Princess Sophia on their deathbeds.[32] The Christian identification of Tharsus with Tarsus combines with the

Renaissance's hazy understanding of its exact location to create confusion and disorientation. It is (as Boemus and Purchas indicate) an alien location under Turkish control, and therefore a place Western Christianity has lost.

Mytilene does not carry the complex resonances of Tharsus, although it was briefly visited by Paul (Acts 20:14), but it clearly belongs to the Greek world under Turkish control during the Renaissance. It is also a city so definitely dysfunctional that its governor, Lysimachus, is a frequent customer at brothels: even his attempted disguise is transparent to Marina's bawd (IV.vi.15–16). Lysimachus, of course, quickly seems to reform, but before he does so, the vivid language of the brothel scenes has convinced us of the pervasive moral decay he has permitted in his realm, and the play provides no indication that Marina's removal from the brothel and Lysimachus's reform have in any way changed the nature of Mytilene: Boult, Bawd, and Pander continue their trade in women 'a man may deal withal, and defy the surgeon' (Iv.vi.24–5), to use Lysimachus's phrase.

Ephesus, well-known from Acts of the Apostles as the location of Diana's temple,[33] similarly receives critical treatment in *Pericles*. Cerimon, the primary human power we see there, is a wealthy man concerned about his social and economic inferiors: the First Gentleman is amazed that Cerimon 'should be conversant with pain, / Being thereto not compelled' (III.ii.25–26). Moreover, he is a magician who has studied 'physic' (III.ii.32), a 'secret art' (III.ii.32) which has taught him of 'the blest infusions / That dwells in vegatives, in metals, stones' (III.ii.35–36) and which has enabled him to revive 'hundreds' (III.ii.44). It is to Cerimon that Thaisa's apparently dead body is brought and he adds her to his list of successful cures, but it is after her resurrection that Ephesus becomes an even more unsettling location for the play's audience.

Pericles's Ephesus is the location of the Temple of the goddess of witchcraft, the Black Diana,[34] but it seems also to be a land of lethargy and resignation, a location that encourages Thaisa to recoil from her responsibilities just as we repeatedly see Pericles reject his role as governor. Quickly after her shipwreck and restoration, Thaisa tells Cerimon: 'But since King Pericles, / My wedded lord, I ne'er shall see again, / A vestal livery will I take me to, / And never more have joy' (III.iv.7–10). Cerimon promptly replies that Diana's temple is nearby and willing to accept her

(III.iv.11–15). Thaisa's decision is motivated by the presumed death of Pericles, a presumption for which she has no evidence. More important than the inaccuracy of her belief is the information she excludes from consideration: she is the only daughter and heir to the kingdom of Pentapolis. As such, her decision to forego her former life is a political act which denies Pentapolis an orderly succession. As a location which encourages and enables Thaisa's decision (and note the speed with which Cerimon offers assistance), Ephesus becomes connected not only with the Turks (as Boemus noted) and witchcraft, but with dangerous and inappropriate political behaviour as well.

In the world of *Pericles*'s audience, Thaisa's culpability should not be underestimated. The problems Queen Elizabeth's childlessness posed for the country were still fresh in the English mind. Moreover, as Bergeron's study has suggested, the isolation of members of the royal family from each other was seen as a troubling act, both for the state as well as the family.[35]

Thaisa's behaviour implicates the political structures of her native Pentapolis as well as those of Ephesus. Pentapolis is typically imagined as 'a group of five cities on the northern coast of Africa', but their exact location remains obscure.[36] Certainly, Pentapolis does not carry the biblical, classical, and contemporary associations of the other of *Pericles*'s cultures. Its obscurity makes it an appropriately idealised setting for the staging of the one liminal site whose government we are asked to imagine positively. King Simonides's kingdom is generally characterised favourably, but the banter of the fishermen who assist Pericles after his shipwreck identifies ambiguities within its political structure:

> 3. Fish   ... Master, I marvel how the fishes live in the sea.
> 1. Fish   Why, as men do a-land: the great ones eat up the little ones. I can compare our rich misers to nothing so fitly as to a whale: a' plays and tumbles, driving the poor fry before him, and at last devours them all at a mouthful. Such whales have I heard on a'th'land, who never leave gaping till they have swallow'd the whole parish, church, steeple, bells, and all.   ...
> 3. Fish   But, master, if I had been the sexton, I would have been that day in the belfry.
> 2. Fish   Why, man?
> 3. Fish   Because he should have swallow'd me too: ... But if the good King Simonides were of my mind. ... we would purge the land of these drones, that rob the bee of her honey.
>
> (II.i.26–47)

While the fishermen lightheartedly discuss the realm of 'good King Simonides', they nonetheless observe that it is a country possessing 'rich misers' who swallow everything in their paths like whales; it is a land of 'drones, that rob the bee of her honey'. It is also a government, like Antioch, in which the royal family is a father–daughter dyad. Simonides's relationship with Thaisa is not incestuous: he does genuinely seem to wish her to wed, but the competition among the six knights and his feigned anger with Pericles present the prince with a challenge analogous to the events in Antioch. In both situations, marriage to the kingdom's heir may occur only after Pericles has victoriously completed a ritual challenge. The experience of Pericles in Antioch should make us, I believe, initially suspicious of Simonides and Thaisa, and Thaisa's seclusion from her political life seems to at least partially justify this doubt.

Nonetheless, Pentapolis is the most positively imagined geographical location in the play, and it is to Pentapolis that Pericles and Thaisa will return at the play's end. As has already been noted, the final disposition of rulers sends Marina and Lysimachus to govern in Tyre. Mytilene, the land which – second to Antioch – seems to need governing most, will lose its governor and will, presumably, be ruled by deputy just as Tyre was during Pericles's travels. No mention is made of Antioch's government after the immolation of Antiochus and his daughter is reported. Tharsus's political position is left similarly ambiguous, although we know that it was the citizenry's moral outrage at Dionyza's attempted murder of Marina that caused hers and Cleon's deaths.

I find these political resolutions troubling, especially in light of the many readings of the play which, like C. L. Barber's, stress the 'transformation of persons into virtually sacred figures who yet remain persons': or, like Tennenhouse's, emphasise the role of the reunited family which, by the end of a Shakespearean romance generally is 'stronger and more pervasive' (i.e., controls more territory) than when the play began; or, like Peterson's, see *Pericles* as a series of events that 'try man's faith in a just and merciful deity'.[37] Instead of sensing a merciful conclusion that unites the action of the play, the political ambiguities with which the play ends confound such a perception: the rulers who have been least willing to govern, Pericles and Thaisa, will control the best of the play's societies; Marina, an inexperienced ruler, and Lysimachus, a reformed 'john' who encouraged moral profligacy in Mytilene, will rule Tyre, a country they have never seen; Tharsus and Antioch's governments are left undefined; Mytilene – the land of Pander, Boult, and Bawd – will be left without a ruler; and Ephesus will, apparently, continue to encourage the magic of Cerimon and the isolation possible within Diana's temple. That all of these locations are part of an ambiguously imagined Asia Minor which resonates with Turkish and 'reprobate'[38] cultures as well as with Christian and classical traditions makes the political resolution of *Pericles* less reassuring and idyllic than much criticism of the play suggests.

The political turmoil present in the play's ending is amplified not only by geographical ambiguities, but also by its relation to the political and familial position of James I. Bergeron sees Shakespeare's romances as concerning 'the need for an heir and a clear successor. With varying degrees of emphasis, each Romance confronts this political-familial problem.'[39] The reunion of Tyre's royal family at the end of *Pericles* may certainly be read in the context of Bergeron's sense of the romances: with the restoration of Marina, the second generation of rule is assured and, as Tennenhouse notes, the geographical area governed by the dynasty increases. Moreover, as Wickham has observed, the approximate date of *Pericles* coincides with the arrival of James's daughter Elizabeth into court: the arrival into London of the teenage daughter who had been raised elsewhere parallels Shakespeare's depiction of the young romance heroine who is restored to her political role.[40]

Yet, I think it is inappropriate to see these correspondences between *Pericles* and James I's political-familial life as supporting James I's government or the unification of Scotland and England. The political structures *Pericles* develops simply do not invite favourable comparisons with Jacobean England. Cumberland Clark, reflecting on the incest and brothel scenes in 1932, suggested that Shakespeare is an unlikely author for the play because if 'Shakespeare had a major hand in it, it would amount to a severe denunciation on his part of the morals of the Greeks.'[41] The denunciation to which he alludes is present in the play, but, because *Pericles* is among the representations of political power which are at least partially influenced by James I's accession to the throne, it is a denunciation not only of Clark's 'Greeks' but of James's reign as well. The unification of Pericles's family and the relief it causes the audience exists simultaneously with the denunciation of the political behaviour of the King whose family achieves this union and political expansion.

Gower's presence in the play amplifies this simultaneous support for and rejection of its action.[42] Gower's dominance as narrator creates a distance between the audience and the play's dramatic content which reinforces the sense of the play as occurring outside the boundaries of English-European existence. Gower is necessary to help the audience imagine the foreign cities and seas, and to ensure that the audience does not forget that what is presented on the stage is a fiction. On the other hand, Gower's role in the history of English poetry and in providing a primary source for the narrative of Shakespeare's play identifies the drama of *Pericles* as an integral part of the audience's cultural history. What, after all, could be more English than a story from the work of the famous – if somewhat tedious – Gower?

Gower's simultaneous function as a means of creating dislocation and identification is mirrored by geography's role in the play. The liminal cultures in which *Pericles* occurs, cultures which simultaneously belong to classical Greek and New Testament traditions – the sources of Western civilisation; and to the infidel, anti-Christian Ottoman Empire – the location of that which is perceived as the non-Western Other, both promote and defeat English identification with the events of the play. This liminal realm permits us to interpret the events of the play as simultaneous rehearsals of the problems and anxieties of James I's 'restoration' of the royal line and expansion of the English kingdom, *and* as an opportunity to increase the power base of the non-Christian cultures centred in Asia Minor and Africa. We must further imagine the restoration which the play's conclusion presents as politically fragmented, as a testament to political inability and retreat, rather than a sign of unification and strength.

All of which returns me to Barnaby Rich's 1606 revision of his *Farewell to Militarie Profession*: his substitution of the 'great Turke' for James I is a telling choice. It suggests a desire to imagine the two figures similarly; it suggests a subconscious sense in which both function to represent that which is alien to English culture. The geographical locations in which *Pericles* occurs suggest a similar identification: the sense in which these cultures are liminal – are both 'us' and 'them' – parallels similar anxiety over the liminal nature of James I.

From *Philological Quarterly*, 7 (1992), 281–99.

NOTES

[Constance Relihan's essay, like Healy's (essay 2), questions the pro-Jamesian reading of *Pericles*, but it also attests to a growing interest in the geopolitical implications of Shakespearean topography, once assumed to be vague, schematic and largely imaginary (especially in the 'romances'). For Relihan, the play's relationship to Jacobean authority is complicated by its setting in a series of liminal sites in Asia Minor, which participated simultaneously in classical Greek and New Testament traditions, and in the infidel, non-European Ottoman empire which threatened seventeenth-century Christendom. The ambiguous cultural associations evoked by these locations help to build a negative picture of their dysfunctional governments and Pericles's abdication of his political responsibilities, which parallels that of James I. Ed.]

1. See David M. Bergeron, *Shakespeare's Romances and the Royal Family* (Lawrence, KS, 1985); Leonard Tennenhouse, *Power on Display: The Politics of Shakespeare's Genres* (New York, 1986), especially p. 147 ff.; and, Glynne Wickham, 'From Tragedy to Tragicomedy: *King Lear* as Prologue', *Shakespeare Survey*, 26 (1973), 33–48, especially p. 34. Any discussion of 'the circulation of social energy' is, of course, indebted to Stephen Greenblatt's *Shakespearean Negotiations: The Circulation of Social Energy in Renaissance England* (Berkeley, CA, 1988).

2. For a survey of discussions of *The Tempest* in relation to geographic and colonial concerns, see Alden T. Vaughan, 'Shakespeare's Indian: The Americanization of Caliban', *Shakespeare Quarterly*, 39 (Summer 1988), 137–53. Vaughan is critical of attempts to read *The Tempest* in relation to American Indians 'because the evidence suggests strongly that Shakespeare's contemporaries and their descendants for nearly three centuries' did not make this connection. He tempers his criticism of such readings, especially those by new historicists, by admitting that the concerns such critics address 'reflect recurrent themes' in American and world history (p. 153).

3. I will not consider here the vexing problem of *Pericles*'s authorship since my focus is on the surviving text, admittedly very corrupt and difficult to identify. Whether Shakespeare revised an earlier play, which seems most likely, or not, does not alter my analysis of the play's political nature. For perspectives on the authorship issue, see Douglas L. Peterson, *Time, Tide, and Tempest: A Study of Shakespeare's Romances* (San Marino, 1973), who sees the play as 'the work of a single controlling intelligence' (p. 104n); Barbara A. Mowat, *The Dramaturgy of Shakespeare's Romances* (Athens, GA, 1976), who excludes *Pericles* from her discussion of the romances because of its disputed status (p. 2); Wickham, 'From Tragedy to Tragicomedy', who accepts the position that Shakespeare revised the final three acts of a

play by George Wilkins (p. 44); and Northrop Frye, *A Natural Perspective: The Development of Shakespearean Comedy and Romance* (Princeton NJ, 1972), who argues that although a marked change in style does occur at the beginning of Act III, 'there is no break in structure corresponding to the break in style' (p. 38). The most interesting recent exchange on the question consists of F. David Hoeniger's 'Gower and Shakespeare in *Pericles*', *Shakespeare Quarterly*, 33 (Winter 1982), 461–79, which posits Shakespeare as the single author who intentionally shifted style to further the audience's sense of Gower's control of the play, and Sidney Thomas's critical response, 'The Problem of *Pericles*', *Shakespeare Quarterly*, 34 (Winter 1983), 448–50.

4. The major literary sources are generally agreed to be Gower's *Confessio Amantis*, Book 8, and Lawrence Twine's *The Patterne of Painefull Adventures* (1576), although its connection to Greek romance and the Latin *Apollonius of Tyre* is pervasive. See Carol Gesner's *Shakespeare and the Greek Romance: A Study of Origins* (Lexington, KY, 1970).

5. Victor Turner, *The Ritual Process: Structure and Anti-structure* (Chicago, 1969), p. 95. See also Arnold van Gennep, *The Rites of Passage*, trans. Monika B. Vizedom and Gabrielle L. Caffee (Chicago, 1960). For literary studies influenced by Turner, see the essays collected in Kathleen M. Ashley (ed.), *Victor Turner and the Construction of Cultural Criticism* (Indiana, 1990).

6. These cultures may also be seen as places where, to use Steven Mullaney's phrase, a 'rehearsal of cultures' is authorised. He argues, in *The Place of the Stage: License, Play, and Power in Renaissance England* (Chicago, 1988), that 'a rehearsal is a period of free-play during which alternatives can be staged, unfamiliar roles tried out, the range of one's power to convince or persuade explored with some licence; it is a period of performance, but one in which the customary demands of decorum are suspended, along with expectations of final or perfected form' (p. 69).

7. For a seminal work in this area, see Edward W. Said's *Orientalism* (New York, 1979).

8. See Martin Bernal's *Black Athena: The Afroasiatic Roots of Classical Civilization*, vol 1. (Livingston, NJ, 1987), a study of the ways in which modern European and American perceptions of classical Greek culture have systematically erased its non-European dimensions. Bernal notes that pre-nineteenth century scholarship recognised the Eastern nature of classical Greece: 'no one before 1600 seriously questioned the belief that Greek civilisation derived from Egypt, or that the chief ways in which it had been transmitted was through Egyptian colonisations of Greece and later Greek study in Egypt' (p. 121).

9. The prayer, titled, 'The Prayer in this Sermon made for the Church, and all the states thereof' is appended to Foxe's *A Sermon of Christ Crucified, preached at Paules Cross the Friday before Easter, commonly called Goodfryday. Written and dedicated to all such as labour and be heavy laden in conscience, to be read for their spiritual comfort*, 1570 (STC 11242. Ann Arbor: University Microfilms, English Books Before 1640, Reel 543). The sermon and prayer were reprinted in 1575, 1577, 1585, and 1609.

10. Samuel Chew, *The Crescent and the Rose: Islam and England during the Renaissance* (1937; reprint, New York, 1965), p. 104.

11. Chew, *The Crescent and the Rose*, p. 101n 1. Christopher Hill, *Antichrist in Seventeenth-Century England* (Oxford, 1971), p. 181, concludes that the identification of the Turks, especially the Great Turk, with Antichrist was more common in Mediterranean cultures than in England; however, he notes that certain English authors, such as Foxe and Aylmer, linked the Turk with the Pope as manifestations of Antichrist on earth. While Foxe considered the Turks to be The New Testament's Antichrist he believed that Christianity would soon be relieved from Turkish attacks (V. Norskov Olsen, *John Foxe and the Elizabethan Church* [Berkeley, CA, 1973], pp. 54–5).

For further discussion of the extremely complex relationships between Eastern and Western cultures in early modern Europe, see ch. 1 of Christopher L. Miller's *Blank Darkness: Africanist Discourse in French* (Chicago, 1985), which explores the historical connections between Orientalism and Western perceptions of African cultures. Simon Shepherd's *Marlowe and the Politics of Elizabethan Theatre* (Brighton, 1986), pp. 142–56, also elaborates on the intricacies of early modern England's attitudes toward the Turks.

12. The full title of Watreman's work is: *The Fardle of Facions conteinyng the aunciente maners, customes, and Lawes, of the peoples enhabiting the two partes of the earth, called Affrike and Asie.* (STC 3197. References are to the microfilmed Huntington Library copy [Ann Arbor: University Microfilms, English Books Before 1640, Reel 281]). Watreman excluded the third section of Boemus's work, which treats European cultures. This work was brought to my attention by Margaret T. Hodgen's *Early Anthropology in the Sixteenth and Seventeenth Centuries* (Pennsylvania, 1964), pp. 131–43. Hodgen notes that between the second, expanded 1536 edition of Boemus's work and 1611, the work was reissued twenty-three times in five languages, including three or four English editions (pp. 132–3). See also Eldred D. Jones, *The Elizabethan Image of Africa* (Washington, 1971), pp. 6–9. Jones calls Watreman's *Fardle* typical of 'sources of popular notions of Africa' during the period (p. 6).

13. Samuel Purchas, *Hakluytus Posthumus or Purchas his Pilgrimes*, 1625, 20 vols (reprint, Glasgow, 1905–7). All references to the text are

to volume and page in this edition. The narratives Purchas collects reflect many of the cultural perceptions current early in the seventeenth century. Although Purchas's work is based, like Hakluyt's *Principle Navigations*, on traveller's reports, the accuracy of these documents is hard to ascertain. Similarly, Hodgen (*Early Anthropology*, pp. 137–8) notes that Boemus's *Omnium Gentium Mores* relies on often unreliable medieval and classical authorities for much of its information. For a discussion of exaggeration and misrepresentation in Renaissance narratives describing Eastern cultures, see especially Jones, *The Elizabethan Image of Africa, passim*.

14. Shakespeare, William, *Pericles, Prince of Tyre*, ed. F. D. Hoeniger (New York, 1963), l.Chor.19. All references to the play are to Hoeniger's edition.

15. In 'Sundrie personall Voyages performed by John Sanderson of London Merchant, begun in October, 1584. ended on October, 1602. With an historicall description of Constantinople.'

16. *The Geneva Bible*, 1560; facsimile reprint, ed. Lloyd E. Berry, (Madison, WI, 1969), Acts 11:26.

17. In R. Mose Hadarson's report, 'Of Tharsis and Tharshish, whether it be the same with Ophir, and both, some indefinite remoter Countrey; whether it be the Sea, or Tartessus, or any place in Spaine.'

18. The map follows Acts of the Apostles. It also locates Tyre, Antioch, and 'Ephes'. It marks but does not name Mytilene. Pentapolis remains unidentified on this, one of the most common maps of the period.

19. In a chapter called, 'Master Brerewoods Enquiries of the Religions professed in the World: Of Christians, Mahumetans, Jewes and Idolaters: with other Philosophicall speculations, and divers Annotations added'.

20. Ed. T. M. Cranfill, *Riche his Farewell to Militarie Profession, 1581* (Austin, TX, 1959), p. lxxiv. See also Cranfill's 'Barnaby Rich and King James', *ELH* 16 (1949), 65–75.

21. Anthony, J. Lewis, '"I Feed on Mother's Flesh": Incest and Eating in *Pericles*', *Essays in Literature*, 15 (Fall 1988), 147.

22. Stephen Dickey, 'Language and Role in *Pericles*', *ELR*, 16 (Autumn 1986), 550–66. Dickey states that Pericles 'constantly retreats from the task of governing' (p. 556).

23. Critics who implicate Pericles in the incest of Antiochus and his daughter include: G. Wilson Knight, *The Crown of Life: Essays in Interpretation of Shakespeare's Final Plays* (Oxford, 1947), p. 38; Howard Felperin, *Shakespearean Romance* (Princeton, NJ, 1972), p. 149; and Cyrus Hoy, 'Fathers and Daughters in Shakespeare's Romances', in Carol McGinnis Kay and Henry E. Jacobs (eds),

Shakespeare's Romances Reconsidered (Lincoln, NE, 1978), p. 84, who argues that the discovery of incest 'leaves its mark' not only on Pericles and the play as a whole, but on 'the dramatist's treatment of father and daughter relations' in all four of Shakespeare's romances. Many students of the play, however, disagree with this position, among them Hoeniger, *Pericles*, p. lxxxi; and Richard Hillman, 'Shakespeare's Gower and Gower's Shakespeare: The Larger Debt of *Pericles*', *Shakespeare Quarterly*, 36 (Winter 1985), 434.

24. These lines also begin to create a sense of Pericles as a character whose 'response to the situations of his life is consistently marked by aphorism and concern for action that announces the lonely virtue of its performer' (Dickey, 'Language and Role', p. 555).

25. The pervasive anxiety over Elizabeth's childlessness and the naming of a successor is well known. For discussion of the effect of this concern in late sixteenth- and early seventeenth-century England see, for example, Bergeron, *Shakespeare's Romances*, pp. 7–8; Marie Axton, *The Queen's Two Bodies: Drama and the Elizabethan Succession* (London, 1977), pp. 11–25; and Carole Levin, 'Queens and Claimants: Political Insecurity in Sixteenth-Century England', in Janet Sharistanian (ed.), *Gender, Ideology, and Action: Historical Perspectives on Women's Public Lives* (Westport, CT, 1986), pp. 59–61.

26. As Dickey ('Language and Role', p. 557) points out, Helicanus's role in Pericles's decision is subject to debate: although Pericles, both in soliloquy and conversation, initially describes the advantages of fleeing Tyre, Helicanus both flatters Pericles by denying the need to flatter him (I.ii.38–48) and suggests that he be left in charge if Pericles does leave the country (I.ii.109–10). Kirby Farrell, *Shakespeare's Creation: The Language of Magic and Play* (Amherst, MA, 1975), p. 197, also raises questions about the nature of Helicanus's role, noting that it is Helicanus's deferential nature which permits Pericles to demonstrate the assertive, decisive, forceful action that was impossible in Antioch. Dickey cautions, however, that the extremely corrupt text of I.ii makes interpretation of the scene and Helicanus's character difficult ('Language and Role', p. 557).

27. Gerald N. Sandy, introducing his translation of *The Story of Apollonius King of Tyre*, states that Tarsus is the 'conventional form' of Tharsus, the name used by the anonymous author of the Latin text (p. 738). See Gerald N. Sandy, trans., *The Story of Apollonius King of Tyre*, B. P. Reardon (ed.), *Collected Ancient Greek Novels* (Berkeley, CA, 1989), pp. 736–72.

28. Support for the former position is considerably greater. For instance, Steven Mullaney calls Pericles's behaviour on Tharsus 'a demonstration of legitimate authority in action' (p. 138), and Tennenhouse terms

Pericles generous (*Power on Display*, p. 178). Dickey, supporting the latter view, calls Pericles's donation to Tharsus a bribe in exchange for his shelter in the city, and he also cites Annette C. Flower's statement that the 'rescue of Tharsus ... demonstrates magnanimity when it is easy for Pericles to be magnanimous' (Flower, 'Disguise and Identity in *Pericles, Prince of Tyre*', *SQ*, 26 [1975], 32; qtd in Dickey, 'Language and Role', p. 556).

29. Jonathan Goldberg suggests that the ritual of giving money to his favourites was central to James's personality. He notes that by 'emptying the royal coffers faster than they could possibly be filled, James acted out a drama of conscience and guilt' (*James I and the Politics of Literature: Jonson, Shakespeare, Donne and Their Contemporaries* [Stanford, CA, 1989], p. 139.) J. P. Kenyon more simply calls James 'pre-eminently a man who liked to be liked' (*Stuart England*, The Pelican History of England, vol. 6 [New York, 1978], p. 55).

30. Hoeniger observes that the inhabitants of Tarsus, the city where Antony and Cleopatra first met, 'had a reputation for being vain, effeminate, and luxurious' (*Pericles*, p. 3).

31. Kay Stockholder emphasises this point by noting that Pericles is typically referred to as 'Prince', not 'King', a choice of title that may reflect 'his inner unreadiness to assume full maturity as a ruler' ('Sex and Authority in *Hamlet*, *King Lear*, and *Pericles*', *Mosaic*, 18 [Summer 1985], 20).

32. Bergeron, *Shakespeare's Romances*, p. 71.

33. See Acts 19.

34. See Leslie Fiedler, *The Stranger in Shakespeare* (Frogmore, 1974), p. 177.

35. One specific example of this separation Bergeron cites, in addition to the gradual estrangement of James I and Queen Anne, is the Venetian ambassador's report that during the Princess Sophia's fatal illness, 'The King is at Theobalds; the Queen at Hampton Court, very sorry about the indisposition of her daughter, to whom the King is very devotedly attached, and it is thought he will give up the chance to go to her' (*CSP Venetian*, 11:39; qtd Bergeron, *Shakespeare's Romances*, p. 39). Of course, James did not interrupt his hunting plans to visit his dying daughter.

36. Cumberland Clark, *Shakespeare and the National Character: A Study of Shakespeare's Knowledge and Dramatic and Literary Use of the Distinctive Racial Characteristics of the Different Peoples of the World* (1932; reprint, New York, 1972), p. 179. Hoeniger, following P. Z. Round's 1890 edition of the play, identifies Pentapolis with Cyrenaica, observing that its Latin name is *Pentapolitanae*

Cyrenaeorum terrae. He adds: 'Cyrene, the first of the five towns from which the district took its name, was the chief Hellenic colony in Africa. But in this play, it is taken to be a city in Greece' (*Pericles*, p. 3).

37. C. L. Barber, '"Thou that beget'st him that did thee beget": Transformation in *Pericles* and *The Winter's Tale*', *Shakespeare Survey*, 22 (1969), 59; Tennenhouse, *Power on Display*, p. 182; Peterson, *Time, Tide, and Tempest*, p. 72.

38. The Dedicatorie to Thomas Newton's *A Notable Historie of the Saracens* (1575) refers to the group of peoples described as 'Saracens, Turks, and other Reprobates'. See the 1977 reprint of Newton's text (The English Experience, no. 863, Norwood, NJ).

39. Bergeron, *Shakespeare's Romances and the Royal Family*, p. 23.

40. Wickham, 'From Tragedy to Tragi-Comedy', p. 43.

41. Clark, *Shakespeare and the National Character*, p. 194.

42. For further discussion of Gower's role in *Pericles* see Hoeniger, 'Gower and Shakespeare in *Pericles*'; Dickey, 'Language and Role in *Pericles*' (551 ff); and, Richard Hillman, 'Shakespeare's Gower and Gower's Shakespeare'.

4

Cymbeline: the Rescue of the King

RUTH NEVO

> All creatures born of our fantasy, in the last analysis, are nothing but ourselves.
>
> (Schiller)

There is a 'plethora of story-lines', as Barbara Mowat puts it, in *Cymbeline*:

> The Snow White tale of a princess, her evil stepmother, a home in the woods and a deathlike sleep; a Romeo-and-Juliet-like tragedy of a banished lover, an unwanted suitor, deaths and near-deaths; a medieval folktale of a chastity-wager and an evil Italian villain.[1]

There are also Roman legions and (real) British chronicle history. The components of these stories are quite regular features of romance narrative, but in *Cymbeline* they generate weirdly replicative configurations: Imogen and Posthumus both survive two lost brothers, both are orphans, and both have been brought up in the same household by a step- or foster parent, as have one set, Imogen's, of lost brothers. We make the acquaintance of a foster father, a bereaved father, a blocking father, a substitute father-mother (Belarius), a surrogate father (Lucius), a father-god, a visionary father-and-mother who appear to Posthumus in a dream or hallucination, and a mother-father in the shape of the King who at the end announces himself, in wonder 'A mother to the birth of three' (V.v.369). A poison disguised as a prophylactic becomes a cordial whose effects appear lethal; into (or out of) the play's orbit floats a trunkless head, a headless trunk, and a false trunk from which a man emerges; Imogen is the victim, twice, of a species of (unconsummated) bed-trick, once with a slanderer sent by her husband to test her, and once with the dead body of her rejected suitor whom she takes to be her husband; she is wakened by an aubade (though she has not been in bed with a lover) and laid to rest with an elegy (though she is not dead); Posthumus changes from Roman to British clothing and back a number of times; and there are more recognitions and revelations in Act V than most readers can confidently count. Would one not be justified in regarding repetition of such high frequency as a kind of representational stutter? Or does the play precisely thus speak of what it can only partly say?

Cymbeline presents some of the knottiest problems in Shakespeare genre criticism, appearing to be neither fish, flesh nor good red herring; readable neither as history, comedy nor romance. Though placed after *Pericles* in the accepted chronology of the final plays, it is in many ways more akin to the earlier *All's Well* than to the other three romances. As in *All's Well*, the heroine sets out in pursuit of an errant husband and the hub of the interest lies in the affairs of the young married couple, who are estranged. Yet much is made of the return of Cymbeline's long-lost sons and the family reunions, as in the romances, which bridge the wide gap of time inserted into the dramatic action by the interwoven desires of two generations. As in *All's Well* it is important that a wasteland-sick king is made well. *Cymbeline* is the last of the plays to make a bold young woman, rather than her father, its main protagonist. In that respect Imogen is more akin to the independent daughters of the earlier courtship comedies than to the thaumaturgic daughters of the three last plays; yet she is far from being free of a controlling parent as are Beatrice, Viola, Olivia and Rosalind. She is what one might call a post-tragic heroine, abused, vilified, hunted, and not in possession of crucial knowledge. She may know what she is doing when she defies her tyrant father ('I beseech you, sir, / Harm not yourself with your vexation, / I am senseless of your wrath' [I.i.133–5]), but she (like everyone else in *Cymbeline*, indeed)[2] is at every point unaware of or deceived about the major facts effecting her situation. Where Rosalind and Viola act out their maverick fantasies with a blithe insouciance, adopting their boy's garb as a ploy to be enjoyed, while it lasts, for the mastery it gives them,

Imogen is driven by desperate straits into hers. She wears, as we shall see, her cap and hose with a difference. It is a difference, I shall argue, which requires for its understanding a radical departure in critical method.

[...]

Suppose we attempt to adapt a hermeneutic of dream analysis, or a model of psychoanalytic discourse for the construing of the 'strangenesses', absurdities, coincidences, improbabilities in this play? Suppose we assume that dramatis personae, like personae in dreams may be composite or split figures, doubles or proxies for each other, and that language ambiguous, or evocatively charged or polysemous or conspicuously figured may indeed mean more, or other than it ostensibly says?[3]

Certainly *Cymbeline* is an excellent text with which to test such hypotheses. We will go far to find a better. It is my project in the following pages to argue that the strange, the outlandish, the incredibly coincidental, the absurd, grotesque or uncanny can be read, not as excrescences to be somehow explained away, but as profoundly meaningful. To ape for a moment the structuralist type of terminology, and to launch a companion to rhemes, semes and phonemes, such oddities could perhaps be regarded as 'dremes' emerging into the ordinary carriage of the plot and the ordinary behaviour of its agents with their own ulterior and covert messages. It is not important, nor is it possible to determine to what extent the author was conscious of them. It is for the purpose of being able to talk about such messages, without determining their status, that we require the notion of a textual unconscious. It is just because *Cymbeline* is replete with representational anomalies, discords and dissonances, presents us with a medley of melodies and chords diverging and converging in a bewildering polyphony, that it can provide a test case for the value of the concept. The question is can we unbind this text, feel our way toward a unifying, organising fantasy which we can deduce as having generated the play and which, made conscious, is capable of reanimating in us a corresponding working through process? A hundred years of psychoanalysis have accumulated a vast archive of instances analogous to the adventurers of our protagonists, and provided a lexicon, but it will not be a matter of deciphering a code or of diagnosing a neurosis in a dramatic character. It is rather a matter of feeling our way into a state of mind, or states of mind, in which the oddities and discrepancies suddenly 'figure'; it is a matter, to add a significant letter to Lacan's dictum, of discovering 'the "unsaid" that lies in the (w)holes of the discourse'.[4]

In the first instance this entails psychological analysis, at whatever level, of the motivations and dispositions of the play's protagonists. 'What does Imogen (or Posthumus, or Cymbeline) want?' is a primary question, but we at once become aware that it is less important to inquire what, for instance, Iachimo or Cloten or Belarius want, than to figure out what they represent within the imagined worlds of the protagonists. Just as dreams are always about the dreamer, so there is always a central ego for a play to be about. It was precisely the reversal of this hierarchy which was witty and intriguing in Tom Stoppard's *Rosencrantz and Guildenstern are Dead*.

Our first oddity, then, is the play's eponym. Why is the drama named for King Cymbeline, when it is not in any strict sense a history play conventionally named after a reigning monarch, and when he himself, save for his initial banishment of Posthumus, is a passive figure, browbeaten and henpecked by his wicked Queen and incomparably less prominent in the play's action than his sorely tried daughter? About her importance there will no doubt be little argument. The Imogenolatry of nineteenth-century Shakespeare criticism,[5] its roots in defensive Victorian (and Renaissance) idealisation to which we no longer subscribe, is still pervasive in the criticism as witness to her centrality, however we may wish to account for it. Yet the King is the pivot and cynosure of all the revelations and recognitions in Act V, suddenly a rival epicentre. The virtual absence of His Majesty the King in the play which is named for him is thus a signifier which demands attention. I believe that the central ego in *Cymbeline* is, ultimately, Cymbeline, but that, for reasons which will presently appear, that ego is in abeyance, in temporary suspension, as it were, behind the three plots through which *Cymbeline* unfolds.

The three plots in *Cymbeline*: the individual marital (Imogen and Posthumus); the familial (the kidnapped brothers); and the national (the rebellion of a province against the Empire) are interlocked with a craft which it is customary to admire; but it is worth noticing that they do not conduct themselves in the least in the way Shakespearean subplots usually do. We are accustomed to three- or even four-tier mirroring structures, as in *A Midsummer Night's Dream*, or *As You Like It*, or *Henry IV*, where goings-on at the socially lower, or more 'foolish' levels counterpoint or comment upon the doings and sayings at the upper level.[6] In *Cymbeline* there is no such ramification or hierarchy. Rather there seem to be issues which find expression over and over again, and so suggest the existence of an obsessive need, a compulsion. The play is like a jigsaw puzzle whose broken-apart and mixed-up pieces must be matched and put together. It is like its families. Children are orphaned, or kidnapped, parents bereaved, a wife and husband separated, siblings parted. The confederation of an empire and its province disrupted. Fragmentation is brought to a phantasmagoric extreme; even bodies are dismembered and not recognised. It is worth noticing that the word 'thing' as an epithet applied to persons – 'Thou basest thing' (I.i.125), 'O disloyal thing' (l.131), 'This imperceiverant thing' (IV.i.14), 'Slight thing of Italy' (V.iv.64), for instance, occurs in *Cymbeline* more often than in any other of Shakespeare's plays. Notice, in contradistinction to this reification, Posthumus' culminating organic image when he finds himself and Imogen: 'Hang there like fruit, my soul' (V.v.263). The personae, disassociated parts of dismembered families, do not recognise each other, or themselves, are confused about their roles, their 'parts', especially Posthumus and Imogen. Or else they are partial persons, clearly projective. The Queen is a poison mother, a projection of infantile fantasy. The King is a *nom du père*, a *non du père*, to borrow Lacan's extraordinarily apt witticism, but in his absence other father figures keep springing up. The recognition scenes at the end, until the very last, are partial, piecemeal, kaleidoscopic; people are, and are not, recognised. The King finds Lucius' page, his daughter, hauntingly familiar. Posthumus sees, though he does not recognise, in the feminine beauty of Belarius' sons the resemblance to their sister, his wife. The family, Meredith Skura notes, 'is so important that characters cannot even imagine themselves without one'.[7] Their problem, however, is how to imagine themselves within one. Hence, in the course of the drama, families keep being reconstituted, partly, or by proxy, in caves, in visions, in disguise.

Let us pursue the fortunes of the initially presented protagonists. We shall not reach the deepest level of fantasy until we have worked through the more manifest meanings and motivations which lead us to what they screen. But it is to the young lovers that the play first solicits our attention.

The story of Posthumus Leonatus, a fatherless youth whose very name orphans him, is the *Bildungsroman* of a young man whose manhood is under inspection. He is of noble lineage but cannot, as yet, be 'delve[d] to the root' (I.i.28). He is put to the

test first of all by the banishment which immediately follows his
marriage. Skura is wrong when she says that Posthumus' first
mistake is to 'usurp his proper place' (in his foster family) 'when
he elopes with Imogen'.[8] He precisely does not elope with her. He
allows himself to be separated from her and leaves her in virtual
imprisonment in Britain. The Gentleman who lavishes praise
upon him, expressing, he says, the general view, announces that
he is a creature such

> As, to seek through the regions of the earth
> For one his like, there would be something failing
> In him that should compare
>
> (I.i.20–2)

The syntax is disorientingly ambiguous. Anyone like him would, by
virtue of the likeness, possess a failing? Anyone assuming to be
compared with him would, by virtue of the comparison, be found
wanting? We settle, of course for the second, but we cannot quite
rid our minds of the other possibility the syntax and lineation
allows. This is followed by a very curious phrase in the Gentleman's
assurance to his interlocuter that he is not exaggerating:

> I do extend him, sir, within himself,
> Crush him together rather than unfold
> His measure duly.
>
> (ll.25–7)

This suggests some malleable object rather than the admired
scion of a noble stock; and we learn, in Pisanio's account of
Cloten's attack upon him, that 'My master rather play'd than
fought / And had no help of anger' (I.i.161–3). What are we being
told, in so devious a manner, about Posthumus the universally
praised? Some doubts about the 'eagle' quality of Imogen's lover
must surely enter one's mind, the more especially since her own
defiance of her father has been outspoken and unequivocal.
Interestingly enough, his own first words to his beloved betray a
self-consciousness about the very question of manliness:

> My queen, my mistress!
> O lady, weep no more, lest I give cause
> To be suspected of more tenderness
> Than doth become a man.
>
> (I.i.92–5)

These two newly-wed quasi-siblings, violently separated, their marriage unconsummated, mark their parting with the gift of significantly symbolic transitional objects. She gives him a diamond, her mother's, to be parted with only after her death, when he will woo her successor; he, invoking death rather than such a possibility, 'imprisons' her arm with a bracelet, a 'manacle of love' (l.122). He needs to 'possess' her (his preoccupation with possessions is evident throughout), and is uncertain of his tenure. She needs to foster and cherish him, but, as we touchingly learn when she relives, with Pisanio, the distancing of his ship, worrying about getting letters, reimagining his diminishing image, envying the handkerchief he kissed and waved, mourning the lost opportunity to bask in a lover's appreciation, she needs him as a mirror in which she can see herself, recognise herself as cherished and valued.

> I did not take my leave of him, but had
> Most pretty things to say. Ere I could tell him
> How I would think on him at certain hours ...
>   or I could make him swear
> The shes of Italy should not betray
> Mine interest and his honor ...
>   or ere I could
> Give him that parting kiss which I had set
> Betwixt two charming words, comes in my father,
> And like the tyrannous breathing of the north
> Shakes all our buds from growing.
>   (I.iii.25–37, passim)

They are buds in their youthfulness, in their youthful narcissism, and they are 'shaken' from growing by the blocking father that Cymbeline is to them. Buds that are kept from growing together, grow apart, revealing fatal dissonances in their relationship, and disequilibrium in their personalities.

That Posthumus allowed himself to be torn from his bride, did not snatch her to him and take flight with her, is, of course, a donnée of the play; but much, and with a certain emphasis, is made of it. In Act II, scene iv Philario asks Posthumus what means he is taking to overcome the King's interdict. 'Not any', is the reply,

> but abide the change of time,
> Quake in the present winter's state, and wish
> That warmer days would come.
>   (ll.4–6)

This is followed by an oxymoron which reads suspiciously like a slip of the tongue. 'In these fear'd hopes,' says Posthumus, 'I barely gratify your love' (ll.6–7). Which emotion, if any, is dominant? fear, hope, doubt? If it is felt that pessimism or trepidation is sufficiently accounted for by a state of fatherlessness, propertylessness and banishment, it is worth recalling that Imogen refers to him 'when he was here' as 'inclin[ing] to sadness, and oft-times / Not knowing why' (I.vi.61–3) and that the sigh that escapes her: 'O, that husband! / My supreme crown of grief ... Had I been thief-stol'n, / As my two brothers, happy!' (ll.3–6), makes her cause of grief anaphorically her husband himself rather than, or at least as well as, his absence; and while it ostensibly refers to the stealing away of her brothers in the past, contains the suggestion of a wished-for stealing away of herself in the present. Posthumus, who speaks very highly of his countrymen as formidable warriors, lacks himself, it seems, sufficient pugnacity to shine as a lover, and it is as a chivalric lover that he is put to the test in Rome by the challenge of a mischief-making Italian.

[...]

There is no question about the provocation. The question that the scene raises is Posthumus' response. For what is, after all, the expected knightly procedure? Surely in such circumstances a man would challenge the slanderer, even the mere doubter of his mistress's honour, to a duel without further ado. It is himself, as against his adversary, that he would put to the test, not his inviolate lady. The scene itself reminds us of this in its reference to the previous occasion, and Philario, nervously attempting to allay the tension: 'Let us leave here, gentlemen' (l.99), 'Gentlemen, enough of this. It came in too suddenly; let it die as it was born, and I pray you be better acquainted' (ll.120–2), has clearly such an outcome in mind. Instead of the 'the arbiterment of swords' (l.49), however, we have the taking of the wager, which places the onus of proof upon the lady, and makes Posthumus' manly honour dependent, not upon an action of his, but upon an action, or non-action, of hers. If Imogen prove faithless, 'I am no further your enemy; she is not worth our debate' (ll.159–60); but the whole chivalric point, surely, is to maintain at sword's point his *belief* in her faithfulness! If she is faithful, *then* he will punish Iachimo – 'you shall answer me with your sword' (l.163). Both these alternatives take refuge in male bonds and relations in which, it seems, Posthumus shelters. The wager makes Imogen a mere object through which a bond with

Iachimo is cemented: either he will become his friend, no woman between them, or his chastiser, again man to man. The wager reflects an inner question, the possibility of which the text has already insinuated into our minds: shall he be (can he?) be a man among men, or a man to a woman?

If Iachimo finds her unassailable, and so not only of supreme worth but also manifestly devoted to Posthumus, this will flatter Posthumus' self-esteem; but what if the cunning, cynical Italian succeeds in gaining possession of 'her dearest bodily part' (l.150), in performing, in other words, as Posthumus' proxy? Does the wager (rather than a duel) fulfil some inner need or desire of Posthumus himself? Is there a secret complicity between inveigler and inveigled?

What for that matter, if Cloten, master of all he surveys in England, gets possession of Imogen? These two are both assailants upon Imogen's chastity, would-be performers of her lover's role, and they are diametrically opposed, sophisticated, cunning, gallant and coarse lout, Queen's son though he be. They are clearly antithetical doubles. If there is an element of cultural comment in the mimetic aspect of their representation – English provincial against Italianate rogue – this remains marginal in the play as a whole. On the other hand the antithesis resonates throughout the whole play and acquires an organising force when we can see it as in some way significantly related to Posthumus himself. Such a relation has been proposed by Murray Schwartz, building skilfully upon Freud's analysis of 'The Universal Tendency to Debasement in the Sphere of Love'.

Iachimo and Cloten, he says, 'represent two related obsessions of a Renaissance personality burdened with the idealisation and worship of women and seeking to establish a stable relationship between platonic sublimation and crude sexual expression'. Both are 'aspects or projections of Posthumus' psyche' which is 'in tense and precarious balance' between alternative sexual modes.[9] 'By following Posthumus carefully through the play we can identify the dreamlike logic (the logic of displacement, condensation, substitution, multiple symbolisation) which underlies its sometimes confusing, over-sophisticated surface', and discover in him 'the tyranny of the superego which would split the psyche into diametric opposites, one part that worships and another that defiles' (p. 236).

We can interpret the play's psychomachia, then, as an inhibition of desire on Posthumus' part which is exhibited in extremely subtle ways through the two proxy suitors, the fastidious Iachimo and the unspeakable Cloten. The following account of this representation of inner conflict owes much to Schwartz' explication, though I do not follow him completely, either in detail or in respect to his conclusions.[10]

Cloten is introduced as early as Act I, scene ii in all his gross, rank, brute libidinality. Pretending to machismo, he is derided by his attendant lords with a flattery the irony of which is so palpable that only a Cloten-fool could miss it. We meet him again immediately before the bedroom scene, when his malodorous presence and his phallic / martial non-exploits are called attention to: 'a pox on't! I had rather not be so noble as I am. They dare not fight with me because of the Queen my mother. Every Jack slave hath his bellyful of fighting, and I must go up and down like a cock that nobody can match' (II.i.18–22). Cloten, says Murray Schwartz, is 'unadulterable phallic aggression' (p. 222), a 'personification of infantile fixations' (p. 226); 'Cloten represents ... uncontrolled phallic wishes that seek their objects relentlessly and without the least regard for otherness' (p. 223). However, Cloten's sexuality is not sheer animal lust, or uninhibited libido. It is disowned by a constant defensive meiosis. The lexis with which he is associated is drawn from a 'south-fog' (II.iii.131) of cloacal, noisome and obscene imagery. As Schwartz puts it, 'He embodies the belief that sexuality defiles its object and drags chastity through the mire' (p. 225). Cloten and Iachimo are not simply two rival evils laying siege to Imogen's integrity and virtue, but secret sharers in the psyche of the absent Posthumus for whom they substitute, and it is this that gives the two personae and the psychomachia they articulate its particular depth and interest. Both Cloten and his counterpart Iachimo ('Cloten in civilised dress', as Schwartz puts it, [p. 227]) represent isolated and split-off parts of an ambivalent and unintegrated personality, the one 'arrogant piece of flesh', pure sexual drive, 'the rebellion of a codpiece' (p. 225), the other, pure, aim-inhibited fantasy as exhibited in the exquisite aestheticism of the bedroom scene.

Cloten, intent upon serenading the object of his desire, is nakedly lewd: 'I am advis'd to give her music a'mornings; they say it will penetrate. ... If you can penetrate her with your fingering, so; we'll try with tongue too' (II.iii.11–15). The aubade opens the scene which follows Iachimo's bedroom visit. The contrast could hardly be more extreme. The aubade is itself readable 'from above' and 'from below': as pretty Ovidian myth or, through its flying, its rising, its steeds watering at the springs of chaliced flowers, its winking Mary-buds that begin to ope their eyes, as veiled coitus. It is ironic in that no night of love has in fact been enjoyed; but it sharpens our perception that in fantasy one indeed has. The 'fingering' and 'tonguing' of Cloten has its marvellously imagined counterpart in Iachimo's soliloquy at Imogen's bedside.

[...]

Iachimo would rather poison Posthumus' mind than possess Imogen's body. So he does not touch her. He denies himself the kiss which he projects onto the 'rubies unparagoned' of her lips: 'How dearly they do't!' (II.ii.17–18). 'Doing', however, is far more than kissing in the imagery which follows. If we allow the language to work its will upon us we will perceive how Iachimo savours every moment of a fantasised sexual act. He begins with the invocation of Tarquin, relishing the latter's menacing tread: 'Our Tarquin thus / Did softly press the rushes ere he waken'd / The chastity he wounded' (ll.12–14). Desire is concentrated in an intensity of seeing, a lust of the eyes. The phallic flame of the taper is itself a voyeur as it 'Bows toward her, and would under-peep her lids' (ll.19–20); the bracelet (an upward displacement) is removed with ease – it is 'As slippery as the Gordian knot was hard' (l.34); the climax, which has brought so many empathetic critics to a similar exalted state, engages a number of primal desires in its minutely observed image. The 'crimson drops / I'th' bottom of a cowslip' (ll.38–9), defloration in an innocently pastoral mask, is transferred to the mole upon her breast, redoubling fantasied pleasure. The soliloquy closes with an orgasm – a rape – completed: 'the leaf's turn'd down / Where Philomel gave up' (ll.45–6), and Iachimo, brought out of his trance by the striking clock (l.51), returns to the trunk with a gnawing sense of guilt.

Iachimo shrewdly exploits vicarious fantasy when he returns with his report, first of her bedchamber 'where I confess I slept not' (II.iv.67), with its tapestry of Cleopatra 'when she met her Roman / And Cydnus swelled above the banks' (ll.70–1), its chimney piece of 'Chaste Dian bathing' (ll.81–2), its winking Cupid andirons, and finally the mole in its 'delicate lodging' beneath her breast, which, he says, he kissed, to the enhancement of an appetite just sated (ll.137–8). Posthumus is sexually aroused by the account. His bitter 'Spare your arithmetic, never count the turns' (l.142) is vividly obscene, as is the tell-tale condensation of images in the rosy 'pudency' (is the lady blushing? or is the sweet view another rosy site?) in his succeeding soliloquy:

> Me of my lawful pleasure she restrain'd
> And pray'd me oft forbearance; did it with
> A pudency so rosy the sweet view on't
> Might well have warm'd old Saturn, that I thought her
> As chaste as unsunn'd snow.
>
> (II.v.9–13)

Just as he 'sees' that rosy 'pudency' so he 'sees' the 'full-acorned' boar which 'Cried "O!" and mounted' (ll.16–17), an image in which high feeding and high sexuality coalesce under the pressure of the imagined scene.

Posthumus, we perceive, is precipitated into his Cloten self, his unreconstructed, for him demeaning sensuality, by Iachimo's machinations. The bracelet is a basilisk – a Medusa's head – that kills him to look on; the metonymic mole a 'stain, as big as hell can hold' (II.iv.140); and in savage reaction he will 'tear her limb-meal!' (l.147), obliterating, in his misogynistic outburst, the threat, and magnet, that is 'the woman's part' (II.v.20). 'The woman's part' is, in analytic terminology, overdetermined. It is the 'dearest bodily part' which his exacerbated fantasy has 'seen'; it is the maternal half of procreation which he would repudiate: 'Is there no way for men to be, but women / Must be half-workers?' (ll.1–2) and upon which he projects all falsities and evils, including his own sense of inauthenticity: his father was, must have been, absent when he 'was stamped', when 'some coiner with his tools / Made [him] a counterfeit' (l.5); and it is, as the woman's part in him – sex, his own repressed sexuality, his own fear of sexual inadequacy, his sexual jealousy – for which he blames women and from which he recoils in rage:

> I'll write against them,
> Detest them, curse them, yet 'tis greater skill
> In a true hate to pray they have their will:
> The very devils cannot plague them better.
>
> (ll.32–5)

Finally, in the letter which informs Pisanio that 'Thy mistress ... hath play'd the strumpet in my bed' (III.iv.21–2), Posthumus, in a perverse, self-contaminating turn, incorporates the woman's part. 'Thy mistress hath play'd the strumpet in my bed: the testimonies whereof lies bleeding in me.' It is he who is the violated virgin since he cannot be the violator that in his present sexual violence he would wish to be.

To illuminate the play's psychomachia from the side of the triad Posthumus, Iachimo, Cloten, however, is to default on half the story. There is another side to the inner conflict in Act II which is plotted through the opposite aspect of the triangle – Imogen, Iachimo, Cloten. The relations can be diagrammed:

                    Iachimo
        Imogen   Posthumus
                    Cloten

These symmetries invite assessment of the protagonists as mirror images of each other. Both are ideal objects to each other; both are victims; both take flight and both seek rehabilitation (literally) in other clothing; and not only Posthumus, but also Imogen, we very soon discover, is in subtle tension or disharmony with her sexuality.

We may have already noticed that Imogen, the fiercely rejected daughter ('Nay, let her languish / A drop of blood a day, and being aged / Die of this folly!' [I.i.156–8]) of a possessive father, chafes at the constraints of being a woman. Hearing of the near-fight between Posthumus and Cloten she says,

> I would they were in Afric both together,
> Myself by with a needle, that I might prick
> The goer-back.
>
> (ll.167–9)

This is odd considering that the 'goer-back', according to Pisanio, was Posthumus himself, and therefore betrays a certain vexation in this abandoned bride. Her reference to her husband as 'My supreme crown of grief … Had I been thief-stol'n, / As my two brothers, happy!' (I.vi.4–6) has already been noted. Imogen is ardent and loving, and not about to admit to any defect in her beloved, but her tongue betrays her.

She is herself hard-pressed. Not only does she remain alone, in virtual imprisonment, in the absence of her lover, beset by the coarse lout she detests as much as she detests his mother, but she is verbally assaulted by the man who comes to her as her husband's friend.

We note her spirited resistance to Iachimo's innuendos in the testing scene, and her repudiation of him when he gives himself away; but it is his giveaway that has saved her. 'My lord, I fear, / Has forgot Britain' (I.vi.112–13) she has just said, dismayed despite herself. It is this perhaps that accounts for the eagerness with which, appeased by Iachimo's retraction, she takes the trunk into custody into her own bedchamber. However, there is, we are invited to infer, another reason. The precious trunk contains jewels purchased by Posthumus: its contents stand therefore, as nearly as any object may, for his bodily presence. It is both in longing and to make amends that she wishes it so close.

Imogen, in the bedroom scene, is an inert, sleeping presence, the object of Iachimo's fantasy, but the references to time which set off and frame Iachimo's soliloquy, mark off a timeless space of fantasy, or dream, for Imogen too. She has been reading for three hours, we learn, before she falls asleep. She prays for protection, as she puts her book aside, from 'fairies and the tempters of the night' (II.ii.9); and when we discover at what episode her reading terminated – in the tale of Tereus, 'where Philomel gave up' (l.46) – we can see why. Wedded, but unbedded, abandoned, in effect, by her husband, her marriage proscribed and herself rejected by her father, beset like Penelope by unwanted suitors, the story of Philomel and Tereus objectifies ambivalent fear and excitement.

[...]

'O for a horse with wings!' Imogen says, when Posthumus' letter summons her to Milford Haven (III.ii.48). And when Pisanio assures her that they can cover no more than a score of miles 'twixt sun and sun' (l.68): 'Why, one that rode to's execution, man, / Could never go so slow' (ll.70–1). This is patent dramatic irony, of course. Pisanio has already read Posthumus' murder letter, and Imogen will hear of it before she gets to her heaven-haven; but if nothing is accidental in the world of the mind then the uttering of such a comparison must indicate the presence of an underlying dread. The manner in which this passionate and high-spirited girl – who has defied her father's fury, who struggles, alone, to resolve the ambivalence of untried sexuality, suffering the absence of her lover with some accusatory vexation, however unacknowledged – responds to the outrage of her husband's misconception of her becomes thus poignantly understandable:

> False to his bed? What is it to be false?
> To lie in watch there and to think on him?
> To weep 'twixt clock and clock? If sleep charge nature,

> To break it with a fearful dream of him,
> And cry myself awake?
>
> (III.iv.40–4)

Outraged and bewildered, her defence against his accusations takes the form of an accusatory injury against herself: she begs Pisanio to kill her – to do his master's bidding – with an image of mutilation, of positive dismemberment:

> Poor I am stale, a garment out of fashion,
> And for I am richer than to hang by th' walls,
> I must be ripp'd. To pieces with me!
>
> (ll.51–3)

This is a turning inward of her anger and her anguish. She sees herself a hunted or trapped creature, a sacrificial lamb or deer, turns feminine sexual submission into masochistic punishment as she tosses away the protective wad of Posthumus' letters in her bosom and invites the sword's penetration: 'Obedient as the scabbard' (l.80). Her first defence against the mortification of Posthumus' treatment of her is a literal mortifying of herself – a mort of the deer, so to speak.

However, Imogen, possessed of remarkable resilience, recovers. Even before Pisanio's suggestion of the page disguise, she has taken heart, and determined, in the first place, not to return to the court:

> No court, no father, nor no more ado
> With that harsh, noble, simple nothing,
> That Cloten, whose love suit hath been to me
> As fearful as a siege.   ...
> Hath Britain all the sun that shines? day? night?
> Are they not but in Britain?
>
> (ll.131–7)

Her response to her plight, like Posthumus' to his, but with opposite effect, is also to reject 'the woman's part' in her, to 'forget to be a woman' (l.154). She embraces Pisanio's idea of the journey to Italy with enthusiasm, is 'almost a man already' (ll.166–7), and will 'abide it with a prince's courage' (ll.183–4); but Imogen's transvestite fantasy solves nothing.

First of all, footsore and weary, she discovers that 'a man's life is a tedious one' (III.vi.1), as she remarks with a wry humour. However, it is her hermaphrodite membership in the reconstituted family of Belarius which makes clear that her flight from her sex will never do. Not only is her real sex only partly concealed – the brothers clearly fall in love with the feminine quality of her beauty (much as does Orsino with Cesario's): 'Were you a woman, youth, / I should woo hard' (ll.68–9) – but also the family likeness between the three is, we infer, only partly concealed. Unavailable to conscious knowledge it is evidently unconsciously registered. For Imogen the vigorous masculinity of the peerless twain is extremely attractive but what it precipitates is a wishful fantasy about her lost brothers, which she invokes to mitigate the defaulting of Posthumus. 'Would ... they / Had been my father's sons' (ll.75–6) she thinks, for then, no longer sole heiress to her father's crown (nor sole object of his possessive love) – her 'prize' would have been less and so 'more equal ballasting' to Posthumus, and their love might have fared better (ll.76–7). As it is, rejected and calumniated she reaffirms that she would rather be a man in their company than a woman to the false Leonatus.

The audience, knowing what it knows, perceives this encounter synoptically. What is (and is not) being recognised by the brothers is Imogen's true gender. What is not (and yet is) being recognised by all three is their kinship. The love which springs up between them is therefore a composite of elements: narcissistic, erotic and familial, a volatile quantity which cannot recognise itself or disentangle its objects.

The rural retreat in Wales is the 'green world' or other place which in Shakespearean comedy is liberating and restorative;[11] but it *is* a retreat – from maturation; a return to infancy, or even beyond, to the shelter of a cave / womb. Belarius is a mother / father – he was a tree 'whose boughs did bend with fruit' until the 'storm or robbery' which 'shook down [his] mellow hangings ... and left [him] bare to weather' (III.iii.61–4). The siblings are androgynous, or sexless – Fidele sings like an angel, and cooks like one too; they all, in fact, cook and keep house like women, though the boys are hunters too. This denial of adult differentiation is, on the one hand, gratifying, healing, a wishful undoing, but the play keeps a stern and monitoring eye on it.

The retreat is glossed in the homilies of Belarius as a beneficient exchange of the sophistries and corruptions of the court for the archaic simplicities of nature, and his contempt for the gates of monarchs, which are 'arched so high that giants may jet through / And keep their impious turbands on without / Good morrow to the sun' (ll.5–7), is a detraction of masculine arrogance. It is subverted by the aspiration of the boys to live the life of the 'full-winged eagle' rather than that of the 'sharded beetle' (ll.20–1), and by Belarius' own approval of their 'wild' violence, which he sees as evidence of an 'invisible instinct' of royalty (IV.ii.177ff). They are precariously poised, in their immaturity, between the noble and the savage, and, all unawares, between innocence and incest since the eruption into their lives of Fidele. The Belarius family romance – designed to 'bar [the king] of succession' (III.iii.102) – represents a barren wish. Belarius' is a fantasy family whose childlike non-differentiation is regressive.

Back at the British court sexual roles are also, in their own way, fruitlessly and damagingly inverted. Cymbeline is patently reluctant to rise against the imperial father figure Caesar, who knighted him and under whom he spent his youth. Patriotic self-assertion is left to the Queen and her son, whose joint monopolisation of the masculine virtues is rendered in interestingly characteristic ways. Cloten, crude as ever, announces that 'we will nothing pay / For wearing our own noses' (III.i.13–14). The Queen describes the British isles as a *hortus inclusus* ('Neptune's park', within its 'salt-water girdle' in Cloten's description [l.80]), a space normally feminine in the symbology of landscapes, but here fortified and lethal:

> ribb'd and pal'd in
> With oaks unscalable and roaring waters,
> With sands that will not bear your enemies' boats,
> But suck them up to th' topmast.
>
> (ll.19–22)

Britain's heirs, cavemen in Wales, are mothered by a man, Britain itself is kinged by a woman, who, if she has her way and her wish for the speedy demise of both Imogen and her father, will soon in fact 'have the placing of the British crown' upon her son's head (III.v.65). The play's central Act has brought the drama to an imminent crisis of intrigue at court, and war over the tribute money. In Belarius' other isle Cloten closes in upon the fugitive Imogen. Appropriately, at the outset of Act IV Fidele, succumbing to grief for her lost love, falls ill.

In Shakespearean tragic structure we regularly find protagonists in Act IV facing a great void, an annihilation of the values which have sustained them. Deprived of their objects of love or faith or hope, they experience despair, so that possible remedy, tantalisingly

just within reach, is occluded from their view, or, if perceived, is
snatched away by the circumstances which have swept beyond
control. In his comic structures, Act IV initiates the remedial phase
of the narrative, exorcising precedent errors and follies by maximil-
ising them to the point of exhaustion. In *Cymbeline*, the most intri-
cately interlocked of the tragicomedies, both vectors coexist, and
are synchronised in the play's most phantasmagoric event – the
mock death of Fidele. In terms of form the bizarre and lurid events
in Wales mark the concatenation of the two contradictory genres in
a grotesque indeterminacy of tragic and comic effects. In terms of
fantasy they mark a turning point in the working through of the
deep conflicts the play articulates.

Imogen, heartsick, takes the potion given her by Pisanio in the
belief that it is remedial, which it is, the malignant will of the
Queen having been outwitted by Cornelius, her physician, who exchanged her poisonous brew for a harmless narcotic. Only
Cornelius, however, knows this. It enables the tragicomic transformation of grave and serious events into restorative and gratifying
ends. Had it been the poison the Queen intended it to be, Imogen's
taking it, on advice from the good Pisanio, would have constituted
the fatal error in a tragic sequence of ironic reversals and disasters.
As it is, it constitutes the mock deception which brings about a sequence of harmless (though painful) errors, mistaken identities and
confusions, which will issue, despite the harm already caused, in a
benign resolution. It is the cause of the (apparent) death which the
play, as comedy, will surmount, while at the same time it is the
cause that the death *is* only apparent, a deathlike trance. It thus
provides for a playing out and working through, in imagination, of
the despairing or destructive urge which drags against the play's
reconstructive thrust.

Cloten, hot-foot on Imogen's track, vicious in his retaliatory
intent to kill Posthumus, ravish her and spurn her home to her
father, is beheaded by Guiderius, and his 'clotpole' sent down the
stream 'in embassy to his mother' (IV.ii.185) in a strange parody of
pagan fertility rituals. As a consequence, the Queen, bereft, so to
speak, of her male organ, declines and dies. This effectively does
away with the evil ones, eliminating sadism and reincorporating it
with its primal source, the voracious mother of infantile fantasy.

That Imogen, who was found in bed by Iachimo, is now found in
her (death) bed with Cloten, reiterates the relationship of these two
to her absent husband: the one representing the repressed libido in

him, the other the repressive superego. Posthumus' next appearance, as we shall see, exhibits him with the violent Cloten-id elements in his personality entirely extinguished, and later he will rout Iachimo in single fight; but we shall return to Posthumus' fortunes presently.

In terms of the emotional dynamic of the play it is a melancholy course that is charted by the sequence from bedroom scene to burial scene. In the bedroom scene eroticism was deviant and devious, but alive. The bedroom scene was accompanied by the aubade, an accolade to love; the burial scene by the dirge, which welcomes death. This haunting lyric envisages a sublime indifference to reed as to oak, to both joy and moan, a placid acceptance of the dust to which golden lads and girls must come. Its desire is for death, for the cessation of being and of vicissitude, a 'quiet consummation' devoutly to be wished. However, Imogen wakes bewildered from her drugged stupor to discover the headless body of Cloten / Posthumus beside her. 'Limb-meal' she inventories her lover's body:

> I know the shape of's leg; this is his hand,
> His foot Mercurial, his Martial thigh,
> The brawns of Hercules; but his Jovial face –
> Murther in heaven?
>
> (IV.ii.309–12)

Throwing herself upon the faceless, headless body she enacts an hysterical incorporation: she smears her cheek with the blood of the corpse, as if to die herself, or, in a gruesome fantasy realisation of Elizabethan 'dying', to match her maidenhead with the violated head of her lover.[12] In this 'consummation' Eros is undone, overwhelmed, by Thanatos, its dark companion.

'I am nothing; or if not, / Nothing to be were better' (ll.367–8) is Imogen's desolate reply to Lucius' question 'What art thou?' (l.366) when he comes upon the scene at the graveside. It is just here that the countermovement to recovery is initiated. Fidele's head was to be laid to the east, we recall, in preparation, we now perceive, for just such a rebirth. 'Wilt take thy chance with me? I will not say / Thou shalt be so well master'd, but be sure / No less belov'd' (ll.382–4), Lucius says, and in response to her vulnerable epicene youthfulness insists that he would 'rather father thee than master thee' (l.395). Imogen, dogged survivor, responds.

Posthumus' progress towards recovery begins with his conscience-stricken, grief-stricken soliloquy at the start of the play's final phase. This is our first meeting with Posthumus since his outburst of misogyny in Act II, scene v. Now he addresses the bloody cloth, evidence, as he believes, of Imogen's death. The great rage is killed in him, and there is a yearning for some form of expression for love, although he is still convinced of Imogen's 'wrying':

> You married ones,
> If each of you should take this course, how many
> Must murther wives much better than themselves
> For wrying but a little! ...
> Gods, if you
> Should have ta'en vengeance on my faults, I never
> Had liv'd to put on this; so had you saved
> The noble Imogen to repent, and strook
> Me, wretch, more worth your vengeance. But alack,
> You snatch some hence for little faults; that's love,
> To have them fall no more ...
> I'll ...
> suit myself
> As does a Britain peasant; so I'll fight
> Against the part I come with; so I'll die
> For thee, O Imogen, even for whom my life
> Is every breath a death
>
> (V.i.2–27, passim)

Is there equivocation in 'the part I come with' (we recall 'the woman's part in him' so bitterly denounced); it is at all events the sadistic, revengeful Cloten part of him which is here repudiated. Later, he routs Iachimo whose 'manhood' has been 'taken off' by 'the heaviness and guilt within [his] bosom' (V.ii.1–2). Neither of the remorseful pair is aware of the other's identity, and there seems little sense, plot-wise, in the dumbshow fight which is superfluous to the conduct of the war and the rescue of the King, the matter at issue at this point in the story. All the more inviting, therefore, is it to see the victory as a symbolic defeat of the Iachimo within.

It is the rescue of the King, however, which serves as focus of the action. It is anticipated by the two boys, given in dumbshow, and then again in Posthumus' vividly detailed account. Three times during the sequence the setting of the heroic feat is described: in a narrow lane (ditched and walled with turf), an old man and two boys (the British forces having retreated in disarray) are defending the King from the oncoming Roman host, when Posthumus joins them. Why the triple insistence? Battle at a narrow entry is, psychoanalytic findings inform us, a classic symbolisation of oedipal conflict. In the context of other subliminal recoveries in this phase of the play, the episode reads like an oedipal conflict reversed, or resolved. No father is killed at a crossroads, or maternal portal, but a king is saved, and by his own sons, together with their other (supposed) father, with Posthumus, the unknown soldier, the foster-son, as partner. The text is underscoring its message, but for Posthumus further realisations are necessary before the catastrophic splits in his personality can be truly healed. Isolated, unknown and bereaved, he is still in despair. His oscillating changes of dress from Roman to British signify that he is a man without an identity, rudderless, directionless, deprived of the will to live. Only death offers a surcease to the pain of loss and the agony of conscience; but he cannot find death 'where [he] did hear him groan, / Nor feel him where he strook' (V.iii.69–70). The more daringly and fearlessly he fights, the more invulnerable he seems.

When he is captured, therefore, this time in Roman clothing, he welcomes his imprisonment, begging the 'good gods' who 'coin'd' his life not to extend his torment, not to be 'appeased', like 'temporal fathers' by his sorrow, and looks forward to his execution with an eagerness which makes the Gaoler remark 'Unless a man would marry a gallows and beget young gibbets, I never saw one so prone' (V.iv.198–9). It is at this point that the death-courting Posthumus has a transforming dream.

The departure from blank verse for the dream and the theophany embedded in it have caused much critical agitation[13] which has simply obscured the insight the dream's substance provides into Posthumus' state of mind. The dream, for Posthumus, is a transparent wish-fulfilment. The parental presences which materialise in the dream are solacing, comforting, approving; 'our son is good' is the burden of their sayings. He fell asleep grief and guilt stricken, invoking the image of the injured Imogen, craving for the punishment, and the relief, of death. In the dream he is embraced, pitied, exonerated by parents and siblings alike. When he awakes to the pain of the loss of this oneiric family, he is nevertheless imbued with a sense of a 'golden chance', of having been 'steep'd in favours' (V.iv.131–2); and although he is still absolute for death even after the dream, and unable to interpret the oracular message, the fantasy of recuperation points to its possibility.

Both Imogen and Posthumus thus experience an annihilating despair, their recovery from which is staged in parallel fashion: through the second-chance gift of protective parents. However, their rehabilitation will not be completely realised until the climactic moment of the blow the unrecognised Imogen receives at Posthumus' hand when she intercedes, in order to reveal herself, at the height of his lament for the woman he has wronged and lost. It is a dramatic moment, but it is more than a mere *coup de théâtre*. This acting out of aggression immediately undone by recognition and forgiveness is therapeutic. The blow is an uninhibited action, spontaneous, unconstrained, passionate, and this is a capacity that his masculinity needs as much as her femininity desires. The shock, moreover, functions for both like a clearing of the air, a clearance of debt or a lovers' quarrel, defusing unconscious resentments which could fester and obstruct, functioning to liberate him from his fear of sexual inadequacy, her from her fear of sexual surrender.

What he says as he hits her is pregnant with dramatic irony bred of all the blindnesses there have been between them, and within them:

> Shall's have a play of this? Thou scornful page,
> There lie thy part.
>
> (V.v.228–9)

This is the last time we shall hear that telling little word 'part'. Fragmentation and self-division are abrogated in the image Posthumus uses when the two at last embrace: 'Hang there like fruit, my soul, / Till the tree die!' (ll.263–4). It is an image which is impossible to dismantle: for we cannot tell whether his own soul or she herself is the anaphoric antecedent of 'my soul', nor whether 'there' is the space within his embracing arms or hers. Does he imagine Imogen hanging like fruit upon his fatherly support? Or does he imagine himself hanging upon her maternal support like a fruit which need never (till the tree die) be detached? This culminating moment annuls the dirge, offers fruit for the latter's dust. Yet it contains its own knowledge of finitude, despite its fantasy of merger and completion of self in other, for even the tree will, one day, die.

The soothsayer's culminating account, to Cymbeline, of his vision of peace is analogous in its mixing of gender. The eagle-Caesar is

indeterminately male and female, so therefore also is radiant
Cymbeline in this mythological union of their powers:

> the Roman eagle,
> From south to west on wing soaring aloft,
> Lessen'd herself and in the beams o'th' sun
> So vanish'd; which foreshow'd our princely eagle,
> Th'imperial Caesar, should again unite
> His favor with the radiant Cymbeline,
> Which shines here in the west.
>
> (ll.470–6)

It is a strange, even monstrous valedictory emblem for a very
strange play. Have we, with the aid of the psychoanalytic insights,
made sense of it? Of any part of it? Has our attempt to 'follow the
path of the signifier', and to tell the other story of *Cymbeline*
thrown light into the shadowy reaches of the textual unconscious
which was our quarry?

The play has been inundated by fantasies of dispersed and re-
assembled families, parents, siblings, marriage partners; of split and
recuperated identities; of 'lopp'd branches, which, being dead many
years, shall after revive, be jointed to the old stock, and freshly
grow' (ll.438–40). Implicit in all these has been an urgent will to
transform the forces making for death and dissolution into a
reaffirmation of procreative life. The *paterfamilias* of Act V, full of
affection and happiness, joyful 'mother to the birth of three' (l.369)
is manifestly not the Cymbeline, the *'nom (non) du père'*, of the beginning, as destructive in his tyrannical possessiveness as he was
submissive to the wife who deceived and enthralled him, and as
patently a projection of oedipal fantasy as was his poison-queen of
an earlier infantile stage of development.

[...]

Nevertheless we may still feel that there remains a gap in our perception of *Cymbeline*. The bits do not cohere. It stays fragmented in
our minds, a bundle of lively, or lurid but disintegrated parts. The
testing question with which this study began is whether we can
close this gap, whether we can move through the Lacanian witticism from ellipse as textual gap to ellipse as transferential circuit in
which text and reader can meet.

Fruitful in this respect is Charles Hofling's reminder that
Shakespeare's mother died the year before *Cymbeline* is generally
held to have been composed, and that in the same year a daughter

was born to his own recently married favourite daughter. The following year Shakespeare returned to Stratford, and to his wife, after the twenty-year absence in London which followed the birth of his third child.[14] This is suggestive, and taken in tandem with the obsessively repetitive imagery of severance, fragmentation and recuperation precipitates a concluding insight.

Freud, in his reflections upon the Triple Goddess – the three significant women figures in a man's life – exhibits an odd amnesia. When he expands upon the story of the three caskets it is mother, wife and burying earth that he names, forgetting a fourth possibility.[15] Shakespeare's romances are, in effect, a riposte. The beloved, thaumaturgic daughters of these last plays supplement Freud's death-dominated triad. The three significant women in a man's life in these late plays are mother, wife and daughter, new life-bringer, who can reverse, at least in fantasy, the decline into death.

Consider the 'death' of Fidele / Imogen. Belarius' 'ingenious instrument' (IV.ii.186) is sounded for the first time since the death of the boys' supposed mother when Fidele dies, and she is to be buried beside the latter's grave. In her mock death she takes the place of Euriphile who took the place of the boys' real mother (who was also her own), whose place was taken by the deathly Queen mother. Lucius announces that no master had a page 'so kind ... so tender ... so nurse-like' (V.v.86–8). She is not only herself symbolically reborn, she is the cause rebirth is in others, that is, in Cymbeline, the absent, occulted father, proxy for his author, the productions of whose imagination are all splinters of the self, of 'His Majesty the Ego'.[16] In this view the motivating, generating fantasy, or perplexity, of the play is located in the figure of the King, and it is this that enables us to move from Lacan's ellipse as a gap in the text, to the ellipse as a circuit connecting text and reader. If we unbind the text in this way, if we see Posthumus as a proxy for Cymbeline in the latter's absence, just as Iachimo and Cloten were proxies for Posthumus in his absence, and behind the whole series of figures a troubled author whose preoccupations the foregrounded stories screen, and while screening reveal, we can suddenly see the whole fable in a new light.

It is a father's deeply repressed desire for his daughter that is relayed through Posthumus, hence he is shackled and hampered in the conduct of his love. Hence the 'killing' of Imogen, sham though it be, and the necrophilia of that nightmarish scene. Hence her rescue by a benign, protective father figure, whom she in turn 'nurses', as Lucius makes a point of telling us. Yet in the recognition scenes there are still painful resonances: Imogen, it seems, deserts her 'father' Lucius; Belarius re-experiences the loss of the children, 'two of the sweet'st companions in the world' (V.v.349) that Cymbeline lost. The severing and re-establishing of parent / grown-child relationships is an arduous and troubled work of transformation, of the dislodging and redeployment of invested emotions, as we may learn from Shakespeare's dramas, if not from life. It is the work of late maturity, no benign retirement, but fraught with layer upon layer of old anxieties and hostilities, layer upon layer of new rivalries and jealousies. This is the work of the oneiric imagination throughout the late plays; and it is to this seedbed of Shakespeare's romances that *Cymbeline* can give us access.

From Ruth Nevo, *Shakespeare's Other Language* (London, 1987), pp.62–94.

NOTES

[In contrast to many previous post-Freudian critics who treated Shakespeare's plays as individual case-studies in neurosis, Ruth Nevo employs a semiotic (Lacanian) mode of psychoanalytic criticism to gain access to the play's 'textual unconscious' through its dream-logic of displacement, condensation and symbolisation. Following 'the path of the signifier' in this way allows her to track the subliminal conflicts worked out in *Cymbeline*: the characters' struggle to define their identities and resolve their ambivalent sexual desires within the context of dismembered and reconstituted families. The play's onion-like layers of substitution are stripped away to reveal its deep 'organising fantasy': a father's repressed desire for his daughter. The text that appears here, with the author's permission, represents a shortened version of the original chapter. Ed.]

1. Barbara A. Mowat, *The Dramaturgy of Shakespeare's Romances* (Athens, GA, 1976), p. 55.

2. Bertrand Evans, *Shakespeare's Comedies* (Oxford, 1960), has shown how the discrepancy between audience knowledge and character knowledge is greater in *Cymbeline* than in any other of Shakespeare's plays. The characters are kept more ignorant and of more essential matters than anywhere else. Hence the accumulation of discoveries in Act V.

3. See Gilbert D. Chaitin, 'The Representation of Logical Relations in Dreams and the Nature of Primary Process', *Psychoanalysis and Contemporary Thought*, II (1978); Pinchas Noy, 'A Revision of the Psychoanalytic Theory of Primary Process', *Int. J. Psycho-Analysis*, 50 (1969); and 'Symbolism and Mental Representation', *Annual of*

Psychoanalysis, I (1973) for useful accounts of primary and secondary processes of thought.

4. Jaques Lacan, *Ecrits*, trans. Alan Sheridan (New York, 1977), p. 93.

5. Most famous of the Victorian adorers is Swinburne who calls Imogen 'the very crown and flower of all her father's daughters ... woman above all Shakespeare's women ... the immortal godhead of womanhood' (*A Study of Shakespeare*, 1880).

6. See Richard Levin, *The Multiple Plot in English Renaissance Drama* (Chicago, 1971).

7. Meredith Skura, 'Revisions and Rereadings in Dreams and Allegories', in *The Literary Freud*, ed. J. H. Smith (New Haven, CT, 1980), p. 205.

8. Skura, 'Revisions', p. 209.

9. Murray M. Schwartz, 'Between Fantasy and Imagination', in *The Practice of Psychoanalytic Criticism*, ed. L. Tennenhouse (Detroit, 1976), p. 231. All further references are included in the text.

10. In general Schwartz' rigorously 'Applied Psychoanalysis' is only partially successful. It suffers from an excessive orthodoxy which attempts to diagnose and schematise exhaustively in accordance with classic psychoanalytic terms and themes. And he tends to see Imogen exclusively as an object of the men's fantasies. 'Shakespeare,' he says, 'forces Imogen to re-enact regressive states we see in Cymbeline and Posthumus. ... In this inverted primal scene Imogen is the "man" who "dies" at the sight of the castrated body, she has become a surrogate for Posthumus, who is "killed" by the sight of the female genitals. The scene works to deny the masculine fantasy by expressing it in an utterly inverted way, (p. 266).

11. See Ruth Nevo, *Comic Transformations in Shakespeare* (London, 1980).

12. Cf. in *Measure for Measure*, IV.ii.1–5 and *Romeo and Juliet*, I.i.21–6.

13. Discussion of the problem and its implications for the question of authorship can be found in J. M. Nosworthy (ed.), *Cymbeline* (London, 1980), pp. xxxvi–vii.

14. Charles K. Hofling, 'Notes on Shakespeare's *Cymbeline*', *Shakespeare Studies* (1965), 133ff.

15. The omission may seem less surprising when one recalls that the Three Caskets essay (1913) does antedate by many years the loving care bestowed upon her ailing father by his 'Anna-Antigone,' as Freud called his own beloved daughter. See *Letters of Sigmund Freud, 1873–1939*, ed. Tania Stern and James Stern (New York, 1960), p. 424.

16. The phrase is Freud's in *Creative Writers and Daydreaming* (1908).

5

The Masculine Romance of Roman Britain: *Cymbeline* and Early Modern English Nationalism

JODI MIKALACHKI

> The birth of the English nation was not the birth of a nation; it was the birth of the nations, the birth of nationalism.
>
> Nations have no clearly identifiable births.[1]

It is somewhat misleading to put the above quotations together, since the first describes the birth of nationalism in England at a specific historical moment (the sixteenth century), while the second invokes the (usually imagined to be) ancient origins of something that has come to be called a nation. I juxtapose them here not simply to imply a wide divergence of scholarly opinion but also to suggest that any discussion of nationalism and early modern England necessarily involves both ways that these quotations read the phenomenon they describe: one places the origins of English nationalism (and perhaps of nationalism more generally) in the early modern period; the other recognises early modern England's own perception of its national origins in antiquity. The quotations do nevertheless represent opposite poles in theories of nationalism. The first introduces Liah Greenfeld's recent study of early modern England as the world's first nation;

assuming the causal primacy of ideas, Greenfeld argues for the idea of the nation as the constitutive element of modernity. The second quotation virtually concludes the last appendix to Benedict Anderson's influential *Imagined Communities*, a study that famously rejects ideological definitions of nationalism, considering it instead alongside anthropological terms like *kinship* or *religion*, and arguing strongly for its emergence in the eighteenth-century Americas. Both works participate in the new social, political, and historical interest in nationalism that developed during the 1980s, just as its subject seemed about to become obsolete.[2]

My own approach emphasises the interplay between historical obsolescence and continuity with the past in the recovery of national origins. I am less concerned to establish whether nationalism did indeed originate in sixteenth-century England (believing, as I do, that nationalism, too, has no clearly identifiable birth) than I am to explore the complexities of early modern attempts to recover English national origins. The tensions of this sixteenth-century project of recovery – its drive, on one hand, to establish historical precedent and continuity and, on the other, to exorcise a primitive savagery it wished to declare obsolete – inform virtually all expressions of early modern English nationalism. These tensions derive from the period's broader social tensions about order, manifested most acutely in anxiety over the nature of familial relations and the status of the family as a model for the order of the state.[3] The centrality of the family and the church to early modern English articulations of the nation suggests that Anderson's anthropological focus might be particularly appropriate to the study of English nationalism in this period. His understanding of nationalism as aligned 'not with self-consciously held political ideologies, but with the large cultural systems that preceded it, out of which – as well as against which – it came into being,[4] informs my own understanding and guides my consideration of how perceptions of national origins reflected and shaped early modern concepts of the English nation.

Greenfeld's intellectual history is not without interest, however, particularly given the prominent role of early modern intellectuals – scholars, poets, visual artists – in developing nationalist icons and narratives in England. One of the great intellectual stumbling blocks to the recovery of national origins in sixteenth-century England was the absence of a native classical past on which to found the glories of the modern nation. Worse yet, the primitive British savagery that purportedly preceded Roman conquest proved antithetical to a fundamental principle of hierarchy in early modern England, for the Britons made no distinction of sex in government.[5] Powerful females loomed large in early modern visions of national origins, from the universal gendering of the topographical and historical 'Britannia' as feminine to the troubling eruptions of ancient queens in the process of civilisation by Rome. Like the unruly women who challenged the patriarchal order of early modern England, these powerful and rebellious females in native historiography threatened the establishment of a stable, masculine identity for the early modern nation.

Recent work on the mutually informing constructs of nationalism and sexuality has defined the former as a virile fraternity perpetuated by its rejection of overt male homosexuality and its relegation of women to a position of marginalised respectability.[6] I would argue that this gendering and sexualising of the nation, generally presented as having emerged in the eighteenth century, had become current by the early seventeenth century in England and involved both an exclusion of originary female savagery and a masculine embrace of the civility of empire. Jacobean dramas set in Roman Britain often conclude with a masculine embrace, staged literally or invoked rhetorically as a figure for the new relation between Rome and Britain. These concluding embraces depend on the prior death of the female character who has advocated or led the British resistance to Rome. The exorcism of this female resistance, constructed as savage, grounds the stable hybrid that crowns these plays with a promise of peace for Britain and wider membership in the Roman world of civilisation. And yet it is precisely the savage females banished from the conclusions of these dramas – ancient queens like Fletcher's Bonduca or the wicked Queen of Shakespeare's *Cymbeline* – who articulate British nationalism and patriotism.

In the following account I shall read Shakespeare's romance of Roman Britain in terms of these issues of gender and sexuality, taking both as constitutive of the nationalism the play articulates. In doing so, I hope not only to revise twentieth-century readings of *Cymbeline* as a nationalist drama but also to explore Renaissance anxiety about native origins and the corresponding difficulty of forging a historically based national identity in early modern England.

I

The Queen's great patriotic speech in Act III, scene i has long been a stumbling block in interpretations of *Cymbeline*. Combining appeals to native topography, history, and legendary origins, it recalls the highest moments of Elizabethan nationalism.[7]

> ... Remember, sir, my liege,
> The kings your ancestors, together with
> The natural bravery of your isle, which stands
> As Neptune's park, ribb'd and pal'd in
> With rocks unscaleable and roaring waters,
> With sands that will not bear your enemies' boats,
> But suck them up to th' topmast. A kind of conquest
> Caesar made here, but made not here his brag
> Of 'Came, and saw, and overcame': with shame
> (The first that ever touch'd him) he was carried
> From off our coast, twice beaten: and his shipping
> (Poor ignorant baubles!) on our terrible seas,
> Like egg-shells mov'd upon their surges, crack'd
> As easily 'gainst our rocks. For joy whereof
> The fam'd Cassibelan, who was once at point
> (O giglot fortune!) to master Caesar's sword,
> Made Lud's town with rejoicing-fires bright,
> And Britons strut with courage.
>
> (III.i.17–34)[8]

The Queen's opening command to remember invokes the restitutive drive of early modern English nationalism. The nation's glorious past – its resistance to the great Julius Caesar, its ancient line of kings, and the antiquity of its capital – depends paratactically on this command, emerging in the incantatory power of names like 'Lud's town' and Cassibelan and in the powerful icon of native topography.[9] Moved by this nationalist appeal, Cymbeline refuses to pay the tribute demanded by the Roman emissaries, thus setting Britain and Rome at war.

As the last of the play's many reversals, however, Cymbeline agrees to pay the tribute and announces his submission to the Roman emperor. In place of the bonfires of victory remembered by his queen, he commands that 'A Roman, and a British ensign wave / Friendly together' as both armies march through Lud's town (V.v.481–2). This volte-face is the more remarkable in that the Britons have just defeated the Romans in battle. Honour, not force, dictates Cymbeline's decision, as he invokes the promise made by his uncle Cassibelan to Julius Caesar, from which, he recalls, 'We were dissuaded by our wicked queen' (l.464). Despite everything else the Queen does to earn this epithet, Cymbeline accords it here in the context of her opposition to the Roman tribute, her disruption of the masculine network of kinship, promises, and honour that binds Cymbeline to Rome. In this final assessment of the political plot, the king's full censure falls on the radical nationalism articulated by 'our wicked queen'.

Critics who wish to read *Cymbeline* as a straightforward celebration of national identity dismiss the Queen's motivation as mere self-interest.[10] By doing so, they fail to interrogate the corporate self-interest that animates nationalism. They further marginalise the Queen by focusing on the oafish Cloten as the main proponent of an objectionable patriotism, thus avoiding the problem of how to interpret her delivery of one of the great nationalist speeches in Shakespeare. Even those who do acknowledge the interpretive difficulties of this scene find ultimately that the patriotic voices of the Queen and Cloten must be rejected in order to effect the play's romance conclusion.[11] G. Wilson Knight's masterful account of Shakespeare's use of Roman and British historiography remains the most instructive in this regard. Knight casts Cymbeline's refusal to pay the tribute, the pivotal national action in the play, as a 'question of Britain's islanded integrity'. While noting Posthumus's early description of British virtue in his reference to Julius Caesar's respect for British courage (II.iv.20–6), Knight nevertheless recognises that the Queen expresses it much more satisfyingly in Act III, scene i. He argues, however, that the Queen and Cloten are types Britain must ultimately reject in order to recognise freely her Roman obligation and inheritance. Writing shortly after the Second World War, Knight comments that the national situation in *Cymbeline* serves, 'as often in real life, to render violent instincts respectable'.[12]

George L. Mosse's argument about nationalism and sexuality, which culminates in an analysis of Nazi Germany, also rests on the term *respectable*. Indeed, in Mosse's analysis an alliance between nationalism and respectability is crucial to the formulation and dissemination of both. He traces naturalised concepts of respectability to the eighteenth century, when modern nationalism was emerging, and finds both to be informed by ideals of fraternity for men and domesticity for women. Men were to engage actively with one another in a spirit of brotherhood, while women were to remain passively within the domestic sphere, exercising a biological maternal function that in no way challenged the spiritual bonding of adult males. 'Woman as a national symbol was the guardian of the continuity and immutability of the nation, the embodiment of its respectability', Mosse observes, adding that the more respectable nationalist movements become, the more respectable their feminine icons look.[13] When Knight notes in 1947 how the national situation in *Cymbeline* serves 'to render violent instincts respectable', he intuits the naturalised alliance between nationalism and respectability that Mosse theorises forty years later.

Cymbeline's Queen is hardly a figure of national respectability. Even her maternal devotion to Cloten can be censured,[14] and the rest of her career as evil stepmother, would-be poisoner, and finally suicide fully earns Cymbeline's concluding approbation of the 'heavens [who] in justice both on her, and hers, / Have laid most heavy hand' (V.v.465–6).[15] Yet Cymbeline's insistence on her political intervention as the mark of her wickedness per se suggests a critique of the nationalism she articulates. This convergence of national and personal wickedness indicates the difficulty of forging national identity before the eighteenth-century alliance of nationalism and respectability. Indeed, the complex and somewhat clumsily resolved romance of *Cymbeline* dramatises the immediate prehistory of that alliance and its constitutive elements. Early modern England certainly had an ideal of respectable womanhood, one that (as in the eighteenth century) rested on the chastity and subordination of women within the patriarchal household. Susan Amussen has demonstrated, however, that the terms of this ideal were not so clear nor so universally accepted in the seventeenth century as has often been suggested. Definitions of wifely obedience in particular were contested by seventeenth-century Englishwomen, despite their general acquiescence to the principle of female subordination. Only by the late seventeenth and early eighteenth centuries are these challenges muted, suggesting that the naturalised ideal of feminine respectability Mosse invokes as an element of nationalism had been fully internalised by women.[16] The difficulties of constructing and ensuring this sexual ideal in the early seventeenth century reveal themselves in the complex formation of a national identity in *Cymbeline*.

If respectable nationalism depends in part on respectable womanhood, someone other than the wicked Queen must embody it. Imogen, so beloved of the Victorians for her wifely devotion and forbearance, might figure as the wicked Queen's respectable double, and she does indeed come to represent an alternative nationalism.[17] Her progress through a series of disguised identities and alliances, not all of them British, indicates the amount of work needed to construct a national icon of feminine respectability, just as the messages from and about the Queen in the final scene assert the impossibility of resolving the drama without invoking her feminine wickedness. This duality of feminine respectability and wickedness reveals how fraught early modern English nationalism was with fears of the unrespectable, or, in the language of the period, the uncivil or barbaric. It also indicates how important gender was as a category for working out these fears.[18] Work that applies Mosse's analysis of nationalism and sexuality to the early modern period notes the identification of the feminine with the barbaric in nationalist discourse. Jonathan Goldberg's reading of *Plimoth Plantation* as the inaugural text of a national American literature notes its persistent alignment of Anglo women with Indians. Although not precisely identical, he argues, they must both 'be effaced in order for history to move forward as the exclusive preserve of white men'.[19]

The collapse of the categories of 'woman' and 'savage' also informs *Cymbeline*. Anxiety about gender, given a nationalist inflection, haunts the drama, emerging particularly in contests over Roman-British relations. If it is most apparent in the caricature of feminine wickedness represented by the Queen, who tries to come between Britain and Rome, it also informs masculine characters in all-male settings. After the Queen's intervention in Act III, scene i, British articulation and enactment of male bonding become increasingly important, from Belarius's reconstitution of an all-male family in the Welsh cave to the princes' further bonding with Posthumus on the battlefield and the ultimate reconciliation of Rome and Britain in the final scene. Although Imogen appears in all these settings, she does so only in boy's dress, a costume she retains to the play's conclusion. I shall discuss the implications of her disguise more fully below but would point out here that it shifts not only her gender but also her status and age from married adult to single youth.[20] These shifts make more apparent the exclusion of adult women, particularly mothers, from the scenes of male bonding in *Cymbeline*.[21] An historiographical concern over originary females seems to be enacted here in familial terms. The construction of the Queen as a figure of savage excess, even if not especially with

regard to her maternity, recalls Goldberg's formulation of the necessary effacement of women and savages 'in order for history to
move forward as the exclusive preserve of white men'.[22] In the
context of *Cymbeline*, one might alter his last words to read
'civilised' or perhaps 'Romanised men'. All roads of male bonding
lead to Rome in this play and, correspondingly, to a place in the
exclusive preserve of Roman history.

Critics reading *Cymbeline* from the perspective of early modern
historiography are divided on the question of Rome's role. Those
who identify the play's romance resolution with the Romans cite
the importance of Rome in British chronicle history and Jacobean
enthusiasm for Augustan analogies.[23] Others argue that in
Cymbeline Shakespeare exorcises his fascination with Roman
history in favour of a more humane British national ethic.[24] Early
modern responses were not so one-sided. In their attempts to recon-
cile ancient British patriotism and a civilised union with Rome,
English historians acknowledged and developed a hybrid nationalist
response to the Roman Conquest. Violently patriotic queens played
an important role in negotiating this hybrid. The hierarchical binar-
ism of gender, fundamental to the construction of early modern
society, also governed that period's construction of the ancient
British relation to Rome. In the section that follows, I shall examine
this phenomenon through the early modern historiography of two
ancient Britons, Boadicea and Caractacus. Although separated
historically by almost twenty years, these two figures of ancient
British patriotism appear side by side in early modern accounts of
Roman Britain. Their dramatic juxtaposition reveals much about
the gendering and sexualising of national origins and identity in
early modern England.

II

Cymbeline's Queen has no direct source in Holinshed's reign of
Kymbeline. She bears a striking resemblance, however, to Voadicia,
or Boadicea, who appears in Holinshed's narrative of Roman
Britain roughly sixty years after the events depicted in
Shakespeare's play.[25] Like Cymbeline's Queen, Boadicea opposed
the Roman conquerors but ultimately failed to free Britain of the
imperial yoke, taking her own life (or dying of 'a natural infirmity')
after a conclusive battle. Also like the wicked Queen, she was

famous for her nationalist stance, especially her great speech on British freedom and resistance to tyranny, where she opposed the payment of tribute to Rome and invoked the same topoi of the island's natural strengths and the glorious history of Britain's people and kings. Ultimately, Boadicea, too, suffered condemnation for her ruthless defence of this position. Although Holinshed acknowledges the legitimacy of her initial grievance (the Romans had seized her late husband's kingdom, raped her daughters, and had her flogged), he finds that her female savagery carried her too far in revenge. Showing no mercy, Boadicea led the 'dreadful examples of the Britons' cruelty' until her undisciplined army of women and men finally met defeat at the hands of a smaller, well-organised band of Romans under the leadership of Suetonius. The editorial summary of her revolt makes explicit both the cause of her failure and the reason for her condemnation: 'the chief cause of the Britons insurging against the Romans, they admitted as well women as men to public government'.[26]

Caractacus, on the other hand, wins unqualified historiographical praise for both his initial resistance and his eventual submission to Rome. In 43 AD he led the western tribe of the Silurians in revolt against Rome. Although he, like Boadicea, was defeated, he did not end his life but was taken to Rome to be led as a captive in the Emperor Claudius's triumphal procession. There he so distinguished himself by the dignity of his speech and bearing that he won freedom and commendation of his manly courage from Claudius himself. Caractacus's manliness, his Roman *virtus*, is the focus of early modern accounts of his uprising. The patriotic oration Caractacus delivers before Claudius is never condemned. On the contrary, the 1587 Holinshed cites it as both laudable and successful, calling it the 'manly speech to the Emperor Claudius, whereby he and his obtain mercy and pardon'. The term *manly* draws an implicit contrast with the earlier condemnation of Boadicea's revolt as an example of feminine government.[27]

The distinction between Caractacus's manly *romanitas* and Boadicea's female savagery became a standard feature of early modern accounts of Roman Britain. Camden begins his collection of 'Grave Speeches and Wittie Apothegmes of woorthie Personages of this Realme in former times' with a thirteen-line citation of the 'manly speech' of Caractacus before Claudius. He follows this with a three-line speech from Boadicea, after which, he reports, she lets a hare out of her lap as a token of the Romans' timidity. This superstitious piece of barbarism meets with the fate it deserves, for 'the successe of the battell prooved otherwise'.[28] As late as Milton's *History of Britain* in 1671, the distinction was maintained. Milton cites in full Caractacus's manly speech and offers him as a classic exemplum of masculine virtue. When he comes to Boadicea's rebellion, however, he refuses to include her oration, saying that he does not believe in set speeches in a history and that he has cited Caractacus only because his words demonstrate 'magnanimitie, soberness, and martial skill'. In fact Milton accuses his classical sources of having put words into Boadicea's mouth 'out of a vanity, hoping to embellish and set out thir Historie with the strangness of our manners, not caring in the meanwhile to brand us with the rankest note of Barbarism, as if in *Britain* Woemen were Men, and Men Woemen'.[29] In this standard pairing of the male and female British rebels against Rome, then, Boadicea represented 'the rankest note of Barbarism', that state in which gender distinctions are collapsed. Caractacus, on the other hand, was a figure of exemplary manliness, invoked to counterbalance the overwhelming female savagery of Boadicea and to reestablish British masculinity.[30]

Fletcher seems to have followed this pattern in composing his drama *Bonduca*. Although he derived most of his historical information from classical sources and Holinshed's *Chronicles*, he also included a character named Caratach, Bonduca's cousin and general of the Britons. Caratach conducts the war by Roman rules, for which he expresses great admiration. He even chastises Bonduca for her extravagant speeches against the Romans, thus anticipating Milton's rejection of her feminine oratory. Because she defied Caratach's order to return to her spinning wheel and instead meddled in the affairs of men, Bonduca is made to bear full responsibility for the Britons' eventual defeat. Despite her eponymous role in the drama, she dies in Act IV, leaving the 'Romophile' Caratach to represent Britain in the last act. During that act he earns the further admiration of the Roman soldiers, who publicly honour and praise him for his Roman virtues. The play ends with his embrace by the Roman commander Swetonius and the latter's words: 'Ye shew a friends soul. / March on, and through the Camp in every tongue, / The Vertues of great *Caratach* be sung.'[31]

Other plays of the period which deal with British rebellion against Rome end with the same masculine embrace. In *The Valiant Welshman*, a dramatisation of Caractacus's rebellion, the character 'Caradoc' is betrayed into Roman hands by the duplicitous British queen Cartamanda and brought before the Emperor Claudius. Claudius then recalls Caradoc's valour in battle, lifts him up from his kneeling posture, and celebrates his valiant name.[32] In William Rowley's *A Shoemaker, a Gentleman*, a disguised British prince twice saves the life of the Emperor Dioclesian and rescues the imperial battle standard in successive clashes with Vandals and Goths.[33] On resigning his trophies to Dioclesian in the next scene with the words 'Now to the Royall hand of Caesar I resigne / The high Imperiall Ensigne of great Rome', the prince is bidden by the emperor to 'Kneele downe, / And rise a Brittaine Knight' (III.v.17–49). *Fuimus Troes, or the True Trojans*, a play about Julius Caesar's conquest, ends in a metaphorical embrace of empire, with the words 'The world's fourth empire Britain doth embrace'.[34] With the exception of Rowley's *Shoemaker*, these plays work toward a reconciliation between Rome and Britain that is exclusively masculine.[35] Any women who might have figured in the action (and they usually do so in invented love plots) have been killed off, leaving the stage free for men to conclude matters of true historic import. With the exclusion of women from the action, the stage of Roman Britain becomes the 'exclusive preserve' of men, both British and Roman. This triumph of exclusion is figured in the masculine embrace that is the dominant trope of these final scenes, invoked as a metaphor of empire and embodied in the stage embraces of male Britons by Roman commanders and in the symbolic merging of their national emblems.[36]

If the masculine romance of Roman Britain delivers Britain from the self-destructive violence of the wicked Queen, however, it also defines the province of Britannia as the passive object of Roman desire. Mosse emphasises the fear of male homosexuality that haunts the fraternal bonding of nationalism.[37] Goldberg expands on this idea in his analysis of *Plimoth Plantation*, citing William Bradford's need to separate the pervasive homosociality of his founding American fantasy of all-male relations 'by drawing the line – lethally – between its own sexual energies and those it calls sodomitical'. Commenting on Bradford's reluctant inclusion of '"a case of buggery"' because '"the truth of the history requires it"', Goldberg sets the unrealisable desire to distinguish originary male bonding from sodomy at the heart of Bradford's history: 'The truth of the history, as I am reading it, is the entanglement of the "ancient members" with and the desire to separate from the figure of the sodomite who represents at once the negation of the ideal and its literalisation.'[38] Fear of homosexuality is neither so clear nor so lethal in early modern constructions of Roman Britain, where female savagery is the primary object of revulsion. When Fletcher and Shakespeare attempt the literalisation of this masculine ideal in terms of a purely British nationalism, however, they produce scenes of male bonding characterised by feminine and domestic behaviour.[39]

The assumption of women's work, speech, and familial roles characterises male bonding among Britons in *Bonduca* and *Cymbeline*. Wales, the last preserve and final retreat of pure Britishness, provides the setting in both cases.[40] In *Bonduca* this nationalist male bonding dominates the last act, where Caratach, hiding from the Romans, cares for his nephew Hengo, last of the royal Iceni after the deaths of Bonduca and her daughters. In doing so, Caratach takes on the maternal role that Bonduca, in her unfeminine lust for battle, has refused to exercise. His whole concern in this last act is the nursing and feeding of the boy Hengo, who is dying of sickness and hunger after the British defeat. Caratach's language to the boy is tender and protective; he tries to shield him from the knowledge of their loss and soothes him with such endearments as 'sweet chicken' and 'fair flower' (V.i.27; V.iii.159). Hengo's name (Fletcher's invention) points to Hengist, the first Saxon ruler in Britain, often used in early modern iconography as the representative of England's Saxon heritage. The moving spectacle of the old warrior nursing the last sprig of British manhood might thus suggest an imaginative attempt to construct a native masculine genealogy proceeding directly from ancient Britain to the Saxon heptarchy, and excluding both women and Rome from the national past. The death of Hengo signals the failure of this fantasy. Only after the collapse of this last hope for the continuation of the British line does Caratach allow himself to be won over by the brave courtesies of the Romans, who promise the boy honourable burial (V.iii.185–8). Caratach's embrace by Claudius follows the failure of this domestic interlude, in which Caratach tries to keep alive the generative fantasy of a purely masculine Britain.[41]

The experiment in an all-male British world is more developed in *Cymbeline*. In the middle of Act III, after ties with Rome have been broken, Shakespeare introduces the Welsh retreat of Belarius, Guiderius, and Arviragus. This idyll represents as full a return to unmitigated Britishness as the wicked Queen's opposition to the payment of tribute. Just as her resistance to Rome fails, causing (in

Cymbeline's view) her own death and that of her son,[42] so, too, does the primitive fantasy of the Welsh cave fail to stave off the ultimate embrace with Rome. In the latter case it is not the death of the British heirs that ends this hope but rather their fear that they will lack a historical afterlife. When Belarius praises the purity of their Welsh retreat, contrasting it with the tales he has told the boys 'Of courts, of princes; of the tricks in war' (III.iii.15), the elder son responds: 'Out of your proof you speak: we poor unfledg'd, / Have never wing'd from view o' th'nest; nor know not / What air's from home' (ll. 27–9). He concedes that the quiet life of their retreat may be sweeter to Belarius than the court but asserts that 'unto us it is / A cell of ignorance' (ll. 32–3). His younger brother then adds:

> What should we speak of
> When we are old as you? When we shall hear
> The rain and wind beat dark December? How
> In this our pinching cave shall we discourse
> The freezing hours away? We have seen nothing:
> We are beastly.
>
> (ll. 35–40)

What the brothers protest is their exclusion from history. They have seen nothing; they are barbaric. Confined to their pinching cave in Wales, they have, quite literally, no history to speak of. This conflict between the princes and their presumed father comes to a head when the brothers want to enter the battle against the Romans. Belarius takes their zeal as an irrepressible sign of their royal blood, which longs to 'fly out and show them princes born' (IV.iv.53–4). It is equally, however, a sign of their desire to enter the world of history. Belarius's own sense of having been painfully shaped by a wider experience only fuels this desire. 'O boys, this story / The world may read in me: my body's mark'd / With Roman swords', he claims (III.iii.55–7), as though his body were a literalisation of the Roman writing of ancient British history. Without fighting the Romans, the princes will have no such marks to read by the winter fire when they are old. The masculine rite of passage such scars represent for them personally is a version of the national entry into history by means of the Roman invasion. For early modern historiographers Britain, too, would have remained outside history had she never entered into battle with the Romans.[43]

This convergence of the personal and the national in the forging of masculine identity offers the possibility of reconciling two of the most important interpretive traditions of *Cymbeline*: the psychoanalytic and the historicist. Where historicists find the battle and its aftermath puzzling and inconclusive in terms of the play's treatment of Roman-British relations, psychoanalytic critics focus on the battle as the play's central masculine rite of passage, interpreting it in archetypal terms that ignore its historiographical complexity.[44] The approach I have been advocating, developed from Mosse's insight about the interrelatedness of nationalism and sexuality, historicises the development of sexual and national identities as it demonstrates their interdependence. Janet Adelman, while recognising the historiographical complexity of Cymbeline's submission to Rome, interprets it in psychoanalytic terms as a result of 'the conflicted desire for merger even at the root of the desire for autonomy'.[45] In historiographical terms, I would argue that in early modern England an originary engagement with Rome was necessary for the formation of an autonomous national identity. Roman Britain came to play a foundational role in the recovery of native origins not only because it provided a context for the male bonding that characterises modern nationalism but also because it enabled exorcism of the female savagery that challenged both the autonomy and the respectability of nationalism.

Engagement with Rome also brought Britain into the masculine preserve of Roman historiography. It is battle with the Romans that affords Cymbeline's sons, the male Britons of the next generation, that historical identity they lacked in their pastoral retreat. In the dramatisation of this episode, they achieve historical status instantly, not because they rewrite Roman history, or win a lasting victory, but rather because that victory is immediately described and preserved in historiographical forms. As soon as the princes' stand with Belarius has been presented dramatically, Posthumus recapitulates it as a historical battle narrative, complete with citations of brave speeches and descriptions of the terrain and deployment of troops (V.iii.1–51). His interlocutor responds by producing an aphorism to commemorate their action, 'A narrow lane, an old man, and two boys' (l. 52), which Posthumus improves into a rhymed proverb: 'Two boys, an old man twice a boy, a lane, / Preserved the Britons, was the Romans' bane' (ll. 57–8). The transformation of the dramatic stand in Act V, scene ii into narrative, aphorism, and proverb in Act V, scene iii represents instant historicisation. This making of history issues directly from engagement with the Romans, which also leads to the princes' restoration as Cymbeline's male heirs. Both the continuance of the masculine British line and the entrance of its youngest branches into written history require abandonment of the purely British romance of the cave in Wales.

III

Imogen alone remains as a possible icon of pure Britishness in the complex of gender, sexuality, and nationalism I have been describing. Surely in her we have an early version of Mosse's icon of respectable womanhood to bless the virile bonding of nationalism.[46] She, more than her father or brothers, presents and experiences Britain, wandering through it, calling up its place names, and describing its natural situation. Imogen's name, invented by Shakespeare for the heroine he adds to his historical material, is derived from that of Brute's wife, Innogen, mother of the British race.[47] And like other ancient queens, Imogen, too, voices a lyrical celebration of the island: 'I' th' world's volume / Our Britain seems as of it, but not in't: / In a great pool, a swan's nest' (III.iv.138–40). The image of the swan's nest is as evocative of national identity as that of Neptune's park in the Queen's speech, suggesting among other things Leland's great chorographic song of the Thames, *Cygnea Cantio*.[48] The context of the speech, however, is quite different from that of the Queen's national celebration in Act III, scene i. In contrast to the Queen's radical 'Britocentrism', Imogen asserts in Act III, scene iv that Britain is only a small part of a larger world, a world from which it is in fact separate. Her line 'Our Britain seems as of it, but not in't' raises the historiographical question of Britain's isolation from the civilised world. At least one critic has suggested that Imogen's line is a version of the Vergilian verse '*Et penitus toto diuisos orbe Britannos*', cited in Holinshed's *Chronicles*.[49] Whether the image is derived from a Roman source or not, it perpetuates the imperial view of Britain's separation from the world identified with civilisation. Rather than lauding this separation, as would Boadicea or the wicked Queen, Imogen suggests that there is a world outside Britain where she may fare better than she will at the hands of the Queen and her son.

As in early modern accounts of ancient Britain, this flight from native isolation leads inevitably to Rome, for Pisanio answers Imogen's speech with the words: 'I am most glad / You think of other place: th' ambassador, / Lucius the Roman, comes to Milford-Haven / To-morrow' (III.iv.141–4). Lucius the Roman and Milford Haven will together shape Imogen's identity for the rest of the play. The mutuality required for them to do so signals how British national identity is formed from the interaction of the Roman invaders with the native land. If there is a magic of place in *Cymbeline*, it is in Milford Haven. The place name takes on an almost incantatory power as Imogen and the other characters make their way to the haven of final recognition and reconciliation.[50] Critics since Emrys Jones have stressed the importance of Milford Haven in Tudor mythography as the place where Henry Tudor landed before marching to defeat Richard III at the Battle of Bosworth Field.[51] They have built on this historiographical reading a sense of Milford Haven as a sacred or enchanted place that saps the strength of Britain's enemies and grounds the resistance of her true defenders. This is very satisfying in terms of Tudor-Stuart mythography, with its claims of Arthurian and British precedence, but it does not explain why Lucius the Roman, rather than Cymbeline, lands at Milford in anticipation of the future Henry VII of England.

The first Britons Lucius encounters on landing are the disguised Imogen and the headless corpse of Cloten in Posthumus's clothes. Lucius's attempt to reconstruct the story of the figure sleeping on the 'trunk ... / Without his top' issues in a series of questions that demand a recapitulation of the play's action which no single character can articulate (IV.ii.353–67) and which will occupy much of the lengthy recognition scene at the play's conclusion. The unreadability of this tableau of headless masterlessness emphasises the confusion of British national identity at this moment, with Cymbeline under the domination of his wicked Queen, Cloten dead in Posthumus's dress, the princes in hiding and ignorant of their royal identity, Imogen disguised and believing Posthumus to be dead, and Posthumus himself at large and still deceived as to his wife's fidelity. Imogen voices this confusion in response to Lucius's final, blunt question, 'What art thou?':

> I am nothing; or if not,
> Nothing to be were better. This was my master,
> A very valiant Briton, and a good,
> That here by mountaineers lies slain. Alas!
> There is no more such masters: I may wander
> From east to occident, cry out for service,

Try many, all good: serve truly: never
Find such another master.

(IV.ii.367–74)

Recalling medieval laments over the dead body of a feudal lord, Imogen presents herself as a youth who has lost all status or place after the death of the 'very valiant Briton' 'he' calls master. In this invented identity she gives voice to the inner despair of her presumed widowhood – her sense of being nothing at the seeming death of her husband – in terms of a nationless wandering from east to west. As in the princes' entry into battle, the personal and the national intersect in Imogen's crisis in Wales.

The upward turn of Imogen's fortunes, and those of her nation, is not far to seek. If there is any straightforwardly respectable character in *Cymbeline*, it is the Roman commander and emissary Lucius. He conducts himself with honour in the council scenes of Act III, scene i and Act V, scene v and succours the disguised Imogen with grace and generosity in Act IV, scene ii. He is also resolutely masculine, deriving his identity from military and political functions, and appearing in such masculine contexts as the council chamber, the march, and the battlefield. Here indeed is a virile antitype of Henry Tudor at Milford, and an ancient predecessor on which to found a stable masculine identity for the nation. When Lucius questions the disguised British princess about her dead 'master's' identity, she gives the latter's name as 'Richard du Champ' (IV.ii.377), suggesting an analogy between his body and the ground. Without putting undue pressure on this analogy, I would suggest that Lucius, in raising Imogen from the ground, also releases her from her quest to reach Milford Haven, from her ritualised laying out by the princes and Belarius, and from her second 'death' on the body of 'du Champ'. In taking her from this multiply constructed British ground, he gives her a new identity in his Roman entourage.

The only constant of Imogen's shifting identity in this scene is her assumed name, Fidele. It is her proper epithet, and yet, for a personification of unwavering marital fidelity, Imogen changes allegiance a remarkable number of times. Her initial defection from her father precedes but informs the play's action; one might even read in her decision to reject the death planned by Posthumus, or in her mistaken abandonment of her marriage while her husband yet lives, a kind of defection from absolute fidelity to him also. Certainly she moves from one allegiance to another in the middle acts of the play, where she leaves the princes and Belarius, abandons the seeming corpse of Posthumus, and ultimately betrays Lucius himself when she refuses to plead for his life before Cymbeline (V.v.104–5). Both in this series of shifts between British and Roman identifications and in the wager plot, the question of Imogen's fidelity is of central importance. Posthumus reviles Imogen and all women for faithlessness when he believes she has betrayed him (II.v.20–35), and Lucius makes a similar generalisation about those who place their trust in girls and boys when she abandons him to his fate (V.v.105–7).[52] By the conclusion of the play, however, Imogen reconciles all her conflicting fidelities. Cymbeline is again her father; Posthumus, her husband; and the princes, her brothers. Last of all these bonds, she restores her relation to Lucius, to whom she says, 'My good master, / I will yet do you service' (ll. 404–5).

This restoration immediately precedes the final reversal of the play, in which Cymbeline restores Britain's tributary relationship to Rome and blames its earlier disruption on the nationalism of his 'wicked queen'. Imogen's final act of fidelity, like her father's, is an acknowledgement of Rome as master, even in defeat.[53] The Latin name Fidele that she assumes as a badge of her wifely constancy suggests the general importance of Rome in the construction of *British* faithfulness. Imogen's quest to prove her marital fidelity becomes involved in the complex question of national fidelity when she decides to follow Lucius. It is Lucius who raises her from ritualised death and failure in Act IV, scene ii, and he who gives her the context in which to reconstruct her identity as Fidele when she acknowledges herself reduced to nothing by the apparent death of Posthumus. Even when she seems to deny Lucius, Imogen reaffirms the Roman bond, telling Cymbeline, 'He is a Roman, no more kin to me / Than I to your highness' (V.v.112–13). While she is disguised, she is constituted as her Latin name Fidele, as though her disgrace could only be lifted, her fidelity reconstructed, in Roman terms.

The role of Fidele involves a shift not only in national identity but also in gender, Lucius's generalisation about those who put their trust in girls and boys being truer than he realises. Her relationship with Lucius thus becomes a version of the other bonds between male Britons and Roman commanders. Like Caractacus, she is lifted from the ground by a Roman leader who celebrates her virtue, and in Lucius's redefinitions of their hierarchical relationship, she becomes increasingly the object of his love, not his mastery. The masculine embrace of Roman Britain is thus figured in the relationship of the disguised Imogen and the Roman Lucius even before the Roman and British ensigns 'wave friendly together' at the play's conclusion. The complexity of what Imogen represents in this embrace, in terms of both gender and sexuality, illustrates the complicated nature of British national identity in the play. Neither her imagined female body nor her boy's disguise offers a stable masculine identity for Britain.[54] The instability of the gender, status, and national identities represented in this figure of disguise and much-questioned fidelity precludes the construction of any stable identity, personal or national.

The resolution of the play's many riddles of identity depends on the deus ex machina of the oracle Posthumus finds on his bosom after dreaming of his family and lineage in Act V, scene iv. This restoration of personal identity has its national analogue. The Roman Soothsayer who explicates the oracle of Posthumus's identity is the same who prophesied the merger of Cymbeline's emblem of the radiant sun with the Roman eagle, as he recalls in the penultimate speech of the play (V.v.468–77). When he reads Imogen into the oracle, he identifies her as 'The piece of tender air ... / Which we call *mollis aer*; and *mollis aer* / We term it *mulier*: which *mulier* I divine / Is this most constant wife' (ll. 447–50). This display of pseudo-etymology recalls the involved and equally fanciful antiquarian derivations of the name *Britain*. (Except for its context, it would stand as a parody of such pedantry, in the style of a Don Armado or a Fluellen.) Camden begins the *Britannia* with a survey of such theories, including Humfrey Lhuyd's derivation of *Britain* from the Welsh *Prid-Cain*, meaning a 'pure white form', a phrase that resonates with the Soothsayer's 'piece of tender air' in its attempt to articulate an ethereal purity.[55] As in the Soothsayer's derivation of *mulier* from *mollis aer*, it also works to disembody and desexualise the loaded term *Britannia*. Even so, by presenting Imogen as a piece of tender air, the Soothsayer completes the separation from the earth begun by Lucius when he lifted her from the ground of Wales and the body of 'du Champ'. This fancy antiquarian footwork restores Imogen to her husband by reconstituting woman, strongly identified with the land in both Imogen and the wicked Queen, as air so that she might take her place in the prophetic new order of Roman Britain.[56]

Imogen never regains the visual trappings of her femininity. If she represents a version of ancient British respectability, it is one riddled with the problems of gender and sexuality which characterise the

British relation to Rome. To the extent that she re-emerges as a respectable ideal at the end of the play, it is through a series of alliances with the male characters, both British and Roman, from whom she derives her identity. Cymbeline's daughter, Posthumus's wife, the princes' sister, and the servant of Lucius, she does not raise the spectre of female autonomy and leadership suggested by the wicked Queen's machinations and the example of Boadicea. The anxieties provoked by these ancient British queens are thus ultimately defused in the series of bonds Imogen has established by the end of the play. These bonds emphasise the necessary subordination of the feminine within the patriarchal structures of marriage and empire. The fact that Imogen re-estab-lishes these bonds while still in her boy's disguise indicates the degree of anxiety about female power to destroy them. Like *Bonduca*, *The Valiant Welshman*, and *The True Trojans*, *Cymbeline* concludes with the image of an exclusively male community.

I would like to close with a word about the relative roles of ho-mophobia and misogyny in early modern constructions of national origins. In Mosse's formulation the greatest threat to the male bonding of nationalism is overt male homosexuality, an anxiety Goldberg discovers as early as the 1630s in *Plimoth Plantation*. Both theorists emphasise the interrelatedness of homophobia and misogyny in the formation of masculine national identity. In the masculine romance of Roman Britain, fears of effeminacy and of women are also intertwined. It strikes me, however, that the latter are much more explicit than the former. A fear of originary female savagery consistently drove early modern historians and dramatists of ancient Britain to find refuge in the Roman embrace. The com-plexities of Britain's position in this embrace certainly raise issues of sexuality, but these seem to me to be subordinated to an overriding concern about the gender of national origins. British origins in all these works emerge as unavoidably feminine, either in the savagery of a wicked queen or in the feminised domesticity and submission of the British male to the Roman embrace. I take the violence with which early modern dramatists and historians rejected the figure of the ancient British queen as an indication of how thoroughly their failure to transform the femininity of national origins disturbed them. Their attempts to avoid this originary femininity led them ultimately to embrace a subordinate status in the Roman empire. While this new status also consigned Britain to a feminised role, it avoided the savagery of the purely British nationalism articulated by ancient queens. It also allowed for a historical afterlife for Britain. In contrast to the ancient queen's savage refusal of empire, the masculine embrace of Roman Britain became the truly generative interaction, producing a civil masculine foundation for early modern English nationalism.

From *Shakespeare Quarterly*, 46:3 (1995), 301–22.

NOTES

[While Jodi Mikalachki shares Nevo's concern (in essay 4) with identity-formation in *Cymbeline*, she seeks to historicise psychoanalytic paradigms. Her essay intervenes in recent critical debates over, first, Shakespeare's contribution to the discursive construction of an English / British national identity (see 'Further Reading', Maley [1999]), and, secondly, the constitutive role that gender and sexuality played in the making of such an identity. As early as the beginning of the seventeenth century, she argues, the recovery of national origins was informed by the premise that a 'respectable nationalism depends in part on respectable womanhood' and the exorcism of its antithesis, 'originary female savagery'. Consequently, the play's quest for a viable national identity requires that the insular version of nationalism championed by Cymbeline's queen (and her powerful female precursors in ancient British history) be rejected in favour of an exclusively masculine alliance with the Roman invaders which would guarantee Britain's membership of the civilised world and entry into history. The endnotes of this essay appear here, with the author's permission, in a shortened form. Ed.]

1. Quotations are taken respectively from Liah Greenfeld, *Nationalism: Five Roads to Modernity* (Cambridge, MA, 1992), p. 23; and Benedict Anderson, *Imagined Communities: Reflections on the Origin and Spread of Nationalism*, rev. edn (London and New York, 1992), p. 205. Anderson's formative study was first published in 1983.

2. For their respective theoretical positions, see Greenfeld, *Nationalism*, pp. 17–21; and Anderson, *Imagined Communities*, pp. 1–7.

3. For studies emphasising the issues of gender and sexuality I take up in this article, see Susan Dwyer Amussen, *An Ordered Society: Gender and Class in Early Modern England* (Oxford, 1988); Amussen, 'Gender, Family and the Social Order, 1560–1725', and D. E. Underdown, 'The Taming of the Scold: the Enforcement of Patriarchal Authority in Early Modern England', both in *Order and Disorder in Early Modern England*, Anthony Fletcher and John Stevenson (eds), (Cambridge, 1985), pp. 196–217 and 116–36.

4. Anderson, *Imagined Communities*, p. 12.

5. In his description of the revolt led by the Iceni queen Boudicca, Tacitus notes this political equality of the sexes and identifies it as one of the defining features of British barbarism: *'neque enim sexum in imperiis discernunt'* (see Tacitus, *Agricola*, trans. M. Hutton, rev. R. M. Ogilvie, in *Agricola, Germania and Dialogus*, 5 vols, Loeb Classical Library [Cambridge, MA, 1970], Vol. 1, Bk. 16.1–3).

6. The most elaborate articulation of this model is George L. Mosse, *Nationalism and Sexuality: Respectability and Abnormal Sexuality in Modern Europe* (New York, 1985).

7. For the historical and land-based nationalism developed by Elizabethan antiquarians, see Richard Helgerson, 'The Land Speaks', *Forms of Nationhood: The Elizabethan Writing of England* (Chicago, IL, and London, 1992), pp. 105–47. G. Wilson Knight includes this Jacobean speech with other Shakespearean examples of what he calls Elizabethan post-Armada sentiment: Hastings's short invocation of the impregnable isle in Act IV of *3 Henry VI*; John of Gaunt's speech in Act II of *Richard II*; and Austria's description of the kingdom he promises to the young Lewis of France in Act II of *King John*. (This last is a somewhat equivocal appeal to nationalism, given its context.) See *The Crown of Life* (London, 1947), p. 136. J. M. Nosworthy's dating of *Cymbeline* as probably 1609 puts it at the peak of popular interest in national history and topography (The Arden Shakespeare *Cymbeline*, ed. J. M. Nosworthy [London, 1955], p. xiv).

8. All quotations of *Cymbeline* follow Nosworthy's Arden edition.

9. For a rich account of nostalgia in Shakespearean appeals to national history and topography, see Phyllis Rackin, *Stages of History: Shakespeare's English Chronicles* (Ithaca, NY, 1990), pp. 86–145.

10. Alexander Leggatt, 'The Island of Miracles: An Approach to *Cymbeline*', *Shakespeare Studies*, 10 (1977), 191–209; Leah S. Marcus, '*Cymbeline* and the Unease of Topicality', in *The Historical Renaissance: New Essays on Tudor and Stuart Literature and Culture*, ed. Heather Dubrow and Richard Strier (Chicago, IL, 1988), pp. 134–68; Robert S. Miola, *Shakespeare's Rome* (Cambridge, 1983), pp. 206–35; Joan Warchol Rossi, '*Cymbeline*'s Debt to Holinshed: The Richness of III.i', in *Shakespeare's Romances Reconsidered*, ed. Carol McGinnis Kay and Henry E. Jacobs (Lincoln, NE, 1978), pp. 104–12; Warren D. Smith, 'Cloten with Caius Lucius', *Studies in Philology*, 49 (1952), 185–94.

11. See Geoffrey Hill, '"The True Conduct of Human Judgment": Some Observations on *Cymbeline*', in *The Lords of Limit: Essays on Literature and Ideas* (London, 1984) and J. P. Brockbank, 'History

and Histrionics in *Cymbeline*' (*Shakespeare Survey*, 11 [1958], 42–9, esp. 44 and 47).

12. Knight, *Crown of Life*, p. 136. For his full reading of *Cymbeline* in this regard, see pp. 129–67.

13. Mosse, *Nationalism and Sexuality*, p. 18.

14. Knight regards the Queen as an extreme figure of motherhood, 'a possessive maternal instinct impelling her violent life' (p. 132).

15. It is not quite clear that the Queen dies by her own hand. As in the historiography of Boadicea described below, the Queen might also be said to have succumbed to an excess of savage emotion. Cornelius's response to Cymbeline's question 'How ended she?' bears both interpretations: 'With horror, madly dying, like her life, / Which (being cruel to the world) concluded / Most cruel to herself' (V.v.31–3).

16. Amussen, *Ordered Society*, pp. 118–23.

17. For an account of Imogen as the pattern of conventional Elizabethan womanhood, see Carroll Camden, 'The Elizabethan Imogen', *The Rice Institute Pamphlet*, 38 (1951), 1–17.

18. Helgerson points in this direction in his brief afterword to *Forms of Nationhood*, 'Engendering the Nation-State', pp. 295–301. For a more developed discussion of how gender anxieties figure in early modern English nationalism, see Jean E. Howard, 'An English Lass Amid the Moors: Gender, race, sexuality, and national identity in Heywood's *The Fair Maid of the West*', in *Women, 'Race', & Writing in the Early Modern Period*, ed. Margo Hendricks and Patricia Parker (London and New York, 1994), pp. 101–17.

19. Jonathan Goldberg, 'Bradford's "Ancient Members" and "A Case of Buggery ... Amongst Them"', in *Nationalisms and Sexualities*, ed. Andrew Parker, Mary Russo, Doris Sommer, and Patricia Yaeger (New York and London, 1992), pp. 60–76, esp. pp. 63–4.

20. Indeed, even before she assumes her boy's disguise, Imogen's status and authority as a married woman are not clear. Anne Barton, in *Essays, Mainly Shakespearean* (Cambridge 1994), has recently pointed to numerous ambiguities in the play's references to the union of Imogen and Posthumus, suggesting that it might have been an unconsummated precontract rather than a solemnised marriage (pp. 19–30). Janet Adelman, in *Suffocating Mothers: Fantasies of Maternal Origin in Shakespeare's Plays, 'Hamlet' to The 'Tempest'* (New York and London, 1992), notes the degree to which Imogen's disguise disempowers her, in contradistinction to the ways it enabled the selfhood of Shakespeare's earlier comic heroines (p. 210).

21. Cymbeline's first queen, mother to Imogen and the lost princes, leaves no other trace in the play than the diamond Imogen gives Posthumus

(I.ii.43). Belarius's wife, Euriphile, nurse to the young princes and mourned by them as a mother, also seems to have been dead for some time (III.iii.103–5). Adelman comments on the need to efface the maternal in the all-male pastoral of Wales (pp. 202–4).

22. Goldberg, 'Bradford's "Ancient Members"', pp. 63–4. Rackin elaborates how women function as 'antihistorians' who resist patriarchal structures of masculine history-writing in Shakespeare's histories ('Patriarchal History and Female Subversion', pp. 146–200). For the particular danger posed by mothers in this regard, see pp. 190–1.

23. Brockbank, 'History and Histrionics', 44–5; David M. Bergeron, '*Cymbeline*: Shakespeare's Last Roman Play', *Shakespeare Quarterly*, 31 (1980), 32–41. Bergeron expands his reading of the play's Augustan elements in *Shakespeare's Romances and the Royal Family* (Lawrence, KS, 1985), pp. 136–57.

24. Robert S. Miola articulates the most radical development of this position in two essays: '*Cymbeline*: Shakespeare's Valediction to Rome', in *Roman Images: Selected Papers from the English Institute, 1982*, ed. Annabel Patterson (Baltimore, MD, 1984), pp. 51–62; and '*Cymbeline*: Beyond Rome', *Shakespeare's Rome*, pp. 206–35. See also Leggatt, 'Island of Miracles', pp. 192 and 204; and William Barry Thorne, '*Cymbeline*: "Lopp'd Branches" and the Concept of Regeneration', *SQ*, 20 (1969), 143–59. Both 'pro-British' and 'pro-Roman' historiographical readings of *Cymbeline* have trouble placing Iachimo and the scenes in Rome in a first-century Roman-British context. The only historiographical sense critics have made of Iachimo is to read his symbolic rape of the sleeping Imogen in Act II, scene ii as a figure for the Roman invasion of Britain. Like the Romans at Milford Haven, Iachimo fails to achieve his conquest yet collects his 'tribute'. The anachronistic intrusion of Renaissance Italy in all its degeneracy may also provide an outlet for anti-Roman sentiment by invoking the early modern context of Rome as the Papacy rather than as the ancient seat of empire. For a brief discussion of Act II, scene ii, see note 46 below.

25. Raphael Holinshed, 'Historie of England' in *Chronicles of England, Scotland and Ireland* (London, 1587), pp. 32–3 and 42–6. Spelling of quotations from Holinshed has been modernised throughout. Brockbank cautiously suggests a resemblance between Cymbeline's Queen and Boadicea ('History and Histrionics', 49, n. 20).

26. Holinshed, 'Historie of England' in *Chronicles*, pp. 44 and 42.

27. Holinshed, 'Historie of England' in *Chronicles*, p. 39. Both evaluations were added to the 1587 edition by its editor, Abraham Fleming.

28. Camden, *Remains Concerning Britain*, ed. R. C. Dunn (Toronto, 1984), pp. 205–6.

29. Milton, *History of Britain*, ed. French Fogle in *Complete Prose Works of John Milton*, gen. ed. Don M. Wolfe, 8 vols (New Haven, CT, and London, 1971), 5: 70–2 and 79–80. Camden, while giving a truncated speech in *Remains*, omits Boadicea's oration from any edition of the *Britannia* published in his lifetime, perhaps for reasons similar to Milton's.

30. Rackin describes a similarly gendered antithesis between Talbot and Joan of Arc in Shakespeare's first Henriad (*Stages of History*, p. 151).

31. John Fletcher, *Bonduca*, ed. Cyrus Hoy, in *The Dramatic Works in the Beaumont and Fletcher Canon*, Fredson Bowers (gen ed.), 8 vols (Cambridge, 1979), Vol. 4, V.iii.201–3.

32. R. A., *The Valiant Welshman, or The True Chronicle History of the life and valiant deeds of Caradoc the Great, King of Cambria, now called Wales*, ed. Valentin Kreb (Leipzig, 1902), V.v.39–58.

33. William Rowley, *A Shoemaker, a Gentleman* in *William Rowley: His 'All's Lost by Lust', and 'A Shoemaker, A Gentleman'*, University of Pennsylvania Series in Philology and Literature 13, ed. Charles Wharton Stork (Philadelphia, 1910), 3.4.

34. Jasper Fisher, *Fuimus Troes, or the True Trojans* in *A Select Collection of Old Plays*, ed. Robert Dodsley, 12 vols (London, 1825), 7: 456.

35. The masculine embrace of *Shoemaker* takes place in the third act rather than at the play's conclusion. Several outspoken female characters, British and Roman, take part in the conclusion to this play, distinguishing it from the all-male reconciliations of the other Roman-British dramas. Indeed, the embrace that closes the play is performed by the newly liberated British queen and her recently restored sons.

36. Just as the Roman and British ensigns 'wave friendly together' at the conclusion of *Cymbeline*, so, too, Cymbeline's emblem of the radiant sun is said to merge with the Roman eagle in the Soothsayer's interpretation of his vision before the battle (V.v.468–77). In this interpretation, the meeting of the emblems becomes the symbol of the right relation between Britain and Rome, vested with the force of destiny, and presented as the key to understanding the play's peaceful resolution.

37. See Mosse, *Nationalism and Sexuality*, chap. 2, 'Manliness and Homosexuality', pp. 23–47.

38. Goldberg, 'Bradford's "Ancient Members"', pp. 67–8.

39. Jones and Stallybrass comment on early modern antiquarian assumptions about national character that linked barbarism with effeminacy in descriptions of the 'Scythian disease', a condition of masculine effeminisation that included impotence and the assumption of women's work, clothing, speech, and other forms of behaviour, represented in national terms by the hereditary effeminacy of the Scythian

royal family. Noting the derivation of Irish origins from the Scythians in some late-sixteenth-century apologies for Irish colonisation, Ann Rosalind Jones and Peter Stallybrass argue for the English need to distinguish their own national identity from this barbaric effeminacy ('Dismantling Irena: The Sexualising of Ireland in Early Modern England', in Andrew Parker et al. [eds], *Nationalisms and Sexualities*, pp. 158–65).

40. For Wales as a place of geographical and sexual liminality in Shakespeare's histories, as 'a scene of emasculation and female power, … the site of a repression in the historical narrative', see Rackin, *Stages of History*, pp. 170–2.

41. Sharon Macdonald, in 'Boadicea: warrior, mother and myth' (*Images of Women in Peace and War: Cross-Cultural and Historical Perspectives*, Sharon Macdonald, Pat Holden, and Shirley Ardener [eds] [London, 1987], pp. 40–61, esp. 49–50), also notes the emphasis on manliness and homoeroticism in *Bonduca*.

42. See, for instance, V.v.462–6; where Cymbeline attributes the deaths of the Queen and her son to divine retribution for her interference in the proper submission of Britain to Rome.

43. The Welsh retreat of the princes has in fact led some critics to conclude that the setting of *Cymbeline* has no historiographical importance and merely enhances the play's romantic qualities. I would argue that the Welsh setting of these scenes is of historical importance precisely because it dramatises the anxiety of being excluded from history. For the opposing readings, see Irving Ribner, 'Shakespeare and Legendary History: *Lear* and *Cymbeline*', *SQ*, 7 (1956), 47–52; and Arthur C. Kirsch, '*Cymbeline* and Coterie Dramaturgy', *ELH*, 34 (1967), 288–306.

44. Most psychoanalytic critics interpret the Welsh cave as a form of maternal protection from which the princes must emerge into battle with the Romans, which restores them to their father and their patrilineal identity. Caesar functions in these readings as the ultimate father, with whom Britain works out its relationship through the Roman conflict and its resolution. See Meredith Skura, 'Interpreting Posthumus' Dream from Above and Below: Families, Psychoanalysts, and Literary Critics', in *Representing Shakespeare*, Murray M. Schwartz and Coppélia Kahn (eds), (Baltimore, MD, 1980), pp. 203–16, esp. 209–14; D. E. Landry, 'Dreams as History: The Strange Unity of *Cymbeline*', *SQ*, 33 (1982), 68–79; and Murray Schwartz, 'Between Fantasy and Imagination: A Psychological Exploration of *Cymbeline*', *Psychoanalysis and Literary Process*, ed. Frederick Crews (Cambridge, MA, 1970), pp. 219–83, esp., 250–9. In contrast, Adelman regards the Welsh retreat as an exclusively male preserve where Belarius can raise Cymbeline's sons free from the tainted

maternity that haunts masculine imagination in the play (*Suffocating Mothers*, pp. 203–4).

45. Adelman, *Suffocating Mothers*, pp. 207.

46. Imogen's identity with Britain has been commented on from a variety of critical perspectives, especially regarding the analogy between the Roman invasion of Britain and Iachimo's invasion of Imogen's bedchamber; see Leggatt, 'Island of Miracles' p. 194; Schwartz, 'Between Fantasy and Imagination', p. 221; and Skura, 'Interpreting Posthumous' Dream', p. 210.

47. Indeed, some recent editors have made a strong argument for 'Innogen' as Shakespeare's intended form of the name. For a summary of this argument, see Roger Warren's *Shakespeare in Performance*: '*Cymbeline*' (Manchester and New York, 1989), p. viii.

48. But see Nosworthy's note to this image in the Arden edition, where he surveys critical concern about the image as undignified or degrading.

49. Brockbank, 'History and Histrionics', 48; Holinshed, 'Description of Britaine', in *Chronicles*, p. 2. The line is from the First Eclogue, translated by H. Rushton Fairclough as 'wholly sundered from all the world'; see *Virgil*, 2 vols, Loeb Classical Library (Cambridge, MA, 1950), 1: 36.

50. Simon Forman, who saw a performance of *Cymbeline* in 1611, mentions Milford Haven several times in his account as the place toward which all the action tends. Nosworthy prints Forman's account in full in the introduction to the Arden edition (pp. xiv–xv).

51. Emrys Jones, in 'Stuart Cymbeline' (*Essays in Criticism*, 11 [1961], 84–99), presents the original and most elaborate reading of the historiographical importance of Milford Haven (93–5). For discussions of the power of Milford developed from Jones's argument, see Landry, 'Dreams as History', pp. 71–3; Leggatt, 'Island of Miracles'; Marcus, '*Cymbeline* and the Unease of Topicality', pp. 148–51; and Frances A. Yates, *Shakespeare's Last Plays: A New Approach* (London, 1975), pp. 47–52.

52. One might even suggest that Posthumus provides a needed vent for the collective masculine anxiety about Imogen's fidelity when he unwittingly strikes his disguised wife onstage (V.v.228–9).

53. Cymbeline's earlier recollection (III.ii.69–73) of having served as a page in Augustus's household (a courtly anachronism culled from Holinshed, 'Historie of England', in *Chronicles*, p. 32) strengthens this parallel.

54. The boy's disguise adds a further complication in that it foregrounds the theatrical convention of boy actors playing female roles.

55. See Holland's translation of this passage in Camden, *Britain*, pp. 5–6.

56. Adelman reads the Soothsayer's linguistic transformation of Imogen as an unmaking of her sexual body that 'does away with the problematic female body and achieves a family and a masculine identity founded exclusively on male bonds' (*Suffocating Mothers*, p. 218). Rackin, noting the importance of Elizabeth of York, Katherine of France, and the infant Elizabeth at the end of Shakespeare's two Henriads and *Henry VIII*, argues that 'the incorporation of the feminine represents the end of the historical process … [and] can only take place at the point where history stops. A world that truly includes the feminine is a world in which history cannot be written' (*Stages of History*, p. 176). From my analysis of *Cymbeline*, I would agree. I would suggest that the converse is also true, that in the romance of national origins, the dis-incorporation of the feminine is the place where history starts.

6

Masculine Authority and the Maternal Body in *The Winter's Tale*

JANET ADELMAN

Within Shakespeare's career, *Antony and Cleopatra* functions as a fragile pastoral moment. Its pastoral is shorn of the power to bring even its modest gains back to the dominating culture: as Egypt's female pastoral is in the end contained and colonised by Rome, so *Antony and Cleopatra*'s moment of festive possibility is largely contained by the surrounding texts. The generative maternal power celebrated in Cleopatra's recreation of Antony is severely curtailed in *Coriolanus*, where maternal presence is once again construed as paternal absence, where mothers are once again fatal to their sons. This construction is, I have argued, the legacy of *Hamlet*, where the mother's sexual body is itself poisonous to the father on whom the son would base his identity; its consequences are variously played out in the problem plays and tragedies that follow from *Hamlet*. Taken together, the romances can be understood as Shakespeare's final attempt to repair the damage of this legacy, in effect to reinstate the ideal parental couple lost at the beginning of *Hamlet*: the idealised mother is recovered in *Pericles* and *The Winter's Tale*, the idealised father in *Cymbeline* and *The Tempest*. But the attempt at recovery itself reinscribes the conditions of loss: in the plays of maternal recovery, the father's authority must be severely undermined and the mother herself subjected to a chastening purgation; in the plays of paternal recovery, the mother must be demonised and banished before the father's authority can be restored.

From beginning to end, the romances reiterate the terms of *Hamlet*, working and reworking his problematic confrontation with the sexualised maternal body: if *Pericles* begins where Hamlet does, in the psychic world poisoned by female sexuality, *The Tempest* answers his need for a bodiless father immune to the female, able at last to control her unweeded garden. Except for a moment in *The Winter's Tale*, when the generative female space of Cleopatra's monument recurs in Paulina's own sheltering monument, the mother and father lost in *Hamlet* cannot be fully recovered together. Instead, the romances oscillate between them, broadly structured by a series of gendered either / or's: either maternal or paternal authority; either female deity or male; either nature or art; either trust in processes larger than the self or the attempt to control these processes.[1] Each play is in effect written in defensive response to the one before it; each destabilises the resolution previously achieved, working and reworking the problematic relationship of masculine authority to the female.

[...]

If *Cymbeline* ends with the magical restoration of paternal authority and the fantasy-accomplishment of a parthenogenetic family in which women need not be half-workers, *The Winter's Tale* begins with the pregnant female body. In its opening lines, the play seems initially to replicate aspects of Belarius's male pastoral, giving us the image of the 'natural' male world from which women have been wholly excluded: in the dialogue between Camillo and Archidamus, the 'rooted' affection (I.i.23) between the brother-kings and the healing powers of fathers' sons take centre stage, with no mention of wives or mothers, and certainly no need for daughters. Though there is tension in this world[2] – the hospitality is distinctly competitive and leaves a residue of anxiety about indebtedness, the kings can 'branch' into 'great difference' from their common root – nonetheless there seems 'not in the world either malice or matter to alter' their love (I.i.33–4). Hermione's entrance – perhaps literally between the two kings? – disrupts this male haven. The visual impact of her pregnant body[3] inevitably focuses attention on her, reminding the audience of what has been missing from the gentlemen's conversation; and her body immediately becomes the site of longing and terror, its very presence disruptive of male bonds and male identity.

Even before Leontes's jealousy makes Hermione's pregnant body the sign of betrayal between the brothers, Polixenes has recast the covert tensions of the first scene in its image:

> Nine changes of the watery star hath been
> The shepherd's note since we have left our throne
> Without a burden. Time as long again
> Would be fill'd up, my brother, with our thanks;
> And yet we should, for perpetuity,
> Go hence in debt: and therefore, like a cipher
> (Yet standing in rich place) I multiply
> With one 'We thank you' many thousands moe.
> That go before it.
>
> (I.ii.1–9)

'Nine changes', 'watery star', 'burden', 'fill'd up': in Polixenes's opening lines, anxieties about indebtedness and separation are registered through the imagery of pregnancy,[4] as though Hermione's body provided the language for the rupture in their brotherhood. In fact, as Polixenes goes on to tell us in his mythologised version of the kings' childhood, the sexualised female body has already been assigned this role:

> **Pol.** We were as twinn'd lambs that did frisk i' th' sun,
> And bleat the one at th'other: what we chang'd
> Was innocence for innocence: we knew not
> The doctrine of ill-doing, nor dream'd
> That any did. Had we pursu'd that life,
> And our weak spirits ne'er been higher rear'd
> With stronger blood, we should have answer'd heaven
> Boldly 'not guilty', the imposition clear'd
> Hereditary ours.
> **Her.**   By this we gather
> You have tripp'd since.
> **Pol.**   O my most sacred lady,
> Temptations have since then been born to's: for
> In those unfledg'd days was my wife a girl;
> Your precious self had not yet cross'd the eyes
> Of my young play-fellow.
>
> (I.ii.67–80)

Once again, the female body disrupts the idealised male pastoral, becoming the sign of 'great difference' between the kings: 'crossing'[5] the eyes of the young playfellows, Hermione and the unnamed woman who will be Polixenes's wife unmake their symbiotic innocence, plummeting them simultaneously into adult differentiation – now there is 'my' and 'your' where there had been only 'we' and 'our' – and into their newly sexualised bodies, in effect recording the fall in them as their phallic spirits are higher reared with stronger blood.[6] Polixenes may call Hermione 'most sacred lady', but he makes her body the locus and the sign of division and original sin, as Hermione herself is quick to note (I.ii.80–2). Moreover, her visible pregnancy stages the submerged logic of his account of original sin: temptations have been born to us, her presence suggests, because we have been born to them, acquiring original sin at the site of origin.

Both in Polixenes's opening speech and in his pastoral myth, the sexualised female body is the sign of male separation and loss. Moreover, in its very fullness, that body becomes the register of male emptiness. The final metaphorics of Polixenes's opening speech bizarrely transform an expression of his indebtedness to Leontes into an expression of chronic male indebtedness to the female in the procreative act: 'like a cipher / (Yet standing in rich place) I multiply / With one "We thank you" many thousands moe / That go before it.' Nothing in himself, he is able to multiply only when he stands in a rich place: his computational joke barely conceals anxiety about the male role in procreation, an anxiety made visible on stage in the rich place that is Hermione's body.[7] But in thus figuring male emptiness and female fullness, Polixenes allows for a transvaluation of sexuality and of the female body. If women are the first temptation, if the phallic rearing of the spirits with higher blood is the sign of the fall in Polixenes's mythologised account of childhood, here it is only by such standing in rich place that man becomes generative: the rich place itself confers value on him. These sharply contrasting attitudes toward sexuality and toward the female body that engenders it mark the trajectory of the play: from an idealised male pastoral to a pastoral richly identified with the generative potential of the female body; from a sterile court in which the maternal body and the progeny who bear its signs must be harried to death to a court in which that body can be restored, its regenerative sanctity recognised and embraced.

If Polixenes's initial speeches give us the image of what must be cured before the play can end happily and hint at the direction from which cure will come, Leontes's psyche is presented as the locus of the disease. Leontes's jealousy erupts out of nowhere and breaks his world apart, as it breaks the syntax and rhythms of his own speeches apart; in the violence and obscurity of its expression, it draws the audience into its own sphere, causing us to snatch at nothings, to reconstruct the world (as Leontes himself does) in a reassuringly intelligible image. Any attempt to explain its strangeness away or to make it wholly coherent violates the dramatic principles through which it communicates itself to us; Shakespeare has deliberately left its expression fragmentary and incoherent, the better to engage us in its processes, making us – like Leontes – communicate with dreams (I.ii.140). But whether or not we think we can pinpoint the onset of the jealousy or the exact progress of its aetiology, it is far from the psychologically unmotivated 'given' of the plot that it is sometimes taken to be.[8] For the jealousy erupts in response to the renewed separation from a mirroring childhood twin and the multiple displacements and vulnerabilities signalled by Hermione's pregnant body;[9] it localises and psychologises the myth of loss embedded in Polixenes's version of Eden. And through it, Shakespeare floods the play with the fantasies that have haunted his male protagonists since *Hamlet*, articulating with astonishing economy and force the anguish of a masculinity that conceives of itself as betrayed at its point of origin, a masculinity that can read in the full maternal body only the signs of its own loss. In Leontes, Shakespeare condenses the destructive logic of tragic masculinity itself; and then, wrenching the play out of the obsessional space of Leontes's mind, he moves beyond tragedy.

In the fantasies given a local habitation in Leontes's jealousy, the fall into original sin is once again registered through the rupture of an idealised mirroring relationship with the brother-twin; genital sexuality once again marks the moment of separation and contamination by women. Polixenes's fantasy of twinship functions in effect as Leontes's prehistory, the shaky foundation from which his jealousy erupts: it is his guarantee of a pure male identity, an identity unproblematised by sexual difference, shaped by a mirroring other who reassuringly gives back only himself;[10] its generative equivalent is the fantasy of male parthenogenesis, with its similar denial of otherness and the woman's part. The alternative to the masculine identity conferred through this mirror is the masculine identity originating in the female and everywhere marked by vulnerability to her: the conflicted identity for which Hermione's pregnant body comes to stand. Either the mirroring twin or the pregnant wife-mother: like Polixenes's fragile pastoral, Leontes's psychic world cannot contain both together. Hence the repeated insistence – visual

and metaphoric – that Hermione's pregnant body comes between
the two kings: as the emblem of a male identity always already
contaminated at its source, that body is the limiting condition to the
fantasy of an identity formed through male parthenogenesis or a
pure male twinship. Its presence in effect forces Leontes to
acknowledge his own maternal origins, immersing him in the
dangerous waters – the contaminated 'pond' (I.ii.195) – of a female
sexuality he can neither excise nor control.

The fantasy of twinship functions in effect to protect Leontes
from immersion in those waters.[11] His jealousy erupts at the first
sign of rupture in that protective mirroring relationship, as though
its loss returned him to the site of his vulnerability to the female;
'At my request he would not' (I.ii.87) is the first sign of danger. As
though newly cast out of his equivalent to the all-male Eden, he
finds in Hermione's pregnant body the sign of all he stands to lose:
remembering their courtship, he remakes her as the unreliable
maternal object, capable of souring the entire world to death by
withholding herself from him (I.ii.102–4). And this withholding is
in his imagination tantamount to annihilation: imagining himself
excluded from her rich place, he responds as though he has become
Polixenes's cipher, flooded with the sense of his own and the
world's nothingness; as he later tells Camillo,

> Why then the world, and all that's in't, is nothing,
> The covering sky is nothing, Bohemia nothing,
> My wife is nothing, nor nothing have these nothings,
> If this be nothing.
>
> (I.ii.293–6)[12]

But this nothingness is not tolerable: and Leontes retaliates against
it, attempting through a monstrous birth of his own – the 'something' born of his affection's copulation with nothing (I.ii.138–43)[13]
– to recreate himself and the world in the shape of his delusion. If
the possibility of Hermione's betrayal first plunges him into the
nothingness of maternal abandonment, it becomes his stay against
nothingness as it hardens into delusion: the world is nothing, he
tells Camillo, *if Hermione is not unfaithful*. Threatened by absolute
loss, he seizes on the fantasy of Hermione's adultery as though it in
itself could give him something to hold on to: better the 'something'
of cuckoldry than the nothingness into which he would otherwise
dissolve. Naming himself a cuckold, insisting on his identity as
cuckold and his community with other men (I.ii.190–200), he finds

in the culturally familiar fiction of female betrayal in marriage both an acceptable narrative for his sense of primal loss and a new adult selfhood. Through the self-born delusion of Hermione's betrayal, he thus gives himself a recognisable place to stand; without it, 'the centre is not big enough to bear / A schoolboy's top' (II.i.102–3).

The fantasy of Hermione's adultery initially seems to serve Leontes well, answering several of his psychic needs at once. Through it, Leontes can attempt to undo his subjection to the rich place of Hermione's body, making her – rather than himself – nothing and securing his 'rest' by giving her to the fire (II.iii.8). His monstrous birth in effect undoes hers: if she is unfaithful, then he can deny his connection to her body, both as husband and as son. Through his delusion, he can imagine her pregnant body as the sign of her infidelity, rather than the sign of his sexual concourse with her; and the baby she carries thus becomes no part of him. For in his mobile fantasy, her pregnant body threatens to display him in the foetus she bears; he keeps dissolving into that foetus. The delusion of Hermione's adultery affords Leontes secure ground in part because it helps him resist this regressive pull back toward her body; in its own way, it serves the same needs as the initial fantasy of twinship. But it is ultimately no more successful than that fantasy; in the end, it returns him to what refuses to stay repressed. In Leontes's fluid formulations, cuckoldry fuses with sexual intercourse and with birth, implicating him once again in the maternal origin he would deny. If Othello and Posthumus conflate adultery with marital sexuality,[14] Leontes conflates both with cuckoldry: all three 'sully / The purity and whiteness' of his sheets (I.ii.326–7). For the sexually mature male body is one with the cuckold's body, both marked by the deforming signs of female betrayal: differentiating himself from Mamillius – 'thou want'st a rough pash and the shoots that I have / To be full like me' (I.ii.128–9) – Leontes identifies the bull's horns with the cuckold's, as though the sexually mature male body were by definition the cuckold's body. And both sexuality and cuckoldry return him to the original site of betrayal: imagining himself a cuckold – 'Inch-thick, knee-deep; o'er head and ears a fork'd one' (I.ii.186) – he simultaneously imagines himself sexually entering Hermione's body between her forked legs[15] and immersed in that body, knee-deep, over head and ears, as though returned to the foetal position. Cuckold, adulterer and foetus fuse in their entry into the maternal womb, the belly that 'will let in and out the enemy, / With bag and baggage' (I.ii.205–6).[16] And the foetus itself becomes that enemy: in the most bizarre and violent of Leontes's conflations – his brutal 'let her sport herself / With that she's big with' (II.i.60–1) – he imagines the unborn baby he would disown as the mother's illicit sexual partner,[17] graphically literalising the sexualised return to the womb.

Deprived of his protective mirroring relationship, thrust back to his origin in the maternal body, Leontes attempts to escape that body through the fantasy of his own cuckoldry; but the fantasy itself betrays him, returning him to his source. But Leontes has simultaneously been pursuing another strategy against nothingness: virtually as soon as his jealousy erupts, Leontes turns toward Mamillius and attempts to recreate a mirroring twin in him.[18] He begins with the familiar patriarchal worry that his son might not be his son: his thrice-repeated assertions of likeness (I.ii.130, 135, 159) serve, first of all, to guarantee his own paternity, as if it were in doubt. But – as in *King Lear* and *Cymbeline* – worries about illegitimacy turn out to be in part a cover for worries about the female role in procreation, legitimate or illegitimate. As Leontes makes clear when he violently separates the boy from his mother – as though she were 'infectious', Hermione says later (III.ii.98) – his fear is not that Mamillius resembles Polixenes, but that he resembles his mother:

> Give me the boy: I am glad you did not nurse him:
> Though he does bear some signs of me, yet you
> Have too much blood in him.
>
> (II.i.56–8)

In this construction of likeness, the signs of Mamillius's difference from him are signs not of an illegitimate father but of his mother's contaminating presence in her son: if he is her child, then he is not fully his father's. Hence the drive toward absolute identity in Leontes's early assertions of the likeness between father and son: those assertions – especially the anxiety-filled assertion that they are 'almost as like as eggs' (I.ii.130)[19] – move from a (just barely) rational concern with paternity toward a deeply irrational attempt to replace the lost twinship by reinstating the fantasy of male parthenogenesis in Mamillius. Leontes's pet names for his son increasingly identify the child as a part – perhaps specifically a sexual part – of his own body, his 'bawcock', a 'collop' of his flesh (1.2.121, 137), as though he could be made without his mother's participation; in effect, those names would make him a split-off portion of his father's masculinity, hence a secure repository for Leontes's threatened identity.[20]

But this defensive fantasy cannot be sustained: like the fantasy of cuckoldry, the attempt at protective identification with Mamillius turns back on itself, ultimately returning Leontes to the corrupt maternal body. Seeing himself in his 'unbreech'd' son may temporarily relieve Leontes of the guilt associated with the use of his own dangerous ornament (I.ii.155, 158), but it must simultaneously recall the period when he himself was not securely differentiated from his mother.[21] For the inescapable fact of maternal origin is always there in Mamillius – as much a part of him as his name, with its unmistakable allusion to the maternal nursery Leontes so dreads.[22] Approaching the boy sitting by his mother's side, Leontes recoils as though he were seeing himself; and he immediately acts to remove the child from her infectious presence. Conflating his own danger with what he imagines to be Mamillius's, he figures Hermione's betrayal as the source of infection in his drink:

> There may be in the cup
> A spider steep'd, and one may drink, depart,
> And yet partake no venom (for his knowledge
> Is not infected); but if one present
> Th'abhorr'd ingredient to his eye, make known
> How he hath drunk, he cracks his gorge, his sides,
> With violent hefts. I have drunk, and seen the spider.
> (II.i.39–45)

'I have drunk, and seen the spider'; 'I am glad you did not nurse him': only eleven lines apart, the phrases echo and explicate one another, identifying Hermione's maternal body with the spider in the cup.[23] In Leontes's infected imagination, maternal nursery is that spider, the infection taken in at the source; his spasmodic attempts to disown Hermione are the psychic equivalents of the violent hefts he images, violent attempts to heave out the internalised mother, the contaminated origin within, like a child spitting up infected – or soured – milk.[24]

Leontes's psychosis illustrates in its purest form the trauma of tragic masculinity, the trauma of contamination at the site of origin. Hermione's pregnant body in effect returns him to this point of origin, and to the sense of contamination culturally registered as original sin; and, despite all his best efforts, the Mamillius in whom he would see himself originally pure gives him back only the reflection of her taint in him. But this taint is ultimately epitomised for Leontes in the baby Hermione now carries; the drama of his expulsion and recovery of the female is thus played out through her. Like everyone else (II.i.17; II.ii.26), Leontes apparently expects this baby to be a boy; that she turns out to be a girl merely confirms her mother's presence in her and hence – according to the familiar logic of illegitimacy[25] – her status as a 'female bastard' (II.iii.174): for Leontes at this stage, 'female' and 'bastard' might as well be interchangeable terms. But her supposed illegitimacy nonetheless serves a defensive purpose. When Paulina brings the baby to him and attempts to make him see himself in her, he reacts with panic, summoning up all the cultural tropes for overpowering women – the shrew, the mannish woman, the husband-beating wife, the witch, the bawd, the midwife – with a nearly comic haste:[26] to see himself in his daughter would be the final blow to his threatened masculinity.[27] Paulina's strategy must therefore backfire: the more convincingly she can represent the baby girl as his likeness, the more desperately he will need to dissociate himself from her, hysterically naming her bastard (seven times within roughly forty lines) and casting her out 'like to itself, / No father owning it' (III.ii.87–8). He has already managed to isolate Hermione with her women, as though their femaleness were catching; now he phobically drives Paulina off the stage and refuses to go near his infant daughter, violently disowning her as though she too could contaminate him.

In casting her out, Leontes begins counter-phobically to remake himself in the shape of the overwhelming mother he most fears: he would dash his infant's brains out with his own hands (II.iii.139–40) or abandon her in a landscape of absolute deprivation (II.iii.175).[28] It is diagnostic of this play's radical re-valuation of the maternal that Leontes should thus appropriate the imagery of Lady Macbeth: here the ultimate source of danger is not the overwhelming mother but the tyrannical husband / father. Localising tragic masculinity in Leontes and decisively moving beyond it, Shakespeare thus recasts the gendered aetiology of tragedy as he had defined it in *Hamlet*, *King Lear*, *Macbeth*, and *Coriolanus*: no longer the province of maternal contamination, it is now the province of the male ego that fears such contamination, the ego that would remake the world in the image of its own desired purity. With the casting out of his baby girl, the death of the son too obviously born of woman, and the apparent death of his wife, Leontes has arrived at this point: he has in effect exorcised female generativity and achieved the all-male landscape he thought he wanted. But he discovers in it not the timeless spring of Polixenes's pastoral fantasy but the landscape of tragedy, an endless winter of barrenness and deprivation the psychic equivalent of the 'barren mountain, and still winter / In storm perpetual' (III.ii.212–13) that Paulina describes as the fitting setting for his repentance. But the same exorcism that locates Leontes in this psychic landscape allows Shakespeare to undertake a radical recuperation of the maternal body: exorcised and banished from the stage, it can in effect be reconstituted and revalued; and thus released from the confines of Leontes's obsessions, the play itself can begin the turn from tragedy to romance.

The first hints of this release come with the birth of Perdita, 'lusty, and like to live' (II.ii.27), herself 'free'd and enfranchis'd' from the womb (II.ii.61). The short scene in which her birth is reported is filled with the promise of release from the tyrannous hold of Leontes's mind. The entrance of Paulina brings not only a new character but a new voice – shrewd, self-assured, funny – strong enough to provide an authoritative countervoice to Leontes's; and from her we hear for the first time of the 'great nature' (II.ii.60), the 'good goddess Nature' (II.iii.103), who will become the presiding deity of recuperation.[29] Through her, Shakespeare begins the move toward romance, simultaneously underscoring a new alliance between gender and genre: her husband allows himself to become the agent of Leontes's delusions (though he recognises the sanctity of the Hermione who appears to him [III.iii.23], he nonetheless believes her guilty); she becomes the advocate for mother and baby, aligning herself firmly with the female forces of recovery.[30] While Paulina sees birth as the promise of freedom and enfranchisement, Antigonus repeats the tragic paradigm linking birth and mortality: in what are virtually his last words – 'poor wretch, / That for thy mother's fault art thus expos'd / To loss and what may follow!' (III.iii.49–51) – he rewrites the baby's exposure not as the consequence of Leontes's phobic delusion but as a parable for birth itself, the exposure to loss that is always the mother's fault.[31] But Perdita lives, while he himself dies as the sacrificial (and gendered) representative of tragedy.[32] And with his death, the play turns decisively away from the tragic paradigm, increasingly aligning its own artistic processes with the good goddess whom Paulina invokes.

Shakespeare achieves the recuperation of the maternal body and the attendant turn from tragedy to romance by immersion in the

fertile space of a decidedly female pastoral. Though the entrance to
the pastoral domain is mediated by a series of male figures – Time,
Polixenes and Camillo, Autolycus – that domain itself is deeply
allied with the fecundity of 'great creating nature' (IV.iv.88); filled
with the vibrant energies of sexuality and seasonal change, it stands
as a rebuke to Polixenes's static and nostalgic male pastoral and to
the masculine identity that would find itself there.[33] And it reaches
back, behind Polixenes, toward the nightmare version of the female
body that could provoke his consolatory dream: the circumstances
of Antigonus's death at the entrance to this pastoral allude to Lear's
great tragic pastoral, replicating its storm and literalising its bear
and sea (*King Lear*, III.iv.9–11), as though signalling that it too
must be revised before the play can proceed. And through Florizel,
Shakespeare hints at just such revision. Lear sees in his pastoral the
emblem of an horrific female sexuality utterly beyond male control;
like Leontes lashing out at the Hermione who 'rounds apace'
(II.i.16), he would attack the generative female body, 'Strike flat the
thick rotundity o' th' world! / Crack Nature's moulds, all germens
spill at once' (III.ii.7–8). Florizel recalls this body in his vow to
Perdita:

> It cannot fail, but by
> The violation of my faith; and then
> Let nature crush the sides o' th' earth together,
> And mar the seeds within!
>
> (IV.iv.477–80)

But he would recuperate what Lear would destroy,[34] aligning his
faith with its generative potential and cherishing the seeds within.

If Leontes founds his masculine identity on separation from the
female, Florizel embraces the female. He has already told Perdita 'I
cannot be / Mine own, nor anything to any, if / I be not thine'
(IV.iv.43–5); now he disowns the ordinary patriarchal identifiers:
'From my succession wipe me, father; I / Am heir to my affection'
(IV.iv.481–2). Mirrored not in an idealised male twin or in a father
but in Perdita – Florizel to her Flora – he founds his identity in his
relation to her, in the process recuperating the word – 'affection' –
that had figured Leontes's monstrous birth. And in return, Perdita
promises him not the static eternity of Polixenes's pastoral but an
aliveness that springs out of the very conditions of his mortality.
She would 'strew him o'er and o'er' with the 'flowers o' th' spring'
that Proserpina let 'fall / From Dis's waggon' (IV.iv.113, 117–18,

129), flowers that allude to the seasonal cycles of birth and death. 'What, like a corpse?' Florizel asks playfully, recapitulating the fears of all those men who find only death in love, only mortality in the sexual body; and Perdita replies,

> No, like a bank, for love to lie and play on:
> Not like a corpse; or if – not to be buried,
> But quick, and in mine arms.
>   (IV.iv.130–2)

In these wonderful lines, Perdita encapsulates the whole process of regeneration enacted by the play, herself becoming the presiding deity of recuperation. Immersed in her pastoral, covered with the flowers that are her sign as Flora, Florizel is immersed in the mortal body: hence the pun on *corpse*. But Perdita does not let that body stay dead. She first rewrites it as the literal ground of love – the bank, for love to lie and play on – and then she revives it, making it 'quick' by taking it into her embrace. *Quick* is the decisive word, in which all the anxieties about maternal origin can meet and be resolved: as he quickens in her embrace, she herself imagistically becomes quick with him; restoring him through the pregnant fecundity of her own body.

If Lear's anti-pastoral storm figures the horrific female body that teaches man his mortality, Perdita's pastoral refigures that body in Perdita herself. Imagining Florizel a bank for love to lie and play on, she remakes herself in the image of Love, the Venus genetrix who is one with great creating nature:[35] her words are in fact anticipated by Shakespeare's earlier Venus ('Witness this primrose bank whereon I lie' [*Venus and Adonis*, 1.151]). Polixenes will later equate the pastoral landscape itself with her body, forbidding his son entrance to both and threatening death to Perdita 'if ever henceforth thou / These rural latches to his entrance open' (IV.iv.438–9).[36] But within her 'rural latches', in the sheltering womb of her pastoral, the mortal body is refigured: death is not denied but embraced and redefined as the condition of the body's aliveness. Perdita's imagistic revival of Florizel turns crucially on her astonishing *or if*, with its acknowledgment that the body is indeed like a corpse: for only what can die can live. Perdita thus reverses the logic of tragedy, restoring aliveness to the mortal body: if Leontes's logic is 'if alive, then dead', the logic of her pastoral is 'if dead, then alive'. As an extension of her body, Perdita's version of pastoral thus repairs the fall implicit in Polixenes's pastoral vision; through it, Shakespeare in effect returns to the source of original sin, rewriting it as the source of wholeness and life.

Florizel stakes his faith on the generative female body, and his extravagant gesture predicts the movement of the play: for with the recovery of the benign maternal body as a source of life comes the recovery of faith, the recovery that enables the play's final restitutions. In its most primitive form, Leontes's crisis has been a crisis of faith.[37] For him as for Othello, doubt is intolerable: the merest possibility of his wife's infidelity spoils her as a source of inner or outer goodness; doubt itself is tantamount to the loss of the sustaining object. Through his doubt, Leontes relives as though for the first time the infant's discovery that the world is separate from him and is not subject to his desires: if his wife can betray him, she is one with the mother who can seduce and betray, souring his inner world as he takes her into himself. All his fantasies of betrayal, of contamination by the female, of spoiling at the maternal site of origin, reflect this fear: in his loss of faith, he can locate only contamination and dread in the female space outside the self. Hence the logic through which he imagines Hermione's betrayal as the spoiling of nurturance: the spider in the cup condenses and epitomises the unreliable outer world that can contaminate the self, the world that is always figured first in the mother's body. Unable to trust in this world, he rejects it, reshaping it in its original form as a promiscuous woman and banishing it, reducing it to nothingness in order to stave off its capacity to hurt him and the contamination he fears from it.

But a world so reduced is a world from which no good can come. As Leontes increasingly manages to do away with the world – casting off wife, friend, children, counsellors, reducing everything external to the level of his dreams (III.ii.81) – he not only reflects but sustains and ensures his own inner hopelessness, his doubt that there is anything good out there. In his panic at the possibility of loss, he unmakes the world; and his cure can come only from the world's refusal to stay unmade. Hence, I think, the primary psychic significance of the play's radical break with Leontes's consciousness: though that break seems to court dramatic discontinuity, it is in fact the only possible antidote to his disease. If Leontes seems to have succeeded in reducing the world to the level of his dreams, what he – and we – need to learn is that the world will go on existing, that it will survive despite his best efforts at destroying it.[38] And the pastoral, first of all, signifies this fact: it is the place neither

he nor we knew about, the place outside the sphere of his omnipotent control. Such a place is by definition dangerous: for Lear, it is
epitomised by his monstrous daughter-mothers and by the overwhelming maternal body of the storm that shows him he is not
ague-proof; and in his disease, Leontes too can see only betrayal
there, in the region beyond his control. But if this place is dangerous, it is also the only place from which hope can come: blotting
out the world, making it nothing, can lead only to the stasis of
Leontes's winter's tale, in which there is no possibility of renewal.
The pastoral of Act IV acknowledges the danger – hence its bear
and storm – but it insists on the possibility of hope: here, the
mother's body is full of promise. Through its association with the
female and its structural position in the play – outside Leontes's
control, outside his knowledge – the pastoral can figure this body,
the unknown place outside the self where good things come from.

If the world's treachery is first figured in the maternal body, then
the recovery of faith requires the recuperation of that body. The
pastoral in effect initiates this recuperation: *The Winter's Tale*
moves from tragedy to romance by demonstrating that this place of
'otherness' can be the source of richness as well as poverty, making
the promise that the world is worth having faith in. And in the end,
Shakespeare's deep intuition makes Leontes's recovery of trust in
the world tantamount to his recovery of the benign maternal body
in the literal form of Hermione: if Leontes's attempt to control the
world by banishing the female had unmade the world for him,
locating him in his own dead inner spaces, Hermione's coming to
life figures the return of the world to him and his capacity to tolerate and participate in its aliveness, with all its attendant risks.[39]
This return is tellingly mediated by a series of female figures, each
beyond the sphere of his control: by Paulina, the archetypically
unruly woman; by Perdita, the daughter who outlives his destructive fantasies, growing beyond his knowledge; and by the 'good
goddess Nature', the 'great creating nature' they both invoke. For
the male effort to make the self safe by controlling the female body
is what must be relinquished before Hermione can return:[40] in this
play's gendering of doubt and faith, faith means willingness to
submit to unknown processes outside the self, processes registered
as female. Hence, I think, the shift in status of the play's ruling
deity: though Apollo is at first clearly the god in charge, his authority diminishes as the play gathers toward an ending; named eleven
times before the end of Act III, scene iii, he is mentioned only twice

after, and not at all in the recognition scenes that ostensibly manifest his power by fulfilling his oracle. We too as audience must learn to trust in the female: control of the play is increasingly given over to the numinous female presence invoked by Paulina and Perdita, the goddess nature who is named eleven times in Act IV, scene iv and Act V, scene ii. The pastoral scene is again the point of transition: there the 'fire-rob'd god' (IV.iv.29) becomes merely one of those subject to the erotic energies of great creating nature; the ceremonious solemnity and unearthliness (III.i.7) of his sacred habitat give way to the profound earthliness of hers, as sacredness itself is redefined and relocated in the female body of the natural world.

The shift from male to female deity thus epitomises the movement of the play: for Apollo stands for the reassurances of male control, including artistic control, conventionally gendered male and set against a female nature;[41] and this control is what Leontes must be willing to give up. The conventional gendering of the art-nature debate thus suits the purposes of Shakespeare's gendering of the process of faith; and given that the crisis of faith is initiated by Hermione's pregnant body, it is no wonder that the debate turns crucially on the issue of breeding. For Polixenes, the prototypical artist is the gardener who manages nature's generativity, marrying 'a gentler scion to the wildest stock', making her 'bark of baser kind' conceive 'by bud of nobler race' (IV.iv.92–5). And though he claims that this artist's power derives from and is subservient to nature herself (IV.iv.89–92), the incipient pun on 'kind' tells a different story: the implicit fusion of class and gender terms – a fusion played out for Polixenes in Perdita's supposedly lower-class body – represents art as the masculine taming of nature's wildness, the ennobling of her base material. But of course Perdita's body turns out not to be base: Polixenes may seem to win this debate; but the structure of the play overturns his temporary victory. In the end, the play decisively rejects the artificial generation of another male artist – Julio Romano, who 'would beguile Nature of her custom' (V.ii.98), outdoing nature by making people in her place. In the context of the gendered art–nature debate, Paulina's introduction to the statue takes on a new emphasis: for the statue who can come alive 'excels' specifically 'whatever ... hand of man hath done' (V.iii.16–17). As Apollo gives way to nature, art gives way to her great creating powers: Leontes asks, 'What fine chisel / Could ever yet cut breath?' (V.iii.78–9).

In Act II, scene i, Leontes's entrance had violently shattered the sheltering female space occupied by Hermione and her ladies; the death of Mamillius was the consequence of that shattering and the attendant loss of maternal presence, without which – his death tells us – we cannot live. Now that space is recreated in Paulina's refuge, which Leontes's long penitential submission entitles him to enter; and here maternal presence can be restored. And the restoration turns on bringing him face to face with exactly what he has done, so that he can undo it step by step, vesting Hermione with life as he has earlier deprived her of it. For the statue grants him what he thought he wanted: the unreliable female body reduced to an icon he could possess forever, static and unchanging; in Othello's words over the Desdemona he has similarly turned to alabaster, 'No more moving' (*Othello*, V.ii.94). Now, in his wife's 'dead likeness' (V.iii.15), he sees the consequences of his inability to tolerate her difference, his attempt at absolute control:[42] confronting in its stoniness both the cold barrenness he has made of the world and the deadness of his own inner world – he has been 'more stone than it' (V.iii.38) – he is overwhelmed by longing for sheer aliveness – hers, and his own – whatever the risks. And in the end, his longing creates her alive for him, recreating aliveness in them both: for the process of her restoration to him has always been interior; all that is required is that he awaken his faith (V.iii.95). Brought through Paulina's ministrations to accept what he knows cannot be true, what is beyond not only his control but his rational understanding, he gives himself over to a magic 'lawful as eating' (V.iii.111): as the spider in the cup had registered the loss of faith in the world, the sanctity of this moment is registered through an image of renewed nurturance. For now 'greediness of affection' (V.ii.102) can be fed in a world made newly trustworthy: in response to his desire, the statue moves, at once embodying and rewarding his faith.

If in his rage and fear Leontes had obliterated the maternal body of the world, his long submission to the female rewards him in the end by returning the world alive to him in the shape of his wife. And though Leontes has – from his point of view – created her aliveness, she is nonetheless alive beyond his need of her: she exists on her own terms, beyond the sphere of his omnipotence. Shakespeare signals her independent existence by insisting that we see her awakening into life from her point of view as well as his: for Hermione awakens only at Paulina's repeated urging (''Tis time; descend; ... approach; ... / Come! ... stir, nay, come away'

[V.iii.99–101]), as though unwilling to risk coming alive; 'Be stone no more. ... Bequeath to death your numbness' (V.iii.99, 102) makes us feel what her transformation feels like to her. And once alive, she remains outside the sphere of Leontes's omnipotence; though she answers his desire with her embrace, she then turns away from him, turns toward Perdita, insisting on her own agency, her own version of her story: 'Thou shalt hear that I ... have preserv'd / Myself to see the issue' (V.iii.125–8). This turning away seems to me extraordinary and wonderful; we need only try to imagine Cordelia turning thus from Lear to see what is at stake. For through it, Shakespeare marks and validates Hermione's separateness as the source of her value, accepting female separateness for himself as well as for Leontes; and he simultaneously opens up a space for the female narrative – specifically the mother–daughter narrative – his work has thus far suppressed. As the mark of his own renewed capacity to tolerate female separateness, he rewrites his own rewriting of one of the governing myths of his imagination, in the process restoring it to its original form: if in *Lear* he occludes the mother–daughter bond central to the story of Proserpina and Ceres, reshaping it as a mother–son or father–daughter narrative, here he restores that bond, as though acknowledging a female continuity and generativity outside the sphere of male desire.

The Hermione who awakens is thus both the creation of Leontes's renewed desire and independent of that desire; she exists at the boundary between inner and outer, self and other. Situated thus, she epitomises the recovery of fruitful relatedness with the world: the relatedness that Winnicott saw modelled in the infant's relation with its first not-me possession, the relatedness that enables creative and recreative play in the potential space that is neither self nor other.[43] And if Leontes is brought to this place, we are brought there, too:[44] in the last moments of the play, Shakespeare aligns his own theatre with Paulina's female space, where we too can 'sup' (V.ii.103), where our desires can be safely fed in recreative play. For the female space of Hermione's recovery is also the space of Shakespeare's theatre: as many have noted, Hermione's aliveness alludes to the risky aliveness of theatre itself, with its moving actors; and like Paulina's, Shakespeare's is a participatory theatre, in which the awakening of our faith is required.[45] Like Leontes, we must first be willing to relinquish control: Shakespeare requires us to give up our position as knowing audience while he transports us to the place we did not know about and gives us the recognition scene we were not looking for, asking that we recreate Leontes's faith in ourselves by our own willingness to believe in what we know cannot be happening. For just this willingness to suspend our own mistrust, to participate in the rich illusionistic play of Hermione's recovery without undue anxiety that we are being played upon, signals the recovery of potential space in us. In the first half of the play we had witnessed the shattering of this space in Leontes, who, in his inability to tolerate the unreliable world outside himself, had retreated to the space of his delusion. From this position of dread, free play across the boundary between inner and outer becomes impossible: any intrusion of the world merely bolsters his conviction that he is being played upon, that his wife's sexual play has forced him to play a role not of his own choosing (I.ii.187–9). We witness the restored possibility of play in the rich festivity of pastoral;[46] now, as we choose with Leontes to make Hermione live, submitting ourselves both to our own desires and to Shakespeare's control of us, we participate in the restoration of the zone of trust, where we discover our own aliveness by allowing the world to come alive for us in the play of her return.

From Janet Adelman, *Suffocating Mothers: Fantasies of Maternal Origin in Shakespeare's Plays* (London, 1992), pp. 193–236.

NOTES

[The thesis of *Suffocating Mothers* (1992), Janet Adelman's magisterial psychoanalytic study from which this extract is taken, is that all Shakespeare's plays from *Hamlet* onwards negotiate 'a psychologised version of the Fall' which represents the maternal sexualised body as the source of contamination, mortality and betrayal, along with the anxieties triggered by the power to make and unmake masculine identity vested in that body. Here she argues that *The Winter's Tale* recapitulates only in order to repair the destructive consequences of this myth. In reading Hermione's pregnancy as 'the sign of male separation and loss', Leontes's fantasies 'illustrate in its purest form the trauma of tragic masculinity'. But by wresting the action away from his tortured psyche and relocating it within the generative space of a 'decidedly female pastoral', the play allows the maternal body to be recuperated and revalued as a sacred revivifying presence. The text and endnotes that appear here, with the author's permission, represent a shortened version of the original chapter. Ed.]

1. My account of this oscillation, like much else in this chapter, is deeply indebted to Richard Wheeler, specifically to his powerful description of the oscillation between trust / merger and autonomy / isolation throughout Shakespeare's tragedies and romances (*Shakespeare's Development and the Problem Comedies* [Berkeley, CA, 1981], esp. pp. 156–7, 200–8, and 213–14).

2. The tension is noted by many; see especially Peter Erickson on the corruption of the male entertainment on which patriarchy rests (*Patriarchal Structures in Shakespeare's Drama* [Berkeley, CA, 1985], pp. 149–51) and Ruth Nevo on the reversible images of estrangement in the kings' togetherness (*Shakespeare's Other Language* [New York, 1987], pp. 100–1).

3. Among those who stress the centrality of Hermione's pregnancy, see especially Erickson (*Patriarchal Structures*, pp. 148–9), Carol T. Neely (*Broken Nuptials in Shakespeare's Plays* [New Haven, CT, 1985], pp. 191–2), and Stanley Cavell (*Disowning Knowledge* [Cambridge, 1987], pp. 208–13). I am particularly indebted to Neely's account here.

4. For many, the pregnancy imagery here primes the audience for Leontes's suspicions; see, e.g., Charles Frey (*Shakespeare's Vast Romance: A Study of 'The Winter's Tale'* [Columbia, 1980], p. 120) and Nevo (*Shakespeare's Other Language*, pp. 101–3). Cavell's extraordinary account of telling, counting, indebtedness, and revenge turns complexly on the imagery of pregnancy and indebtedness here (*Disowning Knowledge*, p. 209).

5. For *cross*, see *OED* 12, *to cross the path of*: 'to come in the way of; often implying obstruction or thwarting', and *OED* 14, 'to thwart, oppose, go counter to'. Shakespeare often uses the word in this general sense: of numerous uses, see, e.g., 3 *Henry VI*, III.ii.127; *Much Ado*, I.iii.59; *Antony and Cleopatra*, I.iii.9; and *Pericles*, V.i.229.

6. For the specifically phallic connotations of *spirit*, see Stephen Booth (*Shakespeare's Sonnets* [New Haven, CT, 1977], pp. 441–3) and *Romeo and Juliet*, II.i.24. Many have noted that Polixenes's version of Eden unorthodoxly exempts the boys from original sin, figuring the sexual woman as temptation and making phallic sexuality equivalent to the fall; see, e.g., Murray M. Schwartz ('Leontes' Jealousy in *The Winter's Tale*', *American Imago*, 30 [1973], 257), Mark Taylor (*Shakespeare's Darker Purpose: A Question of Incest* [New York, 1982], pp. 35–8), Peter Lindenbaum ('Time, Sexual Love, and the Uses of Pastoral in *The Winter's Tale*', *Modern Language Quarterly*, 33 [1972], 7–8), and W. Thomas MacCary (*Friends and Lovers: The Phenomenology of Desire in Shakespearean Comedy* [New York, 1985], p. 203).

7. Howard Felperin notes the imagery of copulation implicit in Polixenes's 'standing' and finds in it evidence of the play's contagious suspicion, its self-conscious representation of the fall from verbal innocence into multivocality or linguistic indeterminacy ('"Tongue-tied our queen?": The Deconstruction of Presence in *The Winter's Tale*', in *Shakespeare and the Question of Theory*, ed. Patricia Parker and Geoffrey Hartmann [New York, 1985], p. 9). In Nevo's wonderfully suggestive account, Polixenes's phrase registers Leontes's 'nothingness, the emptiness of exclusion from a once experienced plenitude' (*Shakespeare's Other Language*, p. 103).

8. Among the many who find the jealousy unmotivated and see in it evidence of Shakespeare's declining interest in verisimilitude and individualistic character, see, e.g., Rosalie L. Colie (*Shakespeare's Living Art* [Princeton, NJ, 1974], p. 266) and Frey (*Shakespeare's Vast Romance*, pp. 28, 45). Psychoanalytic and feminist critics have of course found motive a-plenty. Many see in the jealousy primarily Leontes's generalised fear of sexuality, displaced onto women (e.g., Lindenbaum, 'Time, Sexual Love', pp. 10–11; Patricia Southard Gourlay, '"O my most sacred lady": Female Metaphor in *The Winter's Tale*', *English Literary Renaissance*, 5 [1975], 376, 380; Carol Thomas Neely, 'Women and Issue in *The Winter's Tale*', *Philological Quarterly*, 57 [1978], 182–3, extended in *Broken Nuptials*, pp. 193–4; Mark Taylor, *Shakespeare's Darker Purpose* [New York, 1982] pp. 38–9; Frey, *Shakespeare's Vast Romance*, p. 130; Diane Elizabeth Dreher, *Domination and Defiance* [Lexington, MA, 1986], pp. 150–5). Many follow Stewart in attributing the jealousy specifically to Leontes's attempt to suppress his homoerotic bond with Polixenes (J. I. M. Stewart, *Character and Motive* [New York, 1949], pp. 31–6; John Ellis, 'Rooted Affection: the Genesis of Jealousy in *The Winter's Tale*', *College English*, 25 [1964], 525–7; Leslie A. Fielder, *The Stranger in Shakespeare* [London, 1972], pp. 151–2); for some, that bond itself is a response to oedipal desires and fears (C. L. Barber, '"Thou That Beget'st Him"', *Shakespeare Survey*, 22 [1969], 65, extended in Barber and Richard P. Wheeler, *The Whole Journey* [Berkeley, CA, 1986], pp. 18, 329–30; Stephen Reid, '*The Winter's Tale*', American Imago, 27 [1970], 266–74) or to an underlying narcissistic crisis (Coppélia Kahn, *Man's Estate*, [Berkeley, CA, 1986], pp. 214–17; MacCary, *Friends and Lovers*, pp. 203, 206). For René Girard, the jealousy reflects Leontes's realistic appraisal of the mimetic desire upon which such bonds are based ('Jealousy in *The Winter's Tale*', in *Alphonse Juilland: D'une passion l'autre*, ed. Brigitte Cazelles and René Girard [Saratoga, CA, 1987], pp. 47–57). For others, the motivational centre is less in the male bond than in the fantasised relationship with the mother per se: see especially Schwartz's account of Leontes's response to the fear of separation from an idealised maternal presence and the recovery of that presence through sanctioned communal bonds

('Leontes' Jealousy', pp. 256–73; '*The Winter's Tale*: Loss and Transformation', *American Imago*, 32 [1975], 145–99); Richard Wheeler's account of the loss and recovery of trust in the 'hallowed presence' on which sustained selfhood can be based (*Shakespeare's Development and the Problem Comedies* [Berkeley, CA, 1981], pp. 82–4, 214–21); Erickson's account of the patriarchal transformation and appropriation of an untrustworthy maternal bounty (*Patriarchal Structures*, pp. 148–70); and Nevo's account of the fears of maternal abandonment and annihilation played out in Mamillius's death (*Shakespeare's Other Language*, pp. 104–14). (Among these, Schwartz's seems to me still the fullest and most nuanced psychoanalytic account of the play; I am deeply indebted to it, and to the work of Barber, Wheeler, Neely, Kahn, and Erickson, all of which has influenced my thinking about the play.)

9. In Erickson's elegant formulation, 'The place of Iago is here filled by Hermione's pregnancy' (*Patriarchal Structures*, p. 148).

10. See Schwartz, Kahn, and MacCary for similar readings of the narcissism implicit in the fantasy of twinship.

11. In 'Male Bonding in Shakespeare's Comedies', I argued for this defensive function: the fantasy of twinship 'allows for a new sense of self based on separateness from the mother while maintaining the fluidity of boundaries between self and other characteristic of that first relationship. In that sense it offers protection against engulfment by the mother while allowing for the comforts of union' (in *Shakespeare's Rough Magic: Renaissance Essays in Honor of C. L. Barber*, ed. Peter Erickson and Coppélia Kahn. [Newark, NJ 1985], p. 92).

12. Leontes is ostensibly proclaiming the world something, not nothing, in his speech to Camillo: the world dissolves into nothingness only if he is mistaken in his reading of the signs of Hermione's guilt. But despite this ostensible logic, any audience subjected to the relentless *nothing* of these lines will probably hear in them the pull toward annihilation more clearly than the initial if-clause. For me, at any rate, they are terrifying. See Nevo (*Shakespeare's Other Language*, p. 114), for a similar reading of these lines.

13. The distorted copulative and birth imagery of Leontes's 'affection' speech has often been noted; see especially Schwartz ('Leontes' Jealousy,' pp. 264–5), Carol Neely ('*The Winter's Tale*: The Triumph of Speech', *Studies in English Literature, 1500–1900*, 15 [1975], 325–7), and MacCary (*Friends and Lovers*, pp. 204–6).

14. See Janet Adelman, *Suffocating Mothers: Fantasies of Maternal Origin in Shakespeare's Plays* (London, 1992), p. 213.

15. See *King Lear*, IV.vi.121.

16. Nevo notes the conflation of birth and intercourse here (*Shakespeare's Other Language*, p. 109).

17. See Eric Partridge, *Shakespeare's Bawdy* (New York, 1960), p. 192, for the sexualisation of 'sport'.

18. Neely ('Women and Issue', 183), Kahn (*Man's Estate*, p. 216), and Erickson (*Patriarchal Structures*, pp. 154–5) all note this attempt.

19. Although medical science did not attribute the *ovum* to women until well after Shakespeare's time (see Audrey Eccles, *Obstetrics and Gynaecology in Tudor and Stuart England* [Kent, OH, 1982], pp. 30–2), common observation in the barnyard would suffice to ensure the association of eggs with female generativity.

20. Schwartz notes that Leontes would identify with Mamillius as a 'symbol of phallic integrity' ('Leontes' Jealousy,' p. 268).

21. For the custom of breeching, see Adelman, *Suffocating Mothers*, p. 7. As Maynard Mack notes, the unbreeched Mamillius would have been 'wearing a costume very like [his] mother's' ('Rescuing Shakespeare' [Oxford, 1979], p. 11).

22. As Neely says, 'Mamillius, since not created by some variety of male parthenogenesis, ... is declared infected by his physical connection with Hermione' ('Women and Issue', p. 183). Latin *mamilla* = breast or teat; Schwartz ('Leontes' Jealousy', p. 268) and Kahn (*Man's Estate*, p. 216), among others, note the maternal valence of Mamillus's name.

23. Schwartz's account is the *locus classicus* for the identification of the spider with the catastrophic preoedipal mother, specifically here in the nursing situation ('Leontes' Jealousy', pp. 269–72); Erickson too associates the spider with 'oral contamination' (*Patriarchal Structures*, p. 155). But for MacCary, the spider is the 'sexually insatiable oedipal mother' (*Friends and Lovers*, pp. 209, 215). Whatever their precise interpretations, most psychoanalytically oriented critics find this speech central to Leontes's character.

24. G. Wilson Knight notes this quality in Leontes's linguistic style: 'The spasmodic jerks of his language reflect Leontes' unease: he is, as it were, being sick; ejecting ... something he has failed to digest, assimilate' (*The Crown of Life* [London, 1947], p. 81).

25. See Adelman, *Suffocating Mothers*, pp. 106–7.

26. See Gourlay's fine analysis of their interchange and of the negative stereotypes Leontes invokes ('"O my most sacred lady"', pp. 282–3). D'Orsay W. Pearson argues that Shakespeare invokes and refutes Paulina's association specifically with the stereotypical urban witch throughout the play ('Witchcraft in *The Winter's Tale*: Paulina as "Alcahueta y un Poquito Hechizera"', *Shakespeare Studies*, 12 [1979], 195–213).

27. Schwartz similarly notes Leontes's difficulty in 'equat[ing] himself with his feminine issue' ('*The Winter's Tale*', p. 150). For Frey, daughters always betoken 'a guilty loss of patrilineal procreative power' (*Shakespeare's Vast Romance*, p. 87).

28. Schwartz notes Leontes's identification with the orally catastrophic mother and his echo of Lady Macbeth ('Leontes' Jealousy', p. 268; '*The Winter's Tale*', p. 153).

29. This view has been widely accepted since Knight's powerful expression of it (*The Crown of Life*, esp. pp. 88–90). But there have been at least two important recent *caveats* against the sentimentalising of nature's power in the play: Erickson's analysis of the ways in which the associations of women with 'natural' generative and nurturing processes secure patriarchy and limit gender roles (*Patriarchal Structures*, esp. pp. 158–64), and Marilyn L. Williamson's demonstration of the ideological use of the construct 'nature' to mythologise patriarchal power (*The Patriarchy of Shakespeare's Comedies* [Detroit, 1986], esp. pp. 116–21, 129–30, and 161–4).

30. Of the many who recognise that women and the generative forces associated with them are the agents of recovery in this play, see Gourlay ('"O my most sacred lady"', pp. 377–93) and especially Neely, to whose rich account, both in its original form ('Women and Issue', pp. 181–93) and in its revised form (*Broken Nuptials*, pp. 191–209), I am deeply indebted.

31. For the incipient pun on *fault*, see Adelman, *Suffocating Mothers*, ch. 2, note 26. Hermione playfully evokes the same pun in her dangerous conversation with Polixenes ('If you first sinn'd with us, and that with us / You did continue fault', I.ii.84–5).

32. Among the many who see Antigonus as Leontes's scapegoat, see especially Schwartz ('Leontes' Jealousy', p. 260; '*The Winter's Tale*', pp. 156–9), Erickson (*Patriarchal Structures*, pp. 156, 159), and Nevo (*Shakespeare's Other Language*, pp. 116–18); all three see his fate as a complex reworking of Leontes's delusion.

33. The pastoral is generally seen as a corrective to Leontes's court; Lindenbaum sees it specifically as a corrective to Polixenes's pastoral in its embracing of sexuality and change ('Time, Sexual Love', pp. 14–20).

34. Both Lindenbaum ('Time, Sexual Love', p. 18) and Frey (*Shakespeare's Vast Romance*, p. 73) note Florizel's implicit reversal of Lear's position.

35. Perdita is often identified with nature, Venus Genetrix, or Mother Earth (see, e.g., Lindenbaum, 'Time, Sexual Love', p. 18; Gourlay, '"O my most sacred lady"', pp. 387–8; Kahn, *Man's Estate*, p. 219). But Williamson notes wryly that the natural processes embodied in

Perdita are trustworthy because her noble birth proves them 'socially acceptable' (*Patriarchy*, p. 130).

36. Leontes has already prepared for Polixenes's equation by identifying 'gates' with the female genitalia (I.ii.197).

37. Leontes's crisis of faith is often noted; see, e.g., Frey, *Shakespeare's Vast Romance*, pp. 78–80. Book I of *The Faerie Queene* suggests how readily the loss and regaining of a beloved woman could serve as an analogy for the loss and regaining of faith. But I am thinking less of the loss of any specific religious faith than of the loss of faith in the world outside the self: what Cavell calls 'scepticism's annihilation of the world' (*Disowning Knowledge*, p. 214). In associating this crisis of faith specifically with the mother's body and with the loss of interior aliveness, and the resolution of this crisis with the return of the capacity to play, I am drawing on the work of D. W. Winnicot (*The Child, the Family, and the Outside World* [Harmondsworth, 1964]). Wheeler's wonderfully rich account of the loss and recovery of trust in a 'hallowed presence' (*Shakespeare's Development*, pp. 82–4) is very suggestive for all the romances and is worked out in detail for *The Winter's Tale* (pp. 214–19).

38. My formulation here follows from Winnicott's sense that the object becomes 'usable' only when it survives destruction and thus is placed outside the sphere of omnipotence; its 'use' comes from the recognition of its otherness, which then enables it to contribute to interior richness ('The Use of an Object and Relating through Identifications', *Playing and Reality* [London, 1971], p. 90). Hermione is obviously the primary object that survives destruction; here I am arguing that her return is mediated for Leontes (who recovers her through Perdita) and for the audience by the position of pastoral as the place that Leontes's destruction of the world did not destroy, the place therefore 'usable' because it is outside the sphere of omnipotent control.

39. The last scene presents something of a challenge to those who would see in the play primarily the recuperation of male bonds (e.g., Kahn, *Man's Estate*, pp. 218–19) or the recovery of control over patriarchal issue (e.g., Williamson, *Patriarchy*, pp. 150–2). Keeping us hungry by refusing to show us the reconcilations with Polixenes and Perdita, Shakespeare creates in us the sense that something is missing, so that we too will be ready to go to Paulina's house with 'all greediness of affection' (V.ii.102); and what is missing and longed for is focused in the report of Leontes's cry: 'O, thy mother, thy mother' (V.ii.52–3).

40. The (implicitly gendered) contrast between control and emotion is central to Marianne Novy's understanding of Shakespeare (see *Love's Argument* [Chapel Hill, NC, 1984], pp. 9–10, 16–17); she finds the relinquishing of control characteristic of the romance protagonists and essential to the 'transformed images of manhood' in them (pp. 172–4).

See especially her moving account of the statue's awakening, where 'imagery of warm flesh and cold stone … identifies the contrast between emotion and control with that between life and death' (p. 180).

41. The *locus classicus* for this formulation is Sherry Ortner's 'Is Female to Male as Nature is to Culture?' in *Woman, Culture, and Society*, ed. Michelle Zimbalist Rosaldo and Louise Lamphere (Stanford, CA, 1974), pp. 67–87.

42. My formulation here is very close to Novy's (*Love's Argument*, p. 180) and Neely's ('Women and Issue', p. 191); see also Taylor (*Shakespeare's Darker Purpose*, p. 45) and MacCary (*Friends and Lovers*, pp. 214–15).

43. See D. W. Winnicot, 'Transitional Objects and Transitional Phenomena', *Through Paediatrics to Psycho-Analysis* (London, 1975), p. 230.

44. I use *we* here to register my sense not only of the degree to which Shakespeare demands his audience's participation but also of the degree to which the deepest restorations of the end are relatively uninflected by gender. The most primitive losses and recoveries are prior to gender differentiation: though daughters will probably be less prone than sons to use the language of female contamination to register their sense that the world is alien and potentially overwhelming, both daughters and sons can find in the recovery of the benign maternal body a figure for the recovery of trust in the world.

45. Among the many who see in Hermione's awakening an allusion to Shakespeare's specifically theatrical art, see especially Leonard Barkan ('Living Sculptures': Ovid, Michelangelo and *The Winter's Tale*, *English Literary History*, 48 [1981], 661–2) and Cavell (*Disowning, Knowledge*, p. 218). The role of the audience's faith in bringing the statue to life is commonly acknowledged: see, e.g., Howard Felperin (*Shakespearean Romance* [Princeton, NJ, 1972], p. 242), Frey (*Shakespeare's Vast Romance*, p. 161), R. S. White ('*Let wonder seem familiar*', *Endings in Shakespeare's Romance Vision* [Atlantic Highlands, NJ, 1985], pp. 156–7), Bruce McIver ('Shakespeare's Miraculous Deception: Transcendence in *The Winter's Tale*', *Moderna Sprak*, 73 [1979], 341–51), William C. Carroll (*The Metamorphoses of Shakespearean Comedy* [Princeton, NJ, 1985], pp. 213, 222–3), and especially Nevo (*Shakespeare's Other Language*, p. 127) and Cavell (*Disowning Knowledge*, pp. 218–21).

46. Many note the healing of play in Act IV, scene iv; see especially Frey's lovely description of pastoral play and of the ways in which the pastoral restores our faith a audience, reversing the theatre of suspicion that had preceded it (*Shakespeare's Vast Romance*, pp. 138–44).

7

The Winter's Tale and the Religious Politics of Europe

JAMES ELLISON

I

As Cardinal Wolsey lay dying in Leicester Abbey in November 1530, he sent a last warning to Henry VIII about England's future. He urged the King not to listen to the rising heretics' party, the Protestant reformers. If such men were to be allowed to gain widespread support in the country, Wolsey believed that England would be reduced to the desperate state of contemporary Bohemia, where he thought – quite wrongly – that proto-Protestant rebels had destroyed the very institution of monarchy, and established a communist system: 'by means of which slaughter they have lived all in common like wild beasts, abhorred of all Christian nations'.[1] In his feverish last hours Wolsey may have credited the Bohemia sects with more success than they really enjoyed, but his horror at their experiments with Christian communism did have a basis in reality. There were indeed Christians in Bohemia attempting radically alternative forms of social organisation,[2] and Wolsey viewed their subversive ideologies as the greatest threat that the English monarchical system would have to contend with in the coming years.

Much recent writing on Shakespeare has been concerned with the way the plays treat the operation of power-structures in the society of early modern England, and forms of resistance to that power. Stephen Greenblatt's widely influential essay, 'Invisible Bullets'

(1981), focused attention on the concepts of 'subversion' and 'containment', claiming that '"the very condition of power" for the Tudor state rested in its capacity to *produce* forms of resistance and subversion, both in order to contain them and to use them to its own ends'.[3] Greenblatt gave many readers the impression that he believed *all* forms of resistance in early modern England were surreptitiously co-opted to the service of the state – a charge he later denied[4] – and a storm of criticism descended on him, much of it from critics essentially sympathetic to the cause of New Historicism. Chief among these criticisms have been: that his analysis of early modern English culture is 'monolithic' and 'totalising', creating an absolutist and homogeneous vision of that society which is more appropriate to eighteenth-century France than to Elizabethan and Jacobean society in England; that his approach continues to marginalise the more obviously subversive voices present in sectarian tracts or the anti-court satire of the Jacobean theatre, for example;[5] that he ignores the cultural interplay between individual human agency and the supposedly hegemonic power of the state attempting to engulf it;[6] and finally, that his model is purely synchronic and fails to account for cultural change.[7] As a result, there have been numerous calls for a revised New Historicism which would take these criticisms into account, while remaining faithful to the original conception of a critical approach which distinguishes itself 'from documentary history by its concern to treat the cultural power encoded in and transmitted through textual representations'.[8]

This essay will seek to address some of these concerns by focusing on an area which has to date received only partial coverage in New Historicist studies, that of religion, and especially the politics of religion. Less sophisticated Marxists than Christopher Hill have tended to downplay the revolutionary potential of religion in early modern England; in Greenblatt's writing, religion is seen as largely complicit in the forces which produce the early modern subject, a means of repression by which men's consciences, their innermost thoughts, can be policed and restructured into a condition of obedience and submission.[9] But religion in early modern England was far from being the monolithic force this might imply: on the contrary, it was a hotly contested site, inseparable from politics, and marked by continuing negotiations and rapid change. Religion certainly could be a force for conservatism: but equally, it could be a powerful force for change: many of the most radical political agendas of the age originated with religiously motivated sectarians such as Wolsey's Bohemians. Recognition of this well-documented fact may help to cast light on a central term of New Historicism, 'subversion'. This term has been used to cover a wide range of political positions. To Greenblatt true subversion would seem to imply a complete overthrow of the structures of power built in to the early modern state: most of what appears subversive in the writings of the period is in fact produced and contained by the forces of repression.[10] On the other hand, Jonathan Dollimore uses the term more broadly, to include any kind of anti-government posture: at one point the Earl of Essex can be a 'subversive', although what little we know of Essex's political programme scarcely accords with Greenblatt's definition.[11] Dollimore and others have rightly insisted that there was a broad spectrum of political opinion in early modern England, containing within it a variety of oppositional discourses: but a closer examination of this spectrum will show that it only becomes truly subversive in Greenblatt's sense at the far left extremes.[12]

In broad terms, certain points along the spectrum can be readily identified. On the extreme right would be the discourse of absolutist monarchy favoured by James I and the more royalist Church of England writers; a little to the left of this we might put 'advice to monarchs', humanist-inspired writing which is essentially loyal to the state but offers objective, constructive criticism of the incumbent ruler and his government, rather than flattery; further still to the left we would find parliamentarians such as Sir Edwin Sandys who contested the King's claims to absolute power and defended the ancient rights and privileges of Parliament; still further along the spectrum would be the nascent discourse of republicanism, which at this period, as Blair Worden has shown, has little to do with democracy, and much more to do with an oligarchic system of rule dominated by the aristocracy;[13] somewhere in the middle would be the bitter anti-court satire of Jacobean drama described by Albert Tricomi, which represents not so much a coherent political programme as a general disgust with the current regime; and on the far left we would finally reach the Christian communists of Bohemia and similarly inspired sects, such as the Anabaptists of Münster who for a short time in the 1530s succeeded in establishing a communist state in Germany, and who were only finally 'contained' in the most ruthless and bloody manner by the local princes.[14]

Clearly, from among this wide range of oppositional voices, only the last group, the Christian communists, fulfil Greenblatt's requirements for true subversion, having as their goal the total overthrow of the existing structures of power. The Christian religion was a double-edged sword during this period: it could be a mechanism for state repression, but it could also be the most powerful stimulus of its day towards a rethinking of the whole structure of society.[15] The sectarians who occupied Cardinal Wolsey's final hours also alarmed the Elizabethan government, so much so that in 1593 two English Protestant extremists, Barrow and Greenwood, were declared to be subversives, and brutally executed in a controversial and risky act of political repression.

If we define the sources of true subversion in early modern England in this manner, it is easy to see why they are represented unfavourably in the drama of the time. Sectarians were extreme puritans, and as such likely to be the sworn enemies of the stage-players. It is entirely predictable that the dramatists' references to Brownists, Barrowists, Anabaptists, and the Family of Love, are universally pejorative. From this standpoint, Greenblatt was right: there is no true subversion in the drama of the Elizabethan age, and indeed it is the last place we should expect to find this kind of subversion. But a proper understanding of the extremes to which political subversion could be taken during the period is essential in Shakespeare studies, as it allows us to appreciate how *relatively* conservative he is. There are unmistakable notes of political criticism in Shakespeare's Jacobean writings, but how muted these are compared, for example, with the anti-court satire of Jonson, Chapman, or Day!

On the spectrum outlined above, Shakespeare's position probably comes closest to the humanist genre of 'advice to monarchs': criticisms of the government of the day are openly debated, and grievances aired, but within an essentially pro-monarchist framework. *The Winter's Tale* is an excellent example of this process. In this essay I will offer new evidence indicating that the play was much more closely involved with contemporary politics than has been imagined, and particularly with the controversial foreign policy being pursued by James I. This evidence will allow us to see that Shakespeare celebrates James I's continuing search for European peace in the play, but also reflects tense negotiations between the supporters of this policy and the 'war' party of Prince Henry, negotiations which threatened to undermine the king's whole enterprise.[16] Allusions to the domestic politics of the time have already been recognised in the play, notably a parallel between Leontes' treatment of Hermione and James's behaviour towards Arbella Stuart; more generally a fear of royal absolutism, of the encroaching tyranny which was denounced by the bolder parliamentarians in 1610, has been observed.[17] In this essay I will suggest that to recreate a complete picture of the play's politics, we need to complement these insights with an understanding of how the play comments on James's foreign policies. The key to these references will be shown to lie in the recognition that, to many in Shakespeare's diverse audiences, the Bohemian pastoral would have been recognisable as broadly Protestant in nature; and that this recognition allows the union of Bohemia and Sicily at the end of the play to be seen as emblematic of the hopes of James and his supporters that some kind of reunification between moderate Protestants and moderate Catholics in Europe might be achievable through entirely peaceful means.

II

Throughout his reign, a key tool of James's pacific foreign policy was the negotiation of strategic marriages for his children with European royalty. Contemporary Europe was bitterly divided between Protestants and Catholics. It was a powder-keg, liable to explode at any time: when war finally came, with the outbreak of the Thirty Years' War in 1618, central Europe suffered quite unprecedented devastation. To counter the threat of such a conflagration, James sought to establish alliances across Europe through a balance of Protestant and Catholic marriages for his children. He began this policy as early as 1604, achieving his first success in 1613, with the marriage of James's daughter Elizabeth to Frederick V, the Elector Palatine, who had inherited his father's position as the leader of the German Protestant Union.

The Winter's Tale was probably composed in late 1610 or early 1611; the first performance we know of was in May 1611. By this time, James's policy was well under way, with foreign marriages actively being sought for all three of his surviving children, Henry, Charles and Elizabeth. Clearly there is a superficial parallel to this irenic policy in *The Winter's Tale*: a Bohemian prince, Florizel, marries a Sicilian princess, Perdita, uniting two kingdoms which have become deeply hostile to each other. But a closer look at what Sicily and Bohemia would have represented to Shakespeare's audience will suggest a more exact and interesting parallel. Although *The Winter's Tale* follows its source (Greene's *Pandosto*) unusually closely, it is well known that Shakespeare made the surprising decision to reverse the locations of the countries, Sicily and Bohemia, ruled over by the two kings in Greene's romance: Bohemia becomes the somewhat surprising location of the pastoral in *The Winter's Tale*, rather than Sicily with its suggestion of Arcadia. In the case of Sicily, this geographical switch certainly would have had some significance for the play's first audiences. Leontes is clearly identified as a tyrant in the first half of the play – indeed he is referred to as a tyrant more times than any other Shakespearian character except Macbeth[18] – and Sicily was known for its succession of tyrants: the tyrants of Syracuse were infamous, and were regularly castigated in Renaissance travel-books about the area.[19] In addition, contemporary Sicily was part of the hated Spanish Empire, a by-word for tyranny.

But what of Bohemia? Even if his knowledge of the geographical boundaries of Bohemia was somewhat sketchy, there is one fact about Bohemia that Shakespeare, and many from among his diverse audiences, are likely to have known: that most of its people were Protestant.[20] By the early seventeenth century, approximately 90 per cent of the population of Bohemia counted as Protestant, of one kind or another. The turbulent story of Bohemian Protestantisim was readily available to Shakespeare's contemporaries in the greatest work of Protestant historiography of the period, John Foxe's *Acts and Monuments*, which Shakespeare is known to have used throughout his career. Foxe's work was particularly topical when he was writing *The Winter's Tale*: in 1610 an updated edition was produced, which now included King James himself and the assembled nobility and gentry of the land as near-martyrs, after their narrow escape from the Gunpower Plot of 1605.[21] The *Acts and Monuments* traces the survival of True Religion from the time of Christ, via papal oppression, to the Reformation. In Foxe's tortuous attempts to show a direct line of descent from the original revelation to the men of the Reformation, the Bohemian proto-Protestants, led by Hus, came to occupy a key position. They formed a bridge between the Englishman John Wycliffe ('the morning star of the Reformation') and Martin Luther: Hus had been influenced by Wycliffe, while

Luther in turn had greatly admired the anti-papal achievements of the Hussites.[22] This lineage allowed Protestant historiographers to assign a providential, originating role to England in the events of the Reformation, and this was the line followed by the sixteenth-century Protestant dramatist John Bale (who refers frequently to the Hussites),[23] and by Protestant poets such as Spenser and Michael Drayton.[24]

The Protestantism of the Bohemians was not only a matter of general knowledge among educated Jacobeans; it was also of great interest to James and his government at exactly the time that Shakespeare was writing *The Winter's Tale*. The Kingdom of Bohemia was part of the Hapsburg-dominated Holy Roman Empire, and since the election of the Emperor Rudolf II in 1575, Prague had been the Empire's capital. Although publicly Catholic, the Austrian Hapsburgs were known to be much less closely tied to the ideology of the Roman Catholic Church than their Spanish cousins. The lands of the Holy Roman Empire were torn between Catholicism, Lutheranism, and Calvinism, to say nothing of smaller Protestant sects. The religious divisions within their lands encouraged successive Holy Roman Emperors to speak up for moderation and reunification. This had been the unheeded message from the Emperor at the Council of Trent: Rudolf's predecessor, Maximillian, claimed to be neither Papist nor Lutheran, but Christian. Rudolf himself seems to have held a mix of hermetic and irenic Christian beliefs, seeking to find a middle way between the Reformation and the Counter-Reformation.[25] Rudolfine Prague had become an internationally renowned centre of art, humanist culture, and hermetic magic. Hugh Trevor-Roper has aptly characterised the irenic purpose behind a seemingly cranky occultism:

> This magical world repudiated the formal cosmology of medieval Christendom, and transcended the sectarian differences between orthodox Catholicism and orthodox Protestantism, both of which had returned to that cosmology. At its core, it was ecumenical, tolerant, contemplative, scientific; at its periphery, it ran out into alchemical fantasies, astrological calculations, Pythagorean numerology.[26]

Rudolf's interest in ecumenism was shared by James I, as an important new study has shown.[27] James's first speech to the English parliament in 1604 highlighted the search for a resolution between Protestants and Catholics as a major policy aim,[28] and he went on to call for a General Council to attempt the reunification of Christendom. James knew that the Church of England was claimed by its apologists to represent a *via media* between Geneva and Rome, where Protestantism and Catholicism found their respective extremes: perhaps the *via media* could form the basis of an attempt to reunify the warring churches of Christendom. And so the new English king's approach towards Catholicism was moderate and compromising. His speech to Parliament in 1604 included a remarkable appeal to the Roman Catholic church:

> For if they would leave, and be ashamed of such new and grosse Corruptions of theirs, as themselves cannot maintaine, nor denie to bee worthy of reformation, I would for mine owne part be content to meete them in the mid-way, so that all novelties might be renounced on either side.[29]

Both Rudolf and James seemed to share a desire for a reunited Christendom which would exorcise the demon of religious war from Europe.[30]

From afar, it could seem as though Rudolf was putting these principles into practice: during the first decade of the seventeenth century, he offered (under some duress) increased religious freedom to the Bohemian Protestants, culminating in the famous *Majestätsbrief* ('Letter of Majesty') of 1609 which legitimised Protestant forms of worship within the kingdom.[31] In the same year James made a major pronouncement on the subject of religious reunification, and dedicated it to Rudolf. This was James's long-awaited apocalyptic work, the *Premonition to all most Mightie Monarches, Kings, Free Princes, and States of Christendome*.[32] The origins of this work lay in the Oath of Allegiance controversy which erupted three years earlier. Jesuit writers such as Bellarmine and Suarez had declared that it was legal to assassinate heretical (i.e. Protestant) kings, and as the leading Protestant monarch of Europe, James was a prime target. The conspirators of the Gunpowder Plot were thought to have been directly influenced by this doctrine, and in 1606 James introduced the Oath of Allegiance, aiming to force English Catholics to renounce the Bellarmine doctrine and acknowledge his own legitimacy. The Oath unleased 'a paper warfare in Europe the like of which has never been seen since'.[33] The high-point of this battle has been put at 1609–11, around the time of composition of *The Winter's Tale*, and it involved many of the greatest minds of

Europe. The *Premonition* was James's major personal contribution to the controversy, written as an open letter to Rudolf and the other kings of Europe. In essence it was a warning to them that the Bellarmine doctrine posed a danger to the security of every European monarch, even Catholic ones (as the assassination of Henri IV of France in 1610 by a Jesuit-inspired fanatic was to underline). It exhorted the Catholic monarchs of Europe to cast off their allegiance to the Papacy, and implied they should return to a purified, moderate, Christian church shorn of Papal dominance, such as James believed the Church of England to be. Thus in the years immediately preceding the composition of *The Winter's Tale*, James was attempting to enlist Rudolf in a bloodless project to crush the Papacy, and end the threat of political assassination to himself and other monarchs – it is no coincidence that the wickedness of political assassination is loudly proclaimed in *The Winter's Tale*.[34]

James's diplomatic initiatives towards Rudolf II, coupled with the ongoing Juliers–Cleves crisis of 1610–14 which nearly precipitated a pan-European war between Protestants and Catholics,[35] suggest that the position of the Protestant religion in Europe must have been highly topical when *The Winter's Tale* was composed, and it seems reasonable to ask if Shakespeare included any recognisably Protestant elements in his fictitious Bohemia. The first hint of this comes with Shakespeare's choice of the pastoral genre for the Bohemian peasants. Pastoral was frequently (if by no means exclusively) associated with Protestantism during the English Renaissance. Protestantism was claimed to be a primitive, authentic version of Christianity, from which the Catholic Church had deviated; pastoral could thus be an attractive mode in which to represent Protestant virtues, and this was the line which had been taken by the greatest of Elizabethan Protestant poets, Edmund Spenser, and imitated by a host of his poetic followers. Significantly, in *The Winter's Tale*, Bohemian pastoral is characterised by virtuous behaviour and religious devotion. This is apparent in the first pastoral scene, in which the Shepherd and the Clown rescue the infant Perdita. The Shepherd praises the Clown for burying the remains of Antigonus – 'That's a good deed' (III.iii.131) – and remains uncorrupted by the gold he has found with Perdita: ''Tis a lucky day, boy, and we'll do good deeds by it' (III.iii.136). A little later, the caring Clown, the very model of the Good Samaritan, offers Autolycus money, not knowing Autolycus has already stolen it from him (IV.iii.77). And Perdita herself seems to epitomise the pure, primitive values of her pastoral Bohemian upbringing:

> Per.   Sir, the year growing ancient,
>   Not yet on summer's death nor on the birth
>   Of trembling winter, the fairest flowers o'th'season
>   Are our carnations and the streak'd gillyvors,
>   Which some call nature's bastards: of that kind
>   Our rustic garden's barren; and I care not
>   To get slips of them.
> Pol.   Wherefore, gentle maiden,
>   Do you neglect them?
> Per.   For I have heard it said
>   There is an art which, in their piedness, shares
>   With great creating nature.
>   (IV.iv.79–88)[36]

Despite Polixenes' famous rejoinder to Perdita's claim ('This is an art / Which does mend nature – change it rather'), she will not be swayed from her position: 'I'll not put / The dibble in earth to set one slip of them'. Perdita refuses to grow bastardised hybrid plants, the creation of man rather than nature. In doing so, she seems to favour primitive virtue, memorably advocated by Montaigne, over the incremental corruption created by the human mind. In the same way Protestant theologians claimed to have rediscovered the early days of the primitive Christian Church, uncorrupted by papal accretions.[37] For pastoral Bohemia is exceptionally devout; it has little in common with the earlier pastoral of the Forest of Arden, for example, where Love is the characters' primary concern. Instead, religion is a central part of the characters' lives in Bohemia. In the scene showing the discovery of the infant Perdita and her accompanying gold, the Clown has distinctly Christian words of congratulation for the Shepherd, 'You're a made old man: if the sins of your youth are forgiven you, you're well to live' (III.iii.119–20). Neoplatonic devotion is Perdita's hallmark; she prays to Jove, to Fortune, and to Proserpina. The sheep-shearing scene is a religious festival; it is compared to an English 'Whitsun pastoral' (IV.iv.134), and would have been recognisable to some at least of Shakespeare's audience as exactly the sort of sober popular festival James I sought to encourage in his moderate Church of England, in opposition to puritan tastes.[38] Florizel is portrayed as a chaste lover for whom religion is central to life. His finest love-speech shows this clearly:

> When you speak, sweet,
> I'd have you do it for ever: when you sing,
> I'd have you buy and sell so, so give alms,
> Pray so ...
>
> (IV.iv.136–9)

Not many lovers at the height of their passion imagine their mistresses praying and giving alms to the poor, but Florizel does.

There are other features of the play which connect Bohemia with Protestantism. A fairly minor one is the presence of a puritan in it. In Act IV the Clown plans a choir of rustics, among whom there is a puritan who 'sings psalms to hornpipes' (IV.iii.40).[39] Heraldic history, of the type beloved by the early Stuart courts, also links Bohemia with Protestantism, or least to that would-be champion of Protestantism, Prince Henry. The Prince of Wales's heraldic emblem of three ostrich feathers, accompanied by the motto *Ich Dien*, which is still worn today, was supposed to have originated from Bohemia: the Black Prince was believed to have acquired it at the battle of Crécy (1346) from the defeated King John of Luxemburg, the founder of a new dynasty of Bohemian kings. In 1610, just prior to the composition of *The Winter's Tale*, these facts were referred to by Ben Jonson in the court entertainment *Prince Henry's Barriers*. Jonson describes how the Black Prince

> Like a young lion newly taught to prey,
> Invades the herds – so fled the French – and tears
> From the Bohemian crown the plume he wears ...[40]

Shakespeare's use of Time in *The Winter's Tale* would also have had a strongly Protestant resonance for his audiences. The full title of Shakespeare's source for the play is *Pandosto. The Triumph of Time*, alluding to the Latin tag, *veritas filia temporis*.[41] The idea that truth was the daughter of time was ubiquitous among both Protestants and Catholics during the Renaissance, but for Englishmen it had a special meaning. A pageant of Truth the daughter of Time had been used at the joyous accession celebrations for Queen Elizabeth, after the Catholic persecution of Queen Mary: the peaceful accession of a Protestant monarch was portrayed as Protestant truth restored by the act of Time (the natural death of Queen Mary). These events had been recalled on the London stage in 1606: Thomas Dekker's *The Whore of Babylon*, a virulently anti-Catholic piece written in the aftermath of the Gunpowder Plot, begins with Truth asleep on a rock, her father Time attempting, but unable, to wake her. The funeral cortege of Queen Mary passes across the stage, and Truth miraculously springs to life and rejoices at the accession of the Fairy Queen.[42] Shakespeare's figure of Time who in good Protestant fashion 'makes and unfolds error' (IV.i.2) alludes to the same tradition.[43]

But if the Bohemia of *The Winter's Tale* is Protestant, it also contains a couple of characters who are recognisably Catholic, Polixenes and Autolycus. As far as Polixenes is concerned, I believe that Shakespeare deliberately reflected the religious position of the real Bohemia, where a Protestant majority was dominated by a Catholic elite, by creating a Protestant pastoral world whose ruler is identifiable as a Catholic. Polixenes is defined as a Catholic early in the play. In the lyrical description of his childhood with Leontes, Polixenes makes what one critic has described as a 'theological error':[44]

> We were as twinned lambs, that did frisk i'th'sun,
> And bleat the one at th'other: what we chang'd
> Was innocence for innocence: we knew not
> The doctrine of ill-doing, nor dreamed
> That any did ...
>
> (I.ii.67–71)

To an English Protestant audience, this is certainly an error, as man is fallen and damned from birth in Calvinism, until saved by the grace of Christ. Polixenes states the Catholic position, that through the workings of grace children really could be in a state of innocence.[45] Thus Polixenes, with his erroneous views about the innocence of children, is marked out as a Catholic from the start (Mamillius, with his comic, knowing comments to the court ladies at the start of Act II, seems to underline the Protestant view, that children are already part of the fallen world).[46]

There are also some interesting parallels between Polixenes and Rudolf himself. Polixenes' Bohemia, like that of Rudolf, is poor: at the very start of the play, the Bohemian nobleman Archidamus tells us that Polixenes will not be able to return Leontes' hospitality 'with such magnificence' (I.i.12). Rudolf was generally known to be short of funds. Fynes Moryson visited Prague in 1592, and subsequently commented with disapproval on the Emperor's inability to show princely 'magnificence'.[47] Furthermore, there are a couple of references to the majesty of the Holy Roman Emperor in the play. Florizel swears his love for Perdita is such

> That were I crown'd the most imperial monarch
> Thereof most worthy, were I the fairest youth
> That ever made eye swerve ...
> I would not prize them
> Without her love.
>
> (IV.iv.373–7)

A politically aware audience would have little difficulty in interpreting this as a passing reference to his father's title, that of Holy Roman Emperor; and a little earlier Perdita mentions 'the crown imperial' among her list of flowers (IV.iv.126). Rudolf was also well known as a libertine. John Barclay, a Gentleman of the King's Bedchamber who subsequently was asked by James to translate the *Premonition* into Latin for wider dispersal round Europe, took a similarly dim view of Rudolph's morals: his *Euphormionis lusinini satyricon* (1605–7) 'satirised Rudolf as a diseased libertine and vain alchemist'.[48] Anyone who recognised something of Rudolf in Polixenes may well have found Leontes' irrational jealousy more understandable, and Polixenes' apparent admission in the light-hearted banter with Hermione (I.ii.71–82) that his main sins have been of a sexual nature may be a cautious allusion to Rudolph's well-known failings in this area.

I believe that Autolycus was also recognisable as a Catholic. In Spenser's *Shepheardes Calender* (1579), the poem for May includes a beast-fable in which a wicked fox disguises himself as a tinker:

> But all as a poore pedler he did wend,
> Bearing a trusse of tryfles at hys backe,
> As bells, and babes, and glasses in hys packe.

The contemporary gloss on this passage by the mysterious 'E.K.' explains: 'by such trifles are noted, the reliques and ragges of popish superstition, which put no small religion in Belles: and Babies .s. Idoles: and glasses .s. Paxes, and such lyke trumperies'.[49] As Richard McCabe notes, the fox was widely used in Protestant polemic of the time as an image of crypto-Catholicism.[50] Shakespeare appropriates this language for Autolycus, who is here exultant at his successes during the sheep-shearing festival:

> Ha, ha! what a fool Honesty is! and Trust, his sworn brother, a very simple gentleman! I have sold all my trumpery: not a counterfeit stone, not a ribbon, glass, pomander, brooch, table-book, ballad,

> knife, tape, glove, shoe-tie, bracelet, horn-ring, to keep my pack from
> fasting: they throng who should buy first, as if my trinkets had been
> hallowed and brought a benediction to the buyer ...
>
> (IV.iv.596–603)

Autolycus starts to sound very much like a medieval seller of
indulgences and other religious knick-knacks here. Earlier in the
same scene his sales patter is described in terms of idolatrous
Catholic worship:

> you would think a smock were a she-angel, he so chants to the
> sleeve-hand and the work about the square on't.
>
> (IV.iv.210–12)

Autolycus is corrupting the honest women of Bohemia, as the
Clown bewails (IV.iv.244f); with the Spenserian example in mind,
he is probably intended as a portrait of an adherent of the Old
Religion, attempting to seduce the honest pastoral Protestants with
the sensuous appeal of Catholic worship.

If Polixenes and Autolycus are recognisable as Catholics, so is the
Sicilian King, Leontes. A contemporary audience would naturally
expect the King of Sicily to be a Catholic, but there are two pointers
which specifically associate Leontes with Rome. Firstly, he is associated with religious persecution, an iniquity which Englishmen
identified with Spain and Italy under the Inquisition, England being
claimed to be free of such terrors.[51] Thus Leontes threatens to have
Paulina burned, but she retorts in the time-honoured language of
religious dissidence:

> **Paul.**   I care not:
> It is an heretic that makes the fire,
> Not she which burns in't.
>
> (II.iii.113–15)

Secondly, Leontes' allusion to confession and penitence also marks
him out as a Catholic. When he is trying to persuade Camillo to
murder Polixenes, he recalls his reliance on Camillo in the past:

> I have trusted thee, Camillo,
> With all the nearest things to my heart, as well
> My chamber-counsels, wherein, priestlike,
> Thou hast cleansed my bosom – ay, from thee departed
> Thy penitent reformed.
>
> (I.ii.235–9)

Leontes is referring here to Catholic absolution from sins, delivered by a priest. Protestants, on the other hand, knew that redemption could only come directly from God, via grace, and this is what Leontes undergoes in the second half of the play. There is no intervening priest or friar: instead Leontes comes to understand the true meaning of sin, redemption, penitence, and salvation in a Protestant format, through a direct relationship with grace, symbolised (as we shall see) by Hermione. The only intermediary is the magus-like courtier, Paulina.

But if the pastoral Bohemians of *The Winter's Tale* seem to bear some relationship to the historical Protestants of that region, where might Shakespeare have learned about them? There was, as I mentioned earlier, a great deal of interest in Bohemia at court, and in 1609 we find James appointing an exiled Bohemian, Sir Henry de Gunderrot, to the minor court post of Gentleman of the Privy Chamber, presumably for his expertise on the affairs of Bohemia and the Holy Roman Empire.[52] Another Bohemian connection could have been via Shakespeare's patron, the Earl of Southampton, whose uncle (by marriage) was Thomas Arundell. The latter had fought for Rudolf against the Turks during the reign of Elizabeth I, and had been so successful that Rudolf made him a Count of the Holy Roman Empire in 1595.[53] Shakespeare certainly did know the actor Robert Browne, who had performed extensively across central Europe and Scandinavia from 1592 to 1610, returning occasionally to England: there is some evidence that he led a company of English players to Prague in 1596, and possibly again in 1598.[54] In 1610 he returned to England for good, as a member of the Queen's Men, and Shakespeare probably knew him well, since in 1608 one of the King's Men, William Sly, left Browne his shareholding in the Globe Theatre in his will.[55]

If Shakespeare had sought help with the political geography of *The Winter's Tale*, it was probably readily available to him. Given James's known interest in the region, it would have been sensible to make some enquiries, if only to avoid inadvertently giving offence. The result is a play in which religious affiliations are carefully, albeit subtly, delineated: Bohemian pastoral is Protestant in nature, while Polixenes and Leontes are recognisably Catholic. It remains to consider how this delineation affects our view of the closing scenes, often seen as the key to the play, and how the union of Florizel and Perdita – Bohemia and Sicily – relates to the context of contemporary religious politics.

III

In the final scenes of the play, a Bohemian prince, Florizel, and a Sicilian princess who has been brought up in Bohemia and emphatically represents all that is best in that society, are united, and reunite their warring parents. To a contemporary audience, the union of Sicily and Bohemia would have been easy to interpret as a peaceful victory for the Protestant pastoral values of Perdita and her acolyte, Florizel. I believe that this relates directly to the rise of remarkably ill-founded expectations at about this time that Protestantism would triumph across Europe, and that some kind of reunification with a moderate Catholicism, shorn of dictatorship from Rome, might be possible. Protestantism could point to a number of recent victories. In 1606 Venice separated from the Papal yoke, an event which caused tremendous excitement in England and inaugurated a campaign to convert the Venetians to the Church of England. The Dutch Republic had fought the might of Spain to a standstill, confirmed by the Twelve Years' Truce of 1609. In the same year, as we have seen, the Bohemian Protestants won freedom of worship under their Catholic overlords. In France, the *politique* party of Henri IV were moderate Catholics, asserting their independence from Rome. The Juliers–Cleves crisis of 1610–14, which had threatened to precipitate Europe into a major religious war, was in the process of a resolution which showed the forces of Protestantism in Europe standing firm against the Hapsburg aggressor. To some, it seemed as though a kind of Protestant apocalypse was under way. Stuart apologists such as Gordon and Marcelline looked forward to 'the imminent overthrow of the Anti-Christ and the full re-establishment of the true, ancient British church under James as a natural prelude to the New Jerusalem of Biblical prophecy'.[56] A similar message was conveyed by an apocalyptic masque performed at the wedding of Princess Elizabeth and the Elector Palatine in 1613; and when in 1618 the Elector rashly accepted the offer of the Crown of Bohemia, this too was seen by some English Protestants (including George Abbot, the then Archbishop of Canterbury) in apocalyptic terms 'as the great revolution that would usher in the final struggle between the godly and the papal Antichrist'.[57]

James I was interested in such ideas, always provided they were to be accomplished by peaceful means, and the *Premonition* includes a long apocalyptic digression which looks forward to the rejection of papal domination by the Catholic kings of Europe, and their peaceful conversion to True Religion.[58] Apocalyptic rhetoric during this period is generally thought to express contempt and hatred for Roman Catholicism, but as Anthony Milton has shown, many Church of England writers were able to denounce the Pope as Antichrist while maintaining a moderate and conciliatory view of the Catholic Church.[59] In the *Premonition* James's tone is irenic, despite the occasional violence of the language. He begins by describing St John's vision of the Antichrist as a scarlet woman sitting on a many-headed Beast.[60] An angel explains that the ten horns of the Beast are ten kings, who in turn are interpreted by James as the kings of Europe (Protestant and Catholic):

> I take these ten *Kings* to signifie, all the Christian *Kings*, and free *Princes* and *States* in generall, even you whom to I consecrate these my Labours ... wee shall in the time appointed by GOD, having thus fought with the Lambe, but *being overcome by him*, that is converted by his Word, wee shall then (I say) *hate the Whore, and make her desolate, and make her naked*, by discovering her hypocrisie and false pretence of zeale; and shall *eate her flesh* ...[61]

James predicts the conversion of the kings of Europe ('converted by his Word'), and their rejection of the power of the papacy ('the Whore'). He derives from the Book of Revelation a prophecy of the triumph of True Religion (presumably a kind of moderate Protestantism), accomplished by entirely peaceful means.

These hopes are reflected in the plot and the language of *The Winter's Tale*. Perdita is described as making a powerful impact in Catholic Sicily, an impact of a specifically religious nature. When Florizel and Perdita have landed in Sicily, fleeing from Polixenes' wrath, a servant reports to Leontes on Perdita's beauty:

> This is a creature,
> Would she begin a sect, might quench the zeal
> Of all professors else; make proselytes
> Of who she but bid follow.
>
> (V.i.106–9)

On one level this is merely a conventional adumbration of the princess's beauty, but in the context of the binary Protestant / Catholic opposition in this play, it has a greater significance: Perdita has become a missionary figure, bringing True Religion to Sicily. These lines fit in well with the general tenor of the play's concluding episodes, which adopt a peculiar mixture of apocalyptic and hermetic imagery characteristic of early Stuart court culture. Apocalyptic imagery appears unmistakably in the second half of the play. In the first recognition scene, Leontes and Camillo are said to look 'as they had heard of a world ransomed, or one destroyed' (V.ii.14–15). 'Ransomed' here clearly refers to the Atonement for human sin by Christ, while 'destroyed' refers to the destruction of the old world prior to the building of the New Jerusalem. This line gives us the strongest clue that the play's resolution can be seen in Christian apocalyptic terms. There are a couple of other fleeting references which would not have been lost on the more learned in Shakespeare's audience. Exulting over the ease of his petty victories, the crypto-Catholic Autolycus exclaims: 'I see this is the time that the unjust man doth thrive' (IV.iv.673–4). In apocalyptic terms the 'unjust man' is the Man of Sin whom we have already encountered, in other words the Antichrist. Finally, Hermione's first words in the statue scene would have an apocalyptic ring to them:

> You gods, look down,
> And from your sacred vials pour your graces
> Upon my daughter's head!
> (V.iii.121–3)

To anyone at all familiar with apocalyptic discourse (as Shakespeare certainly was),[62] this line would carry an allusion to the seven vials which James had described in detail in the *Premonition*. The vials are identified in *Revelation* as 'the vials of the wrath of God',[63] and James writes that his period has seen the pouring out of the sixth vial, which brings forth frogs (interpreted as the Jesuits)[64] from the mouth of the Dragon. James and his fellow Christians are living in the period between the sixth and seventh vials, and this is near to the end of time, since the pouring out of the seventh vial will be the Day of Judgement, and the building of the New Jerusalem:

> And thereafter is the latter day described againe (*which must be has-tened for the Elects sake*) and then for the further comfort of the Elect, and that they may the more constantly and patiently endure these temporall and finite troubles, limited but to a *short* space; in the last two Chapters are the joyes of the eternall *Jerusalem* largely described.[65]

Thus when Hermione refers to the 'sacred vials' of the gods at the close of the play, Shakespeare seems to indicate an apocalyptic climax of the play which is in perfect accord with his royal patron's published views. The play's hermetic imagery points in the same direction. The presence of hermetic imagery at the end of *The Winter's Tale* has long been noted by some scholars, but if we put it into the political context I have outlined, its purpose becomes clearer.[66] As we have seen, hermeticism was an international language of tolerance and ecumenism: it almost invariably had a strongly Christian flavour during this period. Christian hermeticism lay behind the hopes of many for religious peace in Europe, offering a broadly based form of Christianity which would be acceptable to all the warring sects of Europe. The leading exponent of such ideas in England had been John Dee, who had grand designs for a universal religion based on Christian hermeticism which would include even the Jews.[67] Moreover, hermeticism provided a direct link between London and Prague from the end of Elizabeth's reign well into the Stuart era: English magi such as Dee, Edward Kelley, and Robert Fludd were all drawn to Prague, while foreign adepts such as Bruno, Michael Maier, and Cornelius Drebbel, sought patronage in both cities.

There are a couple of passing nods in the direction of hermeticism in the play prior to the statue scene. Autolycus, the great transformer of dross into marketable commodities, is the son of Mercury ('littered under Mercury');[68] while Hermione's name suggests a 'herm', a statuesque head of Mercury.[69] But the clearest homage to hermetic magic in *The Winter's Tale* is the statue scene. Several critics have found this reminiscent of the descriptions of the moving statues in the hermetic texts, particularly the *Asclepius* and the *Picatrix*,[70] but Shakespeare did not need to have known a single word of the hermetic texts to have had some familiarity with the magical world of moving statues. Automata, speaking statues, and mechanical marvels were ubiquitous among the creations of Renaissance magi.[71] John Dee had seen the 'wonder rooms' at Rudolf's palace in Prague, with their mechanical marvels, and hermetic engineers such as Cornelius Drebbel exhibited similar wonders in London. In *Lord Hay's Masque* by Thomas Campion (1607), knights metamorphosed into golden trees are brought back to life by the power of Apollo / James.[72] Prince Henry's garden consultant, Saloman de Caus, planned moving statues for an unfinished garden in London, and did actually complete some for the famous

palace at Heidelberg which the Elector Palatine and Princess
Elizabeth had built. And two of the masques to celebrate the
couple's marriage in 1613 included moving statues.[73] Particularly
interesting is the use of moving statues at King James's entrance
into London in 1604, in which actors such as Edward Alleyn stood
motionless in niches, poised to come to life when the king passed
by.[74] In hermetic magic, such statues could emit virtue, and effect
the moral reform of a city: in the *Picatrix*, Hermes was said to have
'placed engraved images and ordered them in such a manner that by
their virtue the inhabitants were made virtuous and withdrawn
from all wickedness and harm'.[75] The tableau of moving statues,
although a traditional feature of civic pageants, would have
conveyed to someone with any knowledge of hermetic ideas a pious
hope for the moral reform of the city of London.

Apocalyptic and hermetic imagery coalesce at the play's
triumphant conclusion: the moving statue is a symbol of hermetic
religious reform, while Hermione's allusion to 'vials' and the earlier
reference to a 'world ransomed, or one destroyed' points to an
apocalyptic event, as we have seen.[76] On one level, this sequence
enacts the salvation of an individual, Leontes. As many critics have
pointed out, Hermione is clearly associated with the term 'grace', a
word which she seems to use at every possible opportunity:
Leontes' reunion with her thus represents his personal salvation
through divine grace. But if we are conscious of Leontes as a
Catholic, as I have suggested we should be, this scene takes on a
further meaning. It shows the conversion of a Catholic monarch to
a recognisably Protestant form of Christianity – from Error to True
Religion. As Stephen Orgel has suggested, Leontes' salvation is
achieved by faith alone, not good works,[77] and his final act of faith
is acted out in front of us:

> **Leon.**   What you can make her do,
>   I am content to look on: what to speak,
>   I am content to hear; for 'tis as easy
>   To make her speak as move.
> **Paul.**   It is requir'd
>   You do awake your faith.
>   (V.iii.91–5)

Paulina's name, invented by Shakespeare, may allude to St Paul, the
favourite theologian of Protestants, as Orgel has also suggested.
Perdita and Florizel, the representatives of Bohemian Protestant

pastoral, look on with approval during this scene. Furthermore, the action of this scene is carefully distanced from Catholic forms of worship by Perdita, who says at one point:

> And give me leave,
> And do not say 'tis superstition, that
> I kneel, and then implore her blessing.
> (V.iii.42–4)

These lines assert that whatever else is happening in this final scene, it is not idolatry or Catholic 'superstition'. Many, if not most, of Shakespeare's audience would have been well versed in Protestant theology to understand that this final scene is the mystical conclusion of the whole work. Shakespeare puts on stage, in a subtle form, the conversion of a leading Catholic king to something like James's moderate Protestantism. This is the apocalyptic conclusion which James had adumbrated in the *Premonition*.

One further piece of evidence for the unseen presence of King James's ideas in this play can be adduced. If the play has a tutelary genius, it is Apollo, who reveals the truth in his Oracle, and punishes Leontes for his obstinacy with the death of Mamillius ('Apollo's angry, and the heavens themselves / Do strike at my injustice').[78] Now there is good reason to suspect that some of Shakespeare's audience would have recognised Apollo as an image of King James. James was exceptionally fond of being depicted as Apollo, *le roi soleil*, as Jonathan Goldberg has shown, and he was frequently represented as such in masques of the period.[79] One such masque was *Oberon, The Fairy Prince*, by Ben Jonson, which had appeared on 1 January 1611; this masque is directly referred to in *The Winter's Tale*, just before the dance of the satyrs in Act IV.[80] In this masque, James *is* Apollo:

> 'Tis he that stays the time from turning old,
> And keeps the age up in a head of gold;
> That in his own true circle still doth run,
> And holds his course as certain as the sun.
> He makes it ever day and ever spring
> Where he doth shine, and quickens everything
> Like a new nature ...[81]

In the context of the international power politics we have found reflected in *The Winter's Tale*, it makes perfect sense to see Apollo as a surrogate for James. James becomes the Oracle of Europe, the fount of wisdom whom the powers of Europe consult in the times of need, and whom they ignore at their peril: very much the role that James sought for himself in Europe. Furthermore there is good reason to suspect that the island on which the Oracle is located is England. The opening of Act III, which shows Cleomenes and Dion returning from the Oracle, is given a surprising degree of solemnity:

> **Cleo.** The climate's delicate, the air most sweet,
>   Fertile the isle, the temple much surpassing
>   The common praise it bears
> **Dion.**   I shall report,
>   For most it caught me, the celestial habits
>   (Methinks I so should term them), and the reverence
>   Of the grave wearers. O, the sacrifice!
>   How ceremonious, solemn and unearthly
>   It was i'th' offering!
> **Cleo.**   But of all, the burst
>   And the ear-deaf'ning voice o'th'Oracle,
>   Kin to Jove's thunder ...
>   (III.i.1–10)

If James was frequently identified with Apollo, he was just as often seen as Jove, hurling his thunderbolts against malefactors and recalcitrant parliamentarians: Shakespeare uses both analogues here.[82] If James is linked to both Apollo and Jove, then his 'temple' is the Church of England, the *via media* between Catholic and Protestant extremes, and Shakespeare's language in this passage reflects this. 'Sacrifice' was commonly used in Anglican poetry to denote Christian prayer,[83] while words like 'ceremonious', 'solemn', 'reverence' and 'grave' amply describe that exceptionally devout form of state religion which the proponents of the Anglican Church advocated. If any further clue that England is being described in this passage is needed, it may finally be noted that Delos ('Delphos' in the play), like the Fortunate Isles, was used as an analogue for England elsewhere in contemporary literature.[84] This passage, then, is a brief glimpse of the ceremonious Jacobean Church, the *via media* around which it was hoped the warring Protestants and Catholics of Europe might unite.

IV

So far I have outlined a reading of *The Winter's Tale* which promotes the foreign policy objectives of Shakespeare's patron,

King James. But *The Winter's Tale* is not purely patronage art, not purely complimentary by any means. There are probing questions inherent in the utopian vision Shakespeare creates in *The Winter's Tale*, which go to the very heart of the policies which we have found represented in the play. The principal difficulty with James's plan, one which as we shall see receives considerable attention in *The Winter's Tale*, was that it involved marrying Prince Henry to a Catholic princess, something he knew would be abhorrent to the strongly Protestant Henry. James's pacific foreign policy had not won universal approval at court, or in the country at large. There was a strong contingent in favour of military intervention on the side of the European Protestants. Prince Henry was the leader of this party, whose traditions were those of Sir Philip Sidney, Ralegh, and Leicester: Protestant, chivalric, and anti-Spanish.[85] The prince had established his own court in deliberate opposition to the drunken, unruly court of his father: his household was like 'a Protestant monastery where swearing was subject to fine and those absent from sermons had their food docked'.[86] He had little admiration for his unheroic father; he looked instead to the example of the reigning King of France, Henri IV, whose extensive military campaigns and skilful diplomacy were famous throughout Europe. The English court became increasingly divided into 'peace' and 'war' parties, coalescing about the king and his son respectively. By early 1611 it was apparent that since Princess Elizabeth would almost certainly marry a Protestant prince, Prince Henry must be married to a Catholic to preserve James's policy of ecumenical balance.[87] Prince Henry mounted a considerable propaganda campaign against his father's plan, which included the commissioning of a diatribe against it from Sir Walter Ralegh, still languishing in the Tower of London.[88] Nonetheless, 1611, the year of *The Winter's Tale*'s composition, saw James seriously entertaining a number of proposals for such an alliance, and it appears that in 1612 he finally accepted a proposal from the Duke of Savoy that Henry marry his daughter Maria, a marriage which was only prevented by the prince's untimely death later in the same year.[89] Indeed a masque seems to have been scheduled for the great celebrations for the marriage of Princess Elizabeth in 1613 which was to have celebrated the religious reconciliation to be achieved through Prince Henry's marriage – Thomas Campion's *The Lord's Masque*.[90]

In *The Winter's Tale* Polixenes, like James, tries to determine whom his son should or should not marry. Polixenes rages at Perdita and Florizel on learning of their marriage plans:

> thou, fresh piece
> Of excellent witchcraft, who, of force, must know
> The royal fool thou cop'st with ...
> I'll have thy beauty scratch'd with briers and made
> More homely than thy state. For thee, fond boy,
> If I may ever know thou dost but sigh
> That thou no more shalt see this knack (as never
> I mean thou shalt), we'll bar thee from succession ...
> (IV.iv.423–30)

Like Leontes, Polixenes threatens to deprive his kingdom of an heir in his mad passion. This careful paralleling of Leontes and Polixenes allows us to see the latter's rage as equally tyrannical and foolish as the former's. At a time when Polixenes' attitude would have been understood and condoned by most of the Jacobean courtiers witnessing the play, Shakespeare portrays it as a form of tyranny.

So this scene probably reflects on the problems of James's policy of irenic marriages for his children, which, in the case of Prince Henry at least, meant forcing his son into an extremely unwelcome alliance. Such an interpretation gains support from the hints contained within the play that the ultimately harmonious plot of *The Winter's Tale* is fanciful and unrealistic. There are deliberate references in Act V to the improbability of the play's conclusion:

> **Sec. Gent.**   This news, which is called true, is so like an old tale that the verity of it is in strong suspicion.
> (V.ii.27–9)

> **Third Gent.**   Like an old tale still, which will have matter to rehearse, though credit be asleep and not an ear open.
> (V.ii.62–4)

> **Paul.**   That she is living,
> Were it but told you, should be hooted at
> Like an old tale ...
> (V.iii.115–17)

From this perspective, the statue scene would not be the product of hermetic magic, but merely an elaborate subterfuge stage-managed

by Paulina. We discover that Paulina has been lying to us since
Act III about Hermione's supposed death:

> O lords,
> When I have said, cry 'woe'! – the queen, the queen,
> The sweet'st, dear'st creature's dead: and vengeance for't
> Not dropp'd down yet.

(III.ii.199–202)

So Shakespeare allows a contrary reading of the play, which
would support the rights of princes to choose their own
princesses. He creates an air of deliberate artificiality which
leaves open the possibility that James's irenic hopes are nothing
more than a pipe-dream, liable to evaporate at any moment (as in
reality they did, at the battle of White Mountain in 1620 when
the rebellious Bohemian Protestants, ignominiously led by the
Elector Palatine, were crushed by Catholic forces). The self-
conscious artificiality of the play, noticed by many critics,[91] is
itself a political statement, allowing an alternative, sceptical view
of the whole irenic enterprise which I have tried to trace in this
essay.

So, if the preceding arguments are accepted, we can begin to see
The Winter's Tale as a play which represents, and comments on,
the foreign policy of the Jacobean government with remarkable
sophistication. This is a play which deals with one of the hardest
strategic questions facing English Protestantism in the early seventeenth century: whether to offer armed support to the embattled
European Protestants, or instead seek a peaceful resolution to the
religious struggle. Much of the play's burden can now be seen as
a celebration of James's preference for a peaceful solution. But
this should not lead us to see the play purely as patronage art, or
as an example of the supposedly monolithic power of the
Jacobean state in action. On the contrary, as I have suggested,
there are counter-voices clearly discernible in the play under-
mining the very heart of the government policies which the play
celebrates. These voices are definitely critical, but they are
scarcely 'subversive': they have little in common with the revolutionary ideas of Cardinal Wolsey's Bohemians. Instead they are
specific comments on the practical realities of daily politics in
Jacobean England, within the framework of an essentially settled

polity. *The Winter's Tale* simultaneously applauds James's foreign policy, and hints at a major moral flaw in it, its dependence on the king's tyrannous marriage plans for his son. Like humanist 'advice to monarchs', Shakespeare's play is pro-government, but avoids outright flattery. The play delivers a mixed report on the king's rule, praising and criticising even-handedly: but its tone is very different from, for example, the anti-Spanish drama of Middleton and Massinger which was to emerge later in James's reign, expressing direct opposition to the king's irenic European policies.[92] Shakespeare remains loyal to the ideal of Jacobean peace he had celebrated in a sonnet which probably dates from the start of the reign:

> Incertenties now crowne them-selves assur'de,
> And peace proclaims Olives of endlesse age.[93]

[James Ellison's essay is published here for the first time.]

NOTES

James Ellison's topical interpretation highlights the play's involvement with the religious politics of early seventeenth-century Europe, a matter of lively concern to Shakespeare's contemporaries which has received surprisingly little attention from historicist critics (Kastan's essay [9] is another exception). Like Relihan (essay 3), Ellison regards the play's 'political geography' as the key to its 'Jacobean' significance. Thus he argues that *The Winter's Tale* pays homage to James I's dream of achieving a peaceful reunification of Christendom by staging the conversion of Leontes (identified as a Catholic tyrant) to the beliefs of Protestant Bohemia and the reconciliation of the two opposing kingdoms (and faiths) through marriage. Notwithstanding its 'relatively conservative' stance, the play is found to be critical of some aspects of James's foreign policy. Ed.]

1. Quoted in René Wellek, 'Bohemia in Early English Literature', *The Slavonic and East European Review*, 21 (1942–3), Pt. 1, pp. 114–46, p. 121.

2. Wolsey was most likely thinking of the Bohemian Adamites, a relatively harmless sect who believed in nudity and free love, and were brutally suppressed by the local authorities.

3. Steven Mullaney, 'After the new historicism', *Alternative Shakespeares 2*, ed. Terence Hawkes (London, 1996), pp. 17–37, pp. 26–7.

4. Ibid., p. 28.

5. For the importance of the sectarian tracts, see James Holstun, 'Ranting at the New Historicism', *English Literary Renaissance*, 19 (1989), 189–225; for subversive drama see Albert H. Tricomi, *Anticourt Drama in England, 1603–1642* (Charlottesville, VA, 1989).

6. Mullaney, 'After the new historicism', p. 37.

7. These criticisms are reviewed at length in Albert H. Tricomi's *Reading Tudor-Stuart Texts Through Cultural Historicism* (Gainesville, FL, 1996), ch. 1.

8. Ibid., p. 17.

9. See Stephen Greenblatt, '*The Tempest*: Martial Law in the Land of Cockaigne', reprinted in Kiernan Ryan (ed.), *Shakespeare: The Last Plays*, (London, 1999), pp. 215–18.

10. For a particularly clear outline of the kind of 'subversive submission' Greenblatt sees even the most rebellious of his chosen Renaissance figures evincing, see Stephen Greenblatt, *Renaissance Self-Fashioning: From More to Shakespeare* (Chicago, 1980), pp. 8–9 and 209.

11. Jonathan Dollimore, 'Introduction: Shakespeare, cultural materialism and the new historicism', in *Political Shakespeare: Essays in Cultural Materialism*, ed. Jonathan Dollimore and Alan Sinfield (Manchester, 1985), pp. 11–12.

12. 'Left' and 'right' are of course anachronistic terms, used here only for the sake of clarity.

13. Blair Worden, *The Sound of Virtue: Philip Sidney's 'Arcadia' and Elizabethan Politics* (New Haven, CT, 1996), pp. 228–9.

14. These pitiful events were described with mock-heroic irony by Thomas Nashe in *The Unfortunate Traveller* (1594): see George Saintsbury (ed.), *Shorter Elizabethan Novels* (London, 1929), p. 284ff.

15. Christopher Hill, *The English Bible and the Seventeenth-Century Revolution* (London, 1993).

16. Martin Butler has recently suggested a similar approach to the court masques; see 'Courtly Negotiations', in *The Politics of the Stuart Court Masque*, ed. David Bevington and Peter Holbrook (Cambridge, 1998), pp. 20–40.

17. See Alvin Kernan, *Shakespeare, the King's Playwright: Theater in the Stuart Court, 1603–1613* (New Haven, CT, 1995), p. 151; and Stuart M. Kurland, ' "We need no more of your advice": Political Realism in *The Winter's Tale*', *Studies in English Literature*, 31 (1991), 365–79.

18. In *Macbeth* there are 18 uses of the word 'tyrant' and variants; *The Winter's Tale* comes second with 10 uses, just ahead of *Richard III* with 9.

19. Michele Marrapodi, '"Of that fatal country": Sicily and the rhetoric of topography in *The Winter's Tale*', in Michele Marrapodi et al. (eds), *Shakespeare's Italy: Functions of Italian Locations in Renaissance Drama* (Manchester, 1993), pp. 213–28, p. 216.

20. Over twenty years ago, Frances Yates wondered if Shakespeare knew more about Bohemia than has been assumed; unfortunately she based this on the very speculative suggestion that Shakespeare might have had some contact with Michael Maier, the alchemical emblematist and court physician in Prague, who visited London in the early years of the century; see Frances Yates, *Shakespeare's Last Plays: A New Approach* (London, 1975), p. 98.

21. John Foxe, *Actes and Monuments ... the sixth time newly imprinted, with certaine additions thereunto annexed: Anno 1610*. Shakespeare was intimately familiar with this encyclopaedic work: he used it for *King John*, the *King Henry VI* plays, and, a couple of years after *The Winter's Tale*, for his play about Henry VIII. See especially Yates, *Shakespeare's Last Plays*, pp. 67–71; and R. A. Foakes (ed.), *King Henry VIII* (London, 1957), p. xxxv and Appendix II.

22. A. G. Dickens, *The English Reformation* (London, 1964), p. 23.

23. Wellek, 'Bohemia', p. 123.

24. Hugh Trevor-Roper, *Catholics, Anglicans, and Puritans* (London, 1987), p. 129.

25. R. J. W. Evans has convincingly claimed that the standard picture of Rudolf as a counter-Reformation persecutor of Protestants often found in histories of the Empire is mistaken. Persecution certainly did occur, but Rudolf seems not to have been behind it (*Rudolf II and his World* [Oxford, 1973, corrected ed. 1984], p. 85).

26. Hugh Trevor-Roper, *Princes and Artists: Patronage and Ideology at four Hapsburg Courts 1517–1633* (London, 1976), p. 99.

27. W. B. Patterson, *King James VI and I and the Reunion of Christendom* (Cambridge, 1997).

28. *The Political Works of James I*, ed. Charles H. McIlwain (Cambridge, MA, 1918), pp. 275–6.

29. McIlwain, ibid., pp. 275–6.

30. See Evans, *Rudolf II*, pp. 80–2 for a description of the similarities between, and shared interests of, Rudolf and James: for other contacts between Rudolph and James, see Robert Grudin, 'Rudolph II of

Prague and Cornelis Drebbel: Shakespearian Archetypes?', *Huntington Library Quarterly*, 54 (1991), 181–205.

31. Jaroslav Pánek, 'The question of tolerance in Bohemia and Moravia in the age of the Reformation', in *Tolerance and Intolerance in the European Reformation*, ed. Ole P. Grell and Bob Scribner (Cambridge, 1996), pp. 231–48, p. 239. Rudolf's concessions to the Bohemian Protestants were made under some duress, since his brother Matthias was also wooing them in his campaign to oust Rudolf.

32. James was widely encouraged by Protestants to see his monarchy in apocalyptic terms. John Napier, the inventor of logarithms, wrote: 'Therefore, it is likewise the dutie of God's servants in this age, interpreters of Prophecies, as well (according to the example of the Prophets) to incourage and inanimate Princes, to be ready against that great day of the Lords revenge, as also to exhort them generally, to remove all such impediments in their cuntries and commonwealths, as many hinder that work, and prove Gods plagues.' From John Napier, *A Plaine Discovery* (Edinburgh, 1593), sig. A6r; quoted in Katherine R. Firth, *The Apocalyptic Tradition in Reformation Britain 1530–1645* (Oxford, 1979), p. 134.

33. McIlwain, *Political Works of James I*, p. lvii.

34. Reflecting on Leontes' command to kill Polixenes, Camillo says:

> If I could find example
> Of thousands that had struck anointed kings
> And flourish'd after, I'd not do't: but since
> Nor brass, nor stone, nor parchment bears not one,
> Let villainy itself forswear't.
>
> (I.ii.357–61)

No one who kills, or attempts to kill, an anointed king will live long himself.

35. See S. R. Gardiner, *History of England from the Accession of James I to the Outbreak of the Civil War 1603–1642*, 10 vols (London, 1884–9), vol. 2, p. 94ff.

36. All line references are to the Arden edition of *The Winter's Tale*, ed. J. H. P. Pafford (London, 1963).

37. The Arden editor includes a passage from Montaigne's *Des Cannibales* which seems to have influenced this play as well as *The Tempest*, although the conflict of Nature and Art was a common Renaissance topic of discussion.

38. James advocated such festivals in *Basilikon Doron*, written before *The Winter's Tale*, and made them official government policy in the *Book of Sports* of 1618; see David Bergeron, '*Richard II* and Carnival Politics', *Shakespeare Quarterly*, 42 (1991), 33–43, p. 34.

39. Shakespeare is alluding to the Reformation custom of singing the metrical psalter of Sternhold and Hopkins to popular secular tunes – mocked as 'Geneva jigs' by their detractors. For the history of English psalm-setting, see Nicholas Temperley, 'Psalms, Metrical: England', in *The New Grove Dictionary of Music and Musicians*, ed. Stanley Sadie, 20 vols (London, 1980), vol. 15, pp. 358–71.

40. Stephen Orgel and Roy Strong, *Inigo Jones: the Theatre of the Stuart Court*, 2 vols (Berkeley, CA, 1973), vol. 1, p. 162.

41. See F. Saxl, 'Veritas Filia Temporis', in *Philosophy and History: Essays Presented to E. Cassirer* (Oxford, 1936), pp. 197–222; also Soji Iwasaki, 'Veritas Filia Temporis and Shakespeare', *English Literary Renaissance*, 3 (1973), 249–63.

42. Thomas Dekker, *The Dramatic Works*, ed. Fredson Bowers, 4 vols (Cambridge, 1953–61), vol. 2, p. 500.

43. For the widespread Protestant characterisation of Catholicism as 'error' see, for example, Edmund Spenser, *The Faerie Queene*, ed. A. C. Hamilton (London, 1977), p. 35 (I.i.18), in which Redcrosse encounters a Catholic dragon of Error.

44. Peter Lindenbaum, *Changing Landscapes: Anti-pastoral Sentiment in the English Renaissance* (Athens, GA, 1986), p. 115.

45. Richard Hooker described the Catholic position on grace thus: 'It is applied unto infants through baptism, without faith or works, and in them it really taketh away original sin, and the punishment due unto it …' (*A Learned Discourse of Justification, Works, and how the Foundation of Faith is Overthrown*, in *Works*, 3 vols, ed. John Keble [Oxford, 1845], vol. 3, p. 488).

46. Polixenes' name may also hint at a connection: by a remarkable coincidence, the first name of the wife of Rudolf's Chancellor in Prague was Polyxena. An allusion to Polyxena Lobkovic could have been intended as an 'in-joke' for the more knowledgeable in the English audience. See Evans, *Rudolf II*, pp. 286–8.

47. Fynes Moryson, *An Itinerary*, 1617, Part 3, Bk. 4, ch. 3, p. 188.

48. Grudin, *Rudolf II of Prague*, p. 184.

49. Edmund Spenser, *The Shorter Poems*, ed. Richard A. McCabe (London, 1999), pp. 79 and 85.

50. Ibid., p. 537.

51. See for example James's claim in the *Premonition* that no one in England suffered for their faith: McIlwain, *Political Works of James I*, p. 158.

52. See *Calendar of State Papers (Venetian)*, Vol. 11, 1607–10, no. 527; for the largely ceremonial role of this function see Neil Cuddy, 'The

Revival of the Entourage: the Bedchamber of James I, 1603–1625', in *The English Court: from the Wars of the Roses to the Civil War*, ed. David Starkey (London, 1987), pp. 173–225, p. 183.

53. The full story is told in G. P. V. Akrigg, *Shakespeare and the Earl of Southampton* (London, 1968), pp. 50–3.

54. Jerzy Limon, *Gentlemen of a Company: English Players in Central and Eastern Europe, 1590–1660* (Cambridge, 1985), p. 107.

55. A. L. Rowse, *William Shakespeare: A Biography* (London, 1963), p. 410.

56. Vaughan Hart, *Art and Magic in the Court of the Stuarts* (London, 1994), p. 49.

57. David Norbrook, '"The Masque of Truth": Court Entertainments and International Protestant Politics in the Early Stuart Period', *The Seventeenth Century*, 1 (1986), 81–110; Simon L. Adams, 'Foreign Policy and the Parliaments of 1621 and 1624', in *Faction and Parliament: Essays on early Stuart history*, ed. Kevin Sharpe (Oxford, 1978), pp. 139–72, p. 146. Abbot commented on the events in Bohemia: 'And methinks I do in this, and in that of Hungary, foresee the work of God, that by piece and piece, the Kings of the Earth that gave their power unto the Beast ... shall now tear the whore, and make her desolate, as St. John in his revelation hath foretold.' (Bodl. Tanner MS. 74, fols. 221–2; quoted in Adams, 'Foreign Policy', p. 147).

58. James was interested in apocalyptic theories all his life. His first work on Revelation was *Ane fruitfull meditatioun*, (Edinburgh, 1588), on Rev. 20:7–10; this was included in the *Workes*, 1616, along with 'A Paraphrase upon the *Revelation*'. The celebration of peace was a ubiquitous theme in Jacobean court culture: see Peter Holbrook, 'Jacobean masques and the Jacobean peace', in *The Politics of the Stuart Court Masque*, ed. David Bevington and Peter Holbrook (Cambridge, 1998), pp. 67–87.

59. Anthony Milton, *Catholic and Reformed: The Roman and Protestant Churches in English Protestant Thought 1600–1640* (Cambridge, 1995), p. 105.

60. Revelation, ch. 17.

61. McIlwain, *Political Works of James I*, p. 147.

62. Similar use of apocalyptic language occurs, for example, in *Richard II*, where the seven sons of Edward III, whose proliferation was to herald such torments for the English nation, are described in apocalyptic terms as 'seven vials of his sacred blood' (*Richard II*, ed. Peter Ure [London, 1956], I.ii.12). Similarly at the start of *Antony and Cleopatra*: 'Then must thou find out new heaven, new

earth' (*Antony and Cleopatra*, ed. M. R. Ridley [London, 1954], I.i.17).

63. Rev. 16: 1.

64. McIlwain, *Political Works of James I*, p. 146.

65. Ibid. p. 149.

66. Yates, *Shakespeare's Last Plays*, p. 89ff; Douglas Brooks-Davies, *The Mercurian Monarch: Magical Politics from Spenser to Pope* (Manchester, 1983), p. 141.

67. Peter J. French, *John Dee: The World of an Elizabethan Magus* (London, 1972), p. 124.

68. From Act IV, scene iii, 24–6. In Book XI of the *Metamorphoses*, Ovid describes how Chione has

> A sonne that hyght *Autolycus*, who provde a wyly pye,
> And such a fellow as in theft and filching had no peere.
> He was his fathers owne sonne right: he could mennes eyes so bleere,
> As for to make ye black things whyght, and whyght things black appeere.

From Arthur Golding, *The Metamorphoses*, ed. W. H. D. Rouse (London, 1961), p. 226.

69. See Julia Gasper and Carolyn Williams, 'The Meaning of the Name "Hermione" ', *Notes and Queries*, 231 (1986), 367, who also note: 'By the seventeenth century, *herma* could mean a statue of a saint in a church ... the saint could be female.'

70. See Yates, *Shakespeare's Lost Plays*, p. 89f; Brooks-Davies, *Mercurian Monarch*, p. 141.

71. Frances Yates, *The Rosicrucian Enlightenment* (London, 1972), pp. 11–13.

72. Brooks-Davies, *Mercurian Monarch*, p. 96.

73. Ibid. pp. 97–9.

74. Jonathan Goldberg, *James I and the Politics of Literature* (Baltimore, MD, 1983; reissued Stanford, CA, 1989), p. 34.

75. Frances Yates, *Giordano Bruno and the Hermetic Tradition* (London, 1964), p. 54. A second hermetic text, one from the *Asclepius*, has some relevance to the statue scene, and to the Renaissance cult of moving statues in general. In it Hermes Trismegistus describes how 'our ancestors invented the art of making gods. They mingled a virtue, drawn from material nature, to the substance of the statues, and since they could not actually create souls, after having evoked the souls of demons or angels, they introduced these into their idols by holy and

divine rites, so that the idols had the power of doing good and evil'; *Bruno*, p. 37.

76. On the political role of hermeticism and neo-platonism in Stuart court culture, see R. Malcolm Smuts, 'Cultural diversity and cultural change at the court of James I', in Linda Levy Peck (ed.), *The Mental World of the Jacobean Court* (Cambridge, 1991), pp. 99–112, p. 100.

77. *The Winter's Tale*, ed. Orgel, pp. 59–60.

78. III.ii.146–7.

79. Goldberg, *James I and Politics of Literature*, p. 25;

80. It is implied that one of the Satyrs at the sheep-shearing festival had previously taken a part in Jonson's masque: 'One three of them, by their own report, sir, hath danced before the king' (IV.iv.336–7).

81. Orgel and Strong, *Inigo Jones*, p. 209.

82. See Leah S. Marcus, '*Cymbeline* and the Unease of Topicality', in Ryan, *Shakespeare: The Last Plays*, p. 135.

83. See for example the opening of 'Mattens' by George Herbert:, 'I cannot ope mine eyes, / But thou art ready there to catch / My morning-soul and sacrifice' (*The Works of George Herbert*, ed. F. E. Hutchinson [Oxford, 1941], p. 62).

84. In Jonson's masques, *The Fortunate Islands* and *Neptune's Triumph* (Orgel and Strong, *Inigo Jones*, p. 375), Delos and the Fortunate Islands are presented as analogues of England.

85. For a description of court factions at this time, see Donna B. Hamilton, *Shakespeare and the Politics of Protestant England* (Hemel Hempstead, 1992), pp. 166–8.

86. Roy Strong, 'England and Italy: the Marriage of Henry Prince of Wales', in *For Veronica Wedgwood: These Studies in Seventeenth Century History*, ed. Richard Ollard and Pamela Tudor-Craig (London, 1986), pp. 59–88, p. 60.

87. Ibid., pp. 67 and 78.

88. Ibid., p. 81.

89. Ibid., p. 80ff.

90. See David Lindley, 'Courtly Play: the Politics of Chapman's *The Memorable Masque*', in *The Stuart Courts*, ed. Eveline Cruikshanks and David Starkey (Stroud, 2000), pp. 43–58, p. 50.

91. See for example Anne Barton, 'Leontes and the Spider: Language and Speaker in Shakespeare's Last Plays', in Ryan, *Shakespeare: The Last Plays*, pp. 22–42, p. 30f.

92. Tricomi, *Anticourt Drama*, pp. 153–4. Examples of this drama are Massinger and Fletcher's *The Tragedy of John Van Olden Barnavelt* (1619), Massinger's *The Maid of Honor* (1622), and Middleton's *A Game at Chess* (1624).

93. William Shakespeare, *Shakespeares Sonnets Never Before Imprinted*, 1609, Sonnet 107, sig. G3r. On the dating of this sonnet to 1603, and its connection with the release of the Earl of Southampton from the Tower by the new king, see e.g. Akrigg, *Shakespeare and the Earl of Southampton*, pp. 254–5.

8

Caliban versus Miranda: Race and Gender Conflicts in Postcolonial Rewritings of *The Tempest*

JYOTSNA G. SINGH

Caliban and decolonisation

I cannot read *The Tempest* without recalling the adventures of those voyages reported in Hakluyt; and when I remember the voyages and the particular period in African history, I see *The Tempest* against the background of England's experimentation in colonisation ... *The Tempest* was also prophetic of a political future which is our present. Moreover, the circumstances of my life, both as colonial and exiled descendant of Caliban in the twentieth century is an example of that prophecy.[1]

There is just one world in which the oppressors and oppressed struggle, one world in which, sooner than later, the oppressed will be victorious. Our [Latin] America is bringing its own nuances to this struggle, this victory. The tempest has not subsided. But *The Tempest*'s shipwrecked sailors, Crusoe and Gulliver, can be seen, rising out of the waters, from terra firma. There, not only Prospero, Ariel, and Caliban, Don Quixote, Friday and Faust await them, but ... halfway between history and dream – Marx and Lenin, Bolivar and Marti, Sandino and Che Guevara.[2]

Since Caliban first appeared on the stage in Shakespeare's *The Tempest* in 1611, he has been theatrically reincarnated in many different forms. Most recently, Prospero's 'misshapen knave' and 'demi-devil' has been transformed into a third world revolutionary. Revisionary histories of colonialism – especially since the 1960s – frequently evoke the figure of Caliban as a symbol of resistance to colonial regimes in Latin America, the Caribbean, and Africa. These revisions interrogate the so-called 'discovery' of the Americas to trace a history of the Caliban myth in the early encounters between the European colonisers and natives. Crucially, they challenge the veracity of Columbus' account of 'cannibals' in his diary, suggesting that the term 'cannibal' – for which Caliban is an anagram – is itself a deformation of the name *Carib*, an Indian warrior tribe opposed to the Europeans or a variant of another tribal name, *Kanibna*. Furthermore, they argue that while there is limited and conflicting evidence backing Columbus' association of caribs / cannibals with people who eat human flesh, the image of the cannibal easily elided with Shakespeare's Caliban, ideologically holding in place the European distinction between their own 'civilised' selves and the 'savage' others they encountered in the New World.³ Cheyfitz lays down the boundaries of this revisionary reading as follows:

> Whatever the actual linguistic case may be, however, we have cause to wonder, as Columbus himself apparently did from time to time, at Columbus' association of the cannibals with eating human flesh. He did not have any empirical evidence, and his assertion that the Arawaks themselves told him is contradicted by Columbus' own admission that neither the Indians nor the Europeans knew each other's language. If we try to imagine the use of gestures in this case, we have not gotten around the problem of translation, but only embedded ourselves more deeply in it ... [however] after the association Columbus elaborated in his journal, cannibal ... [became] a part of a diverse arsenal of rhetorical weapons used to distinguish what they conceive of their 'civilised' selves from certain 'savage' others, principally Native Americans and Africans.⁴

Such contemporary interrogations of the so-called originary moment of European colonialism in Columbus' 'discovery' of the Americas have stirred considerable interest in earlier, native revisions of colonial history. Today, as we question Prospero's heroic qualities within the providential code that had previously designated the play a pastoral romance, we can also recognise why Caribbean and Latin American writers, in the wake of decolonisation in the

1960s, imaginatively identify with Caliban in their rewritings of Shakespeare's play. Roberto Fernandez Retamar recalls a history of a variety of Latin American responses to *The Tempest* through this century – some of which valorise Ariel as a native intellectual – and argues that new readings from a genuinely non-European perspective were only enabled by the gradual emergence of 'third world' nations.[5] Thus, writing in 1971, Retamar declares

> Our symbol then is not Ariel ... but rather Caliban. This is something that we, the *mestizo* inhabitants of these same isles where Caliban lived, see with particular clarity: Prospero invaded the islands, killed our ancestors, enslaved Caliban, and taught him his language to make himself understood. What can Caliban do but use that same language – today he has no other – to curse him ... I know no other metaphor more expressive of our cultural situation, of our reality ... what is our history, what is our culture, if not the history and culture of Caliban?[6]

These identifications with Caliban, and an accompanying unease about his alien language, typify numerous Latin American and Caribbean responses, especially in their articulations of Caliban's revolutionary potential against Prospero's linguistic authority. The Barbadian writer George Lamming, while assuming his people's identification with Caliban, often returns to the impasse of the coloniser's language in his pioneering essay of 1960:

> Prospero has given Caliban language: with all its unstated history of consequences, an unknown history of future intentions. This gift of language meant not only English, in particular, but speech and concept as a way, a method, a necessary avenue towards areas of the self which could not be reached any other way ... Prospero lives in the absolute certainty that Language, which is his gift to Caliban, is the very prison in which Caliban's achievements must be realised and restricted.[7]

Writing some years later, the Martinique writer and founder of the Negritude movement, Aimé Césaire, is more unequivocal in his play, *A Tempest*, casting Caliban as a successful revolutionary who persistently repudiates Prospero's (European) version of history:

> **Caliban**   ... I am telling you [Prospero] ... I won't answer to the name Caliban ... Call me X. That would be best. Like a man without a name. Or, to be more precise, a man whose name has been stolen. You talk about history ... well, that's history, and everyone knows it! ... Uhuru.[8]

These and other such third world identifications with Caliban have clearly occasioned a paradigm shift among Western audiences and critics who in the past 'tended to listen exclusively to Prospero's voice; [who] after all ... speaks their language'.[9] And in his stage manifestations too, Caliban has come a long way from appearing as the eighteenth-century primitive or the nineteenth-century Darwinian 'missing link' to be accepted as a colonial subject or an embodiment of any oppressed group.[10] Undoubtedly, these anti-colonialist rewritings of Shakespeare's *The Tempest* question the play's seemingly aesthetic concerns, crucially relocating it within a revisionist history of the 'discovery' of the Americas and the struggles for decolonisation in this region. However, while these historicisations of Prospero's mistreatment of Caliban *make visible* the colonial contexts of Shakespeare's play, they often simply signal a *reversal* of the roles of the oppressor and the oppressed, typically demonstrated by Césaire in *A Tempest* when he depicts the relation between Prospero and Caliban as an endless and inevitable Hegelian struggle between the master and slave. Despite leaving open the possibility of a constant negotiation of power between the two men in alternating roles, the play does little to question the inevitability of hierarchical structures.

Therefore, ironically, Prospero refuses to return to Europe at the end of Césaire's play. He threatens a freed and defiant Caliban: 'I will answer your violence with violence', but concludes almost tamely: 'Well Caliban, old fellow, it's just us two now, here on the island ... only you and me', while Caliban shouts: 'Freedom Hi-Day, Freedom Hi-Day'.[11] Finally, in his anti-colonial version of Shakespeare's play, Césaire leaves Prospero and Caliban at an impasse: locked in a continual, potentially violent struggle while sharing the otherwise uninhabited island.

In Lamming's reading of *The Tempest*, the writer also frequently lapses into psychologising universals when defining the Prospero / Caliban polarity (in which Miranda has a peripheral role):

> [According to Lamming, while] Caliban is [Prospero's] convert, colonised by language, and excluded by language ... Prospero is afraid of Caliban. He is afraid because he knows that his encounter with Caliban is largely his encounter with himself. The gift [of language] is a contract from which neither participant is allowed to withdraw ... [yet] Caliban is a child of Nature ... [and] Miranda is the innocent half of Caliban.[12]

In such formulations, Prospero is the dominant force in a natural psychic struggle between Self and Other, namely, between Prospero and Caliban – and Miranda as the object of desire functions to define and keep this rivalry alive.

Lamming and Césaire exemplify a tendency among the anti-colonial appropriations of *The Tempest* to reverse the roles of oppressor and oppressed. And more importantly, in doing so, they view the identities of the women – of Miranda and of the missing 'native' woman, Sycorax – simply as an aspect of the Prospero / Caliban opposition rather than in terms of the complex *sexual ideologies* underpinning colonialism. I wish to look afresh at the relation between Miranda and Caliban, specifically at the way in which Shakespeare's play intersects with postcolonial reappraisals of it, which, I believe, do not adequately address the interactions between race, sexuality, and political struggle. At the centre of my concerns lies the *gendering* of these postcolonial discourses of revolution in which Caliban as the prototype of a male revolutionary becomes a convenient, homogenising symbol for decolonisation. What these writers do not acknowledge is that their focus on Caliban 'generates a self-conscious, self-celebrating male paradigm' that often posits a utopia in which women are marginalised or missing.[13] Retamar imagines such a male utopia in his vision of a tempest, 'halfway between history and dream', which will unify the former oppressors and oppressed: Prospero, Caliban, and Ariel figure alongside Friday, Don Quixote, Marti, and Guevara, among others, but Miranda (as well as her dead mother) and Sycorax are missing.[14]

Postcolonial theorists (both in Western and non-Western locations) have frequently critiqued narratives of 'discovery' for the way in which they gender 'the New World as feminine, [while] sexualising … its exploration, conquest, and settlement'.[15] Some have also traced a history of this feminisation of the various non-European cultures, whereby they exude a 'full blown … sensuality' of a 'sweet dream' in which the West had been wallowing for more than four centuries.[16] From these examples it is evident that critics resisting colonialism have been quick to note how gender is crucial in mapping the signification of power relations in the West – especially in relation to its native others. It is surprising, however, that in their rewritings of *The Tempest*, non-Western writers like Lamming, Césaire, and Fanon have created liberationist, third world narratives oddly oblivious to the dissonances between race and gender struggles. Thus, ironically, their anti-colonial discourse produces the liberated 'Black Man' via the erasure of female subjectivity. For instance, they acknowledge Miranda, but only as the property of the European masters, and therefore, in their eyes, a desired object to be usurped and claimed in the service of resistance. It is Fanon's alienated black male who best expresses this contradiction in the agenda of decolonisation, when he declares: 'I marry white culture, white beauty, white whiteness. When my restless hands caress those white breasts, they grasp white civilisation and dignity and make them mine.'[17] Such assertive, and potentially forcible, claims on the European woman are never questioned by Fanon or others, while the possibility of a fruitful partnership with a native woman – a native mate for Caliban – is never given serious consideration.

In *The Pleasures of Exile*, for instance, 'resistance and liberation are an exclusively male enterprise'.[18] Lamming attempts to understand the relation between Miranda and Caliban who, in his version, share 'innocence and incredulity' but differ in 'their degree of being'.[19] Ultimately, however, he privileges 'Caliban's history ... [which] belongs to the future'.[20] Miranda, in contrast, is made to depend on her father's view of history and await her future within a patriarchal lineage, whereby 'the magic of birth will sail [her], young, beautiful, and a virgin, into the arms of the King's only son'.[21] Furthermore, and more crucially, as Paquet mentions in her foreword, '[finally] like Melville's Ishmael, Caliban is left alone on the island [without the promise of a mate]' and 'Sycorax, as a symbol of a landscape and a changing human situation, is a memory, an absence, and a silence ... [as] Lamming consciously postpones consideration of Sycorax and Miranda's mother as contributing subjects of Caribbean cultural history'.[22]

Aimé Césaire's play, *A Tempest* (which I will discuss at length later), also celebrates Caliban's linguistic and political appropriations of Prospero's power, but once again, without radically altering the terms of a patriarchal power struggle in which the woman's presence is incidental or abstract: namely to perpetuate her father's noble lineage by marrying Ferdinand, the ruler of Naples. And Caliban's mother, the 'native' Sycorax, figures in the play as a *symbolic* Earth Mother embodied in the natural elements of the island. As a result, while the experience of the play foregrounds a seemingly gender-neutral struggle between master and slave, it is, in effect, predicated on the marginalisation of the female figures. Before analysing the gender politics of Césaire's play any further, I would like to examine the discourse of sexuality in Shakespeare's

The Tempest and explore how it offers the crucial nexus for Prospero's colonial authority. An analogy for Prospero's imposition of cultural and political organisation on the sexuality of his subjects – Miranda, Caliban, and to a lesser extent, Ferdinand – can be found in the structure of the exchange of women as gifts in earlier, 'primitive' societies – a structure which served as an idiom for both *kinship* and *competition* among men. In this I hope to show that while Césaire rewrites Shakespeare's play as a third world manifesto of decolonisation, he leaves intact the intractable system of gender categories that are the centrepiece of Prospero's ostensibly benevolent mastery.

Desiring Miranda

Miranda   Why speaks my father so urgently? This
  Is the third man that e'er I saw; the first
  That e'er I sighed for ...
Ferdinand   O, if a virgin
  And your affection not gone forth, I'll make you the
  Queen of Naples.
                        (Shakespeare, *The Tempest*, I.ii.445–9)[23]

On the occasion of Ferdinand and Miranda's first meeting, arranged and controlled by Prospero, in Act I, scene ii of Shakespeare's play, a curious and telling exchange takes place between the three of them. Miranda articulates her desire for Ferdinand by distinguishing him from the other two men she has known: her father and Caliban. Here, Miranda is unaware of her father's apparently 'magical' control of this moment, even as she articulates her desire as a personalised, autonomous experience of sighs and longings. Ferdinand, however, does not look to his heart to understand his attraction for her; instead, he quickly reveals a connection between his sexual desire and the requirements of a patriarchal lineage: 'if a virgin', he asks her, 'I'll make you / The Queen of Naples.' Prospero, the presiding deity, controls their feelings as he finds his power slipping – 'this swift business / I must uneasy make' (I.ii.451–2) – while cautioning Miranda against her limited judgement: 'Thou think'st there is no more such shapes as he, / Having seen but him and Caliban. Foolish wench! / To th' most of men this is a Caliban, / And they to him are angels' (I.ii.479–82).

In eliding Caliban and Ferdinand in vague comparison to 'most of men' – while rhetorically suggesting an identity and difference between them – Prospero points out how he uses Caliban as the less-than-human other in order to define gender (and racial) identity in conveniently elusive terms of what it is *not*. In this gesture, Prospero unwittingly reveals that not only does he fear Caliban's potential for miscegenation with Miranda, but that every man who desires his daughter is potentially a Caliban, unless that desire can be channelled to fulfil the demands of an aristocratic lineage.

While noting the dynamics of Prospero's fatherhood, critics often have observed the play's ambivalence toward motherhood. For instance, Coppélia Kahn notes that '[Prospero's] only mention of his wife is highly ambivalent, at once commending and questioning her chastity before his daughter: "The mother was a piece of virtue, and / She said thou wast my daughter (I.ii.56–7)" '.[24] David Sundelson reiterates this point by suggesting that the 'reverence for father Prospero does not extend to mothers. Whatever ambivalence toward them is hidden in Prospero's tale of expulsion, the one mother in the play is unmistakably demonic: Sycorax.'[25] She is a 'foul witch' (I.ii.263), a 'damned witch ... banished for mischiefs manifold, sorceries terrible / To enter human hearing' (I.ii.264–5). Sundelson then argues, 'This demon mother's rage is "unmitigable" (I.ii.276); only a father could end the torture.'[26] Stephen Orgel also persuasively reads the effects of Prospero's ambivalence toward wives / mothers: 'The absent presence of the wife and mother in the play constitutes a space that is filled by Prospero's creation of surrogates and a ghostly family: the witch Sycorax and her monster child Caliban ... the good child / wife Miranda ...'[27]

Caliban as the offspring of this 'demon' mother serves appropriately as an other. Thus, Prospero's (and the play's) view of Caliban as a potential rapist illustrates how the discourse of sexuality underpins colonial authority. That Prospero assumes authority in terms typical of colonialist discourse is recognised by most postcolonial critics. As one critic states, 'Colonialist discourse does not simply announce a triumph for civility, it must continually *produce* it [through a struggle with rather than an assimilation of its others].'[28] Hence, interpellated within Prospero's narrative of sexual and racial control, the identities of both Caliban and Miranda must constantly be *produced* in terms of sexual struggle in which, as Prospero's subjects, their sexuality comes under constant surveillance, even as one enables the repression of the other. Both race and gender conflicts come into play in this three-way dynamic, inhering within the same system of differences between coloniser and colonised, yet not without some *dissonances* within the systemic forces. Miranda, who knows no men (other than her father) between whom she can distinguish, responds unequivocally to Caliban's different appearance, which seems an inherent sign of his 'villainy'. In Act II, scene ii she declares to her father: ' 'Tis [Caliban] a villain sir, / I do not love to look on' (I.ii.309). Yet, like a typical coloniser, she also reveals her civilising impulses toward Caliban: 'I pitied thee, / Took pains to make thee speak, taught thee each hour / One thing or another' (I.ii.353–5) – simultaneously holding out little hope of improvement for his 'vile race'.

Neither Prospero nor Miranda allow Caliban an identity as a desiring subject who wishes to gain sexual access to Miranda for the legitimate aim of 'peopl[ing] … This isle with Calibans' (I.ii.350–1). However, given Prospero's manipulation of Ferdinand's 'wooing', it is clear that he decides which man is to have access to his daughter. Though Miranda has a position of colonial superiority over Caliban, she nonetheless has a marginal role within a *kinship* system in which all the three males are bonded through their competing claims on her. According to Lévi-Strauss, Mauss, and others, one of the most striking features of this system among so-called primitive societies was the practice of giving and receiving gifts as a part of social intercourse; within this system, the gift of women was the most profound because the exchange partners thereby enacted a relationship of kinship.[29] Significantly, however, gift exchange could confer upon its participants a special solidarity as well as a sense of competition and rivalry. From the perspective of some feminist anthropologists, this system had far-reaching implications for women:

> If it is women who are being transacted, then it is men who give and take them who are linked, the woman being a conduit of a relationship rather than a partner to it. The exchange of women does not necessarily imply that women are objectified … But it does imply a distinction between gift and giver. If women are the gifts, then it is the men who are exchange partners. And it is the partners, not their presents, upon whom the reciprocal exchange confers its quasi-mystical power of social linkage … [Thus] women are *given* in marriage, *taken* in battle, exchanged for favours, sent as tribute, traded, bought, and sold.[30]

Several contemporary anthropologists recognise the danger of attributing a timeless universality to this concept of a kinship system. For instance, they point to the gender inflections of Lévi-Strauss' reasoning when he says that women should be exchanged as the only way of overcoming the contradiction by which the same woman is, on the one hand, the object of personal desire, and, on the other, the object of the desire of others and a means of binding others through alliance with them. Such a naturalised definition of a woman's role also, critics argue, does not account for some matrilineal, non-Western societies that neither hold proprietorial attitudes toward women nor use them as a means of social and sexual exchange. Despite these limitations of Lévi-Strauss' gendered language, the notion of the exchange of women is nonetheless useful in demonstrating, when applicable, how a specific cultural paradigm organises and shapes female sexuality and subjectivity.[31]

It is apparent, then, that underlying the dynamics of Prospero's power struggle with Caliban and, to a lesser extent, with Ferdinand, over the two men's sexual claims to Prospero's daughter, lies the social grid of the kinship system. Thus, desiring Miranda makes the noble Ferdinand a suitable exchange partner for her royal father. She is to be the means whereby the royal descendants of the two men will be related by blood. Ferdinand makes apparent that this arrangement is, in effect, an exchange of Miranda's virginity (which her father must guard) for the throne of Naples. This is reinforced at the end of the play, when Ferdinand retrospectively asks *his* father's permission for his marriage to Miranda: 'I chose her when I could not ask my father / For his advice' (V.i.190–1).

The marriage of Ferdinand and Miranda typically exemplifies the theory of reciprocity in kinship systems. Marriages are the most basic form of gift exchange, whereby the woman whom one does not take is offered up as a precious gift. Caliban, the seeming outsider among kin, nonetheless has a role within the system of gender differences underpinning gift exchanges among men. His desire for Miranda leads him to imagine a kinship with Prospero, even if it means *taking* her forcibly: 'Would't had been done! / Thou didst prevent me; I had peopled else / This isle with Calibans' (I.ii.349–51). In this scenario, Caliban not only wishes to create a blood tie with Prospero, but also to use Miranda as a means of producing male children – a population in the image of Caliban rather than of Miranda. When Prospero prevents Caliban from violating the 'honour of [his] child' (I.ii.348), he in turn assumes a proprietorial control over his daughter as a sexual gift, which he will later *give* to the royal Ferdinand.

A central feature of the traditional kinship structure is that *all* levels and directions in the traffic of women, including hostile ones, are ordered by this structure. Thus, gift exchange could be an idiom of rivalry and competition and marriage itself could be highly competitive.[32] In this context, while Prospero believes that Caliban exists outside of any civilised social forms, the latter is nonetheless Ferdinand's rival in desiring Miranda, and on the basis of this claim is bonded with the two other men; an acknowledgement and denial of his desire by Prospero ironically serves to legitimate Caliban's position as a rival within the structures of gift exchange. Prospero and Miranda may consider Caliban 'a thing most brutish', but from his perspective, the coloniser has withheld from him the gift of woman in order to maintain the hierarchical boundaries between them. The basis of the power struggle between Prospero and Caliban, then, is an implicit consensus about the role of woman as a gift to be exchanged.

Miranda's role as a gift is further complicated by Prospero's implicit (and European) fear of a monstrous progeny that could result from a misplaced gift exchange with a man who is racially marked as other. In Prospero's eyes the imaginary 'Calibans' who could 'people' the isle would connect his lineage to that of Sycorax, whom *he* describes as the 'damned witch' whose 'sorceries terrible' banished her from 'Argier' (Algiers). For Prospero (and for European audiences), her magic is antithetical to his supposedly beneficent Art because she embodies an aberration of nature, both in terms of her sexuality (her impregnation by an incubus) and her racial identity as a non-European. While Prospero claims to know the history of her life, his only source is Ariel, and as one critic points out, 'we have no way of distinguishing the facts about Caliban and Sycorax from Prospero's invective about them'.[33] Given his demonising rhetoric, it is not surprising that a fear of miscegenation is a crucial trope that structures Prospero's 'plot' of selective inclusion and exclusion in which Miranda, Ferdinand, and Caliban figure as prominent characters.

We get a fuller sense of Sycorax's demonisation if we consider *The Tempest*'s relation to the poetic geography of the Renaissance (derived from classical and medieval sources), in which European identity is frequently contrasted with images of otherness. According to John Gillies, Sycorax's mythic journey from Algiers to the New World is motivated not so much to find a new 'howling wilderness' as to *make* one. Her adoption of 'Setebos', a New World 'devil' ('my Dam's god'), evokes associations with the name of the demonised god of the 'heathen' Patagonian Indians. Thus, in her role as the non-Western other in the collective European imagination, she is like 'Ham, progenitor of the Caananite, the Negro and other supposedly bestial and slavish races, ... an outcast from the world of men, a wanderer beyond bounds and an active promoter of the degeneracy of her "vile" race'.[34]

Prospero's plot of a 'happy end', however, does not accommodate the figure of Claribel, who haunts the margins of *The Tempest*. In fact, it is telling that Shakespeare's play, unlike Prospero's script, does not resolve the contradiction between the anxiety of miscegenation from Miranda's potential union with Caliban and the political imperative for a European like Alonso to give his daughter in a marriage across racial lines. References to the forced marriage of Claribel to the King of Tunis in North Africa, which appear early in the play, strike a discordant note in the emerging racial ideology that leads European audiences to rejoice at the play's 'happy' marriage at the end – a marriage that preserves the purity of European lineage in the union of Naples and Milan.

That Claribel's match deviates from the cultural norm is made evident by Sebastian when he chides Alonso 'That would not bless our Europe with your daughter / But rather loose her to an African' (II.i.129–30) and reminds him that his daughter was divided by her 'loathness' for the Tunisian and 'obedience' toward her father. Furthermore, Gonzalo's unexplained identification between Claribel and Dido, Queen of Carthage, complicates our view of the racial and gender politics involved in the match. For instance, the fate imposed upon Alonso's reluctant daughter is the one violently resisted by Dido who chose to die rather than marry an African King, Iarbus. According to Peter Hulme, to recall Carthage 'is to bring to mind several centuries of punishing wars with Italy ... when presumably Claribel has been a gift to fend off a dangerous new power in the central Mediterranean'.[35] The references to Dido also evoke contradictory images: that of the widow, and 'a model at once of heroic fidelity to her murdered husband and the destructive potential of erotic passion'.[36] Overall, while the meanings of this allusion are multiple and remain ambiguous, references to North Africa encroach upon the boundaries of the imaginary Italian states of the Renaissance that defined their culture against 'barbarians' like the offspring of the Algerian Sycorax, or in another instance, the 'bar-barian Moor'. While images of the Tunisian queen do not intrude into Prospero's plan of social and sexual organisation, they nonetheless open up an imaginary space for viewers (and readers) of the play to imagine the (impossible or repressed) possibility of miscegenation in the service of political expediency, even as the woman's subjectivity continues to be shaped by her status as a gift.

Some political, especially feminist, readings of Shakespeare's *The Tempest* try to open up the play to such dissonances that remain unaccommodated by the play's 'happy' conclusion. One such strat-egy is to read an implicit affinity between Caliban and Miranda in relation to the overarching power of Prospero, whom they desig-nate as a racist patriarch. While acknowledging that historically European women have been complicit with their men in producing the non-European man as a demonised Other and a potential rapist, they attempt to read against the grain of such polarisations. Lorrie J. Leininger's landmark essay, despite its essentialism, is useful in exploring a relationship between Miranda and Caliban, not in sexual terms, but in the context of a mutual recognition of the pos-sibilities of resistance.[37] Thus, Leininger creates an imaginary riposte by Miranda to her father in which she both reveals and dis-rupts colonial hierarchy as well as the kinship system: 'My father is no God-figure. No one is a God-father' (p. 291). Calling for respect for Caliban's non-European ancestry, she also refuses to be used as a means of his oppression:

> ... men are reminded of Indians when they first see Caliban; he might be African, his mother having been transported from Algiers ... I will not be used as the excuse of his enslavement ... I need to join forces with Caliban – with all those who are exploited ...[38]

Furthermore, Leininger's Miranda repudiates the value placed on her 'virginity' both by the kinship system – as a gift exchanged or withheld – and by the colonial institutions based on the 'protection' of European women: 'I cannot give assent to an ethical scheme that locates all virtue symbolically in one part of my anatomy. My virginity has little to do with the forces that will lead to a good harvest or to greater social justice.'[39] Such insights offered by femi-nist revisions of *The Tempest* make visible the structural contradic-tions in Miranda's subject-position as 'the sexual object of both the Anglo-American male and the native other'.[40] And while Miranda ultimately aligns herself to the colonising father and husband, the play and Leininger also gesture toward an alliance, however problematic, in a childhood 'prehistory' when Miranda taught Caliban language, or in a utopian, egalitarian future.

Such feminist possibilities and insights rarely figure in third world, postcolonial versions of the play. A call for decolonisation and revolution in a play such as Aimé Césaire's *A Tempest* ironically shows that race and gender struggles occur in antithetical, rather than cooperative relationships. The play enacts a breakdown of colonial hierarchy, but leaves intact the system of kinship between men.

A postcolonial 'brave new world'

Prospero   Good God, you tried to rape my daughter!
Caliban   Rape! Rape! Listen you old goat, you're the one that put
those dirty thoughts in my head. Let me tell you something: I
couldn't care less about your daughter, or about your cave for that
matter.[41]

Aimé Césaire's Caliban is clearly the protagonist of *A Tempest*. In this telling exchange between him and Prospero, he strongly repudiates the identity of a rapist that he claims *is produced* by his master. Caliban's almost perfunctory dismissal of any possibility of sexually desiring Miranda is put to question in Act II, scene i by her description of that 'awful Caliban who keeps pursuing me and calling out my name in his stupid dreams' (p. 35). Except for these two moments that leave a lingering sense of ambivalence, the play largely leaves unexplored the issue of power and sexuality as it concerns the relationship between Prospero, Miranda, and Caliban. The latter moment, in effect, seems to deny his identity as a desiring subject, shrugging off 'dirty thoughts' not of his own making to become a single-minded prototype of a third world revolutionary. Does his rejection of Miranda as a sexual prize signal a 'brave new world' in which the patriarchal kinship bonds between men are dissolved?

Before responding to this rhetorical question, let me first establish *A Tempest*'s dramatic and political credentials. First published in French in the wake of decolonisation in 1969, it revised the history of the Caribbean. Calling for a troupe of black actors performing their own version of Shakespeare's play, it was initially produced in

Africa, the Middle East, and the Caribbean, as well as in France. It was translated into English by Richard Miller in 1985 and was introduced to New York audiences in a successful, though politically restrained, production in 1991. The spirit of the play derives from the Negritude movement, of which Césaire was one of the founders, with its aim being to reverse the political and linguistic oppression of blacks within colonialism.

Set in a colony – a prototype of a Caribbean or African setting – in the throes of resistance and unrest, the play initially focuses on Caliban's verbal attacks on Prospero's control over language and representation. Here Césaire is clearly sensitive to the way in which the name Caliban / cannibal appears in Shakespeare's play – and in colonial history – 'through an imperial and colonial act of translation'.[42] Thus, Césaire has Caliban declare his independence in Swahili, 'Uhuru!'. To which Prospero mutters, 'Mumbling your native language again! I've already told you, I don't like it' (p. 11). He wants his native subject to 'at least thank (me) for having taught you to speak at all. You, a savage ... a dumb animal, a beast I educated, trained, dragged up from the Bestiality that still clings to you' (p. 11). Césaire's Prospero is the familiar proponent of the 'civilising mission'; thus, Caliban's rebellion is rightly aimed at Prospero's power of 'naming' when he declares, 'I don't want to be called Caliban any longer ... Caliban isn't my name' (p. 15).

Accompanying Caliban's disruptions to the coloniser's language are intimations of an actual resistance movement (as Prospero tells Ariel in Act III, scene iii: 'Caliban is alive, he is plotting, he is getting a guerrilla force' [p. 50]), as well as of an impending black independence in Ariel's concluding resolve to sing 'notes so sweet that the last / will give rise to a yearning / in the heart of the most forgetful slaves / yearning for freedom ... and the lightened agave will straighten [into] / a solemn flag' (p. 60). Prior to his articulation of this 'unsettling agenda', Ariel, who is labelled a 'Mulatto', plays the historical part of those mixed races, often in the middle of the colonial hierarchy, more able to accept their somewhat limited oppression. Ariel declares that he and Caliban are 'Brothers in suffering and slavery ... and in hope as well ... [but] have different methods' (p. 20); yet Ariel's vision of brotherhood includes Prospero, and for him any fight of freedom is for his master too – 'so that Prospero can acquire a conscience' (p. 22).

The play does not end with an unequivocal victory leading to the expulsion of the coloniser. Rather, it posits a Hegelian dialectic in which Prospero and Caliban remain on the island, with Prospero declaring his power as well as a curious, almost natural bond. 'Well Caliban, old fellow, it's just us two now, here on the island' (p. 68). Given this ending, *A Tempest* is commonly staged as a 'political comedy' with a humorous rhetorical play on language.[43] However, one cannot overlook the political message of the play: to promote 'black consciousness' and rewrite the script of colonial history. At least imaginatively, if not literally, the play creates a different kind of 'brave new world' in which the struggle for political and cultural independence is in *process*.

Undoubtedly, Césaire's postcolonial vision (incorporating the philosophy of Negritude) challenges the categories of representation defining the non-European races as inferior and in need of civilisation. But while it celebrates a revolution of brotherhood, it holds in place a kinship system in which women figure as gifts or objects of exchange. Caliban's somewhat ambivalent repudiation of Miranda seems to free him from hostility and rivalry toward Prospero and Ferdinand, but in another sense, his gesture can also be read as a symbolic rejection of a potential gift – a daughter who is to be given to some man in marriage. Unlike feminist critics such as Leininger, Césaire, in his revision of Shakespeare's play, makes no attempt to reconceptualise the relationship between Caliban and Miranda, or to suggest any possibilities of a shared resistance to the patriarch. Anxieties about possible miscegenation, so crucial to Prospero's demonisation of Caliban in Shakespeare's play, are repressed by Césaire in his diminishment of Miranda's role. Caliban's summary dismissal of any desire to possess Miranda sexually is a convenient structural device for mobilising an all-male revolution – one which recapitulates the kinship structure in its most basic form, giving a minimal presence to Miranda.

Thus, a play celebrating the emerging freedoms of the 1960s does not change Miranda's fate. Her marriage is once again *arranged* in a gift exchange that will ensure future peace and stability in a growing nation that will now combine two European city states. Prospero articulates this to Ariel at the outset: 'These are men of my race and of high rank ... I have a daughter. Alonso has a son. If they were to fall in love I would give my consent. Let Ferdinand and Miranda marry, and may that marriage bring us harmony and peace. That is my plan. I want it executed' (p. 16). Though Prospero wilfully stays on this island to continue his 'civilising mission,', he ensures the consolidation of his kingdom through the alliance of Naples and Milan via the marriage of his daughter. Hence, while Césaire empowers Caliban to cry out unfailingly, 'Freedom Hi-Day', we never find out how Miranda's 'brave new world' turns out after all.

While Miranda's circumscribed role conveniently fulfils the requirements of a European patriarchy, it is telling that Césaire does not introduce a woman who can be Caliban's 'physiognomically complementary mate'. Writing in the context of the history of the Americas, and specifically from the perspective of Caribbean women, Sylvia Wynter criticises Shakespeare's play for its absence of Caliban's mate:

> [The] question is that of the most significant absence of all, that of Caliban's Woman, of Caliban's physiognomically complementary mate. For nowhere in Shakespeare's play, and in its system of image-making, one which would be foundational ... to our present Western world system, does Caliban's mate appear as an alternative sexual-erotic model of desire ... an alternative system of meanings. Rather there, on the New World island, as the only woman, Miranda ... [is] contrasted with the ontologically absent, potential genetrix – Caliban's mate – of another population of human, i.e., of a 'vile race' 'capable of ill-will'.[44]

Reading this absence historically, Wynter (citing Caribbean writers like Maryse Condé) suggests that 'the non-desire of Caliban for his own mate, Caliban's "woman" is ... a founding function of the "social pyramid" of the global order that will be put in place following upon the 1492 arrival of Columbus in the Caribbean'.[45] In this first phase of Western Europe's expansion into the Americas, given the expanding slave trade out of the 'Europe-Africa-New World triangular traffic', Caliban as 'both the Arawak and African forced labour, [supposedly] had no need / desire for the procreation of his own kind'.[46] It is ironic that these criticisms, revealing the limitations of Shakespeare's play, are also applicable to Césaire's revisionary version. Caliban's revolt can have little impact as long as the absence of a native woman as his sexual reproductive mate functions to negate the progeny / population group comprising the original owners / occupiers of the New World lands, the American Indians.

In conclusion, if Aimé Césaire's *A Tempest* is widely read as an allegory of decolonisation, it fails to address adequately the relationship between liberation movements and the representations of sexual difference. Instead, it shows that if resistance movements are 'imagined communities', then such imaginings are frequently based upon particular, and often disempowering, constructions of women's sexuality.[47] As gifts of exchange, or conduits of homosocial desire between men, women taking part in the movements for real national liberation could not escape the determinations of earlier kinship structures. Reflecting this historical trend, Césaire conveniently represents Miranda as the property of the colonisers, but more significantly, displaces the sexual, maternal identity of the 'native' woman, Sycorax, onto the idealised abstraction of the Earth as Mother, while denying Caliban a potential union with a Caribbean woman. Finally, Césaire's call for a revolution lacks credibility as he prevents Prospero's former slave from peopling the isle with Calibans.

From Valerie Traub, M. Lindsay Kaplan and Dympna Callaghan (eds), *Feminist Readings of Early Modern Culture* (Cambridge, 1996), pp. 191–207.

NOTES

[Jyotsna Singh's essay is part of a growing corpus of work investigating the complex ways in which colonial discourse intersects with gender and sexual ideologies (see 'Further Reading', Loomba [1989], Wynter [1999]). Reappraising the numerous rewritings of *The Tempest* from the perspective of the colonised subject that appeared in the wake of decolonisation, she argues that the radical edge of their revisionism is blunted by a failure to recognise the connection between racial and sexual forms of oppression and thus to imagine the possibility of shared resistance to patriarchal rule on the part of Miranda and Caliban. Consequently while Caliban has been reinvented as the male prototype of a 'third world revolutionary', Miranda's fate as an object of exchange between men remains unaltered in postcolonial appropriations of *The Tempest*. Ed.]

1. George Lamming, *The Pleasures of Exile* (1960; Ann Arbor, MI, 1992), p. 13.

2. Roberto Fernandez Retamar, *Caliban and Other Essays*, trans. Edward Baker (Minneapolis, 1989), p. 55.

3. For fuller accounts of *The Tempest* and decolonisation, see Eric Cheyfitz, *The Poetics of Imperialism: Translation and Colonization from The Tempest to Tarzan* (Oxford, 1991), pp. 42–58. To follow

the production of the term, 'Cannibal', see Peter Hulme, *Colonial Encounters: Europe and the Native Caribbean 1492–1797* (London, 1986), pp. 1–3. Also see Roberto Fernandez Retamar, *Caliban and Other Essays*, pp. 6–21.

4. Cheyfitz, *The Poetics of Imperialism*, p. 42.

5. Retamar, *Caliban and other Essays*, pp. 6–21. Retamar offers a detailed history of the changing political images of Caliban in Latin American history through decolonisation.

6. Ibid., p. 14.

7. Lamming, *The Pleasures of Exile*, p. 14.

8. Aimé Césaire, *A Tempest: An Adaptation of The Tempest for Black Theatre*, trans. Richard Miller (New York, 1969), p. 15.

9. Francis Barker and Peter Hulme, 'Nymphs and Reapers Heavily Vanish: The Discursive Con-Texts of *The Tempest*', in *Alternative Shakespeares*, ed. John Drakakis (London, 1985), p. 204.

10. Virginia Vaughan, ' "Something Rich and Strange": Caliban's Theatrical Metamorphoses', *Shakespeare Quarterly*, 36:4 (Winter 1985), 390–405.

11. Césaire, *A Tempest*, pp. 67–8.

12. Lamming, *The Pleasures of Exile*, p. 15.

13. Sandra Pouchet Paquet, foreword to George Lamming, *The Pleasures of Exile*, pp. xxi–xxiv, offers a feminist critique of Lamming's postcolonial vision. Specifically, her focus on the missing Sycorax identifies the limitations of the postcolonial revisions of the original.

14. Retamar, *Caliban and Other Essays*, p. 55.

15. See Louis A. Montrose, 'The Work of Gender in the Discourse of Discovery', in *New World Encounters*, ed. Stephen Greenblatt (Berkeley, CA, 1993), pp. 177–83, for a look at the ways in which the early colonial discourses were gendered, thus feminising the 'New Worlds'. His analysis offers a useful model for a rhetorical analysis of the structure of colonial narratives.

16. Malek Alloula, *Colonial Harem* (Minneapolis, 1987), p. 3.

17. Frantz Fanon, *Black Skin White Masks* (1952), trans. Charles Lamm Markmann (New York, 1967), p. 63.

18. Paquet, foreword, Lamming, *The Pleasures of Exile*, pp. xxi–xxii.

19. Lamming, *The Pleasures of Exile*, p. 114.

20. Ibid., p. 107.

21. Ibid.

22. Paquet, foreword, ibid., p. xxii.

23. William Shakespeare, *The Tempest* (1610–11), Signet Classic / Penguin edition (New York, 1987). All quotations are taken from this edition.

24. Coppélia Kahn, 'The Providential Tempest and the Shakespearean Family', in *Representing Shakespeare: New Psychoanalytic Essays*, ed. Murray A. Schwartz and Coppélia Kahn (Baltimore, MD, 1980), pp. 217–43.

25. David Sundelson, ' "So Rare a Wonder'd Father": Prospero's *Tempest*', in ibid., pp. 33–55.

26. Ibid.

27. Stephen Orgel, 'Prospero's Wife', in *Rewriting the Renaissance: The Discourses of Sexual Difference in Early Modern Europe*, ed. Margaret W. Ferguson, Maureen Quilligan, and Nancy Vickers (Chicago, 1986), p. 51.

28. I base my analysis of the structure of colonial discourse on Paul Brown's formulation, in ' "This Thing of Darkness I Acknowledge Mine": *The Tempest* and the Discourse of Colonialism', in *Political Shakespeare*, ed. Jonathan Dollimore and Alan Sinfield (Ithaca, NY, 1985), pp. 48–54.

29. My application of the exchange of women in kinship systems is indebted to Gayle Rubin's feminist, anthropological analysis, 'The Traffic in Women: Notes on a Political Economy of Sex', in *Toward an Anthropology of Women*, ed. Reyna R. Reiter (New York, 1974), pp. 157–210. For a fuller discussion of Mauss' and Lévi-Strauss' theories by Rubin, see pp. 171–7.

30. Ibid., pp. 174–5.

31. Eleanor Burke Leacock, *Myths of Male Dominance* (New York and London, 1981), pp. 229–41. Leacock discusses the gender inflections of Lévi-Strauss' formulations as well the tendencies of other anthropologists 'to seek universals in relations between the sexes', pp. 231–3.

32. Rubin, 'The Traffic in Women', pp. 172–4.

33. Orgel, 'Prospero's Wife', p. 55.

34. John Gillies, *Shakespeare and the Geography of Difference* (Cambridge, 1994), pp. 140–4. He locates Sycorax within the poetic geography of the period, by drawing on associations (made by Renaissance and earlier geographers and ethnographers) between her and other non-European others.

35. Hulme, *Colonial Encounters*, pp. 111–12.

36. Orgel, 'Prospero's Wife', p. 51.

37. Lorrie Jerrell Leininger, 'The Miranda Trap: Sexism and Racism in Shakespeare's *The Tempest*', in *The Woman's Part: Feminist Criticism of Shakespeare*, ed. Gayle Green, Ruth Swift Lenz, and Carol Thomas Neely (Urbana, IL, 1980), pp. 285–94.

38. Leininger, 'The Miranda Trap', pp. 291–2.

39. Ibid., p. 292.

40. Laura Donaldson, *Decolonizing Feminisms: Race, Gender, and Empire-Building* (Chapel Hill, NC, 1992), p. 17.

41. Césaire, *A Tempest*, trans. Richard Miller, Act I, scene ii, p. 13. All subsequent quotes will be taken from this edition. Page numbers are noted in parenthesis within the text.

42. Cheyfitz, *The Poetics of Imperialism*, p. 41.

43. D.J.R. Bruckner, Review of *A Tempest*, *New York Times*, 16 October 1991, p. B 1.

44. Sylvia Wynter, 'Beyond Miranda's Meanings: Un / silencing the Demonic Ground of Caliban's Woman', in *Out of the Kumbla: Caribbean Women and Literature*, ed. Carole Boyce Davies and Elaine Savoury Fido (Trenton, NJ, 1990), p. 360.

45. Ibid., pp. 360–1.

46. Ibid., p. 361.

47. I am indebted to the 'Introduction' to *Nationalisms and Sexualities*, ed. Andrew Parker, Mary Russo, Doris Sommer, and Patricia Yaeger (London, 1992), p. 13, for this formulation of 'imagined communities' derived from Bendict Anderson's usage. Several essays, under the section 'Women, Resistance, and the State', examine the relationship between resistance movements and social constructions of women's bodies, pp. 395–424.

9

'The Duke of Milan / And his Brave Son': Old Histories and New in *The Tempest*

DAVID SCOTT KASTAN

> Every image of the past that is not recognized by the present as one
> of its own concerns threatens to disappear irretrievably.
> (Walter Benjamin)

It is, of course, *The Comedy of Errors* that alone among
Shakespeare's plays mentions 'America' (which the Syracusan
Dromio exuberantly locates 'upon [Nell's] nose, all o'er embellished
with rubies, carbuncles, sapphires, declining their rich aspect to the
hot breath of Spain'[1]), but it is Shakespeare's other comedy observing the unities of time and place, *The Tempest*, that has almost
inescapably become his play of Europe's engagement with the New
World. Since Malone in 1808 first called attention to the play's relation to the Virginia Company pamphlets, offering the closest
thing we have to something that might be thought of as a source for
The Tempest, the experience of Thomas Gates and his men in
Bermuda has been taken to give a local habitation and a name to
the stereotypical narrative of shipwreck and deliverance articulating
the play's romance form.[2]

Following Malone, critics have long claimed that the accounts of
the miraculous escape of Gates's ship from 'the most dreadful

tempest', as Strachey's report terms it, that drove it from the Virginia coast provided the material that stimulated Shakespeare's dramatic imagination. The texts of the various reports from Virginia have come to seem the determining source and subtext of the play itself. In 1901, Morton Luce, editor of the first Arden edition, argued that the wreck of the *Sea-Venture* 'must have suggested the leading incidents of *The Tempest*'; 'indeed', he continues, 'we may fairly say that fully nine-tenths of the subjects touched upon by Shakespeare in *The Tempest* are suggested by the new enterprise of colonisation.'[3] And critics have continued to insist, as John Gillies has recently put it, that the play is 'vitally rather than casually implicated in the discourses of America and the Virginia Company', whose directors included the Earl of Southampton, to whom Shakespeare dedicated *Venus and Adonis* and *The Rape of Lucrece*, and the Earl of Pembroke, one of the dedicatees of the First Folio, making such a connection to Shakespeare plausible if not absolutely compelling.[4]

Recently, of course, criticism of *The Tempest*, while reasserting the New World context, has effectively wrested the play from the idealisations of romance (as Gillies's word 'implicated' no doubt signals). The experience of the Virginia colonists is no longer merely a timely reminder of the timeless structures of a romance mode in which the world of 'mortal accident' is discovered to 'suffer a sea-change / Into something rich and strange' (I.ii.403–4), in which the hand of 'great creating nature' can be felt organising the turbulence of earthly existence, re-establishing love and human continuance. No longer is *The Tempest* a play of social reconciliation and moral renewal, of benevolent artistry and providential design; it now appears as a telling document of the first phase of English imperialism, implicated in the will-to-power of the Jacobean court, even as an 'instrument of empire' itself.[5]

Prospero is no longer an inspiring magus but an arrogant and ill-tempered magistrate (not even the 'good, authoritarian Governor' that Geoffrey Bullough saw[6]); and the romance form is no longer a utopian spectacle of wonder but itself a participant in the ideological activity of imperialism – performing the necessary act of colonialist legitimation by naturalising domination as the activity of a 'Providence divine' (I.ii.159). Coleridge found *The Tempest* to be one of those plays 'where the ideal is predominant',[7] but for us the 'ideal' usually now seems only the name that the powerful give to their desire. In our anxious postcolonial moment, the power of

Prospero's art, once confidently viewed as benevolently civilising, has become the coloniser's technology of domination and control. Prospero's magic in the play now appears, in Stephen Greenblatt's phrase, as 'the romance equivalent of martial law', or, in Peter Hulme's version, marking out 'the space really inhabited in colonial history by gunpowder'.[8] And Caliban and, if somewhat less truculently, Ariel are the natives of the new world who have been unwillingly subjected to the coercive power of European knowledge.

This is the current orthodoxy of *Tempest* criticism, but not, it should be said, of *Tempest* performance, which most often has chosen, for obvious reasons, to emphasise the theme and spectacle of artistry, even as it has come to recognise the contradictions and stresses of the text. Nonetheless, there have been memorable 'colonial' interpretations, such as Jonathan Miller's production of the play at the Mermaid in 1970, casting black actors as Caliban and Ariel and explicitly depending, as Miller wrote, on 'the whole colonial theme as knowledge which the audience brought to bear on Shakespeare's play'.[9] But though undoubtedly 'colonial', this was not a 'new world' *Tempest*. Miller was thinking explicitly of the then current political situation in Nigeria, and he based his characterisations upon Octave Mannoni's analysis in *La Psychologie de la colonisation* (1950) of the 1947 revolt in Madagascar. And, more recently, George Wolfe's 1995 *Tempest* in Central Park (and then on Broadway), starring Patrick Stewart, did stage the play as a third-world fantasy and made its colonial theme explicit, if uncertainly located both temporally and geographically. But these productions are, in any case, more the exception than the rule.

If on stage *The Tempest*'s relation to the new world is still optional, the critical assertion of the play's relation to the colonial enterprise in the Americas is now seemingly inescapable, even historically extendable, as in Leslie Fiedler's claim that in the play 'the whole history of imperialist America has been prophetically revealed to us'.[10] Fielder at least has the good grace not to see the play as solely a document of *English* imperialism; but clearly for Fiedler, as for most of us who have read it in his wake, the play unsettlingly defines the encounter of the old world with the new, of the powerful with the powerless, its bad faith evident in Prospero's bitter denunciation of Antonio's usurpation of his dukedom but his complete blindness to his own usurpation of the sovereignty of the island. 'This island's mine,' protests Caliban, 'by Sycorax my mother, / Which thou tak'st from me ... I am all the subjects that you have, / Which first was mine own King: and here you sty me / In this hard rock, whiles you do keep from me the rest o'th' island' (I.ii.333–46). Prospero responds angrily: 'thou most lying slave', not, however, angry about Caliban's claim of alienated sovereignty but at his assertion of undeserved hard-treatment: 'I have us'd thee, / Filth as thou art, with human care; / and lodg'd thee / In mine own cell, till thou didst seek to violate / The honour of my child' (I.ii.346–50). What Prospero calls a lie is only the claim that he is an oppressor; Caliban's claim that he is a usurper is not contested, indeed, not even heard, so fully does Prospero feel his own right to rule to be beyond any question.

No doubt Prospero's bad faith (a bad faith not cancelled out by the fact that Caliban's sovereign claim is itself based upon his Algerian mother's parallel domination of a native 'spirit' population) is relevant to any understanding of the encounter with the new world, whose native inhabitants could have said to their putative 'discoverers', no less tellingly than Prospero to Miranda, ''Tis new to thee' (V.i.184). But it is worth reminding ourselves how thin is the thread on which the play's relation to the new world hangs.

The play is obviously set in the old world; the tempest is called up as the Italian nobles are returning from Africa to Italy, and those who have escaped the storm are said to return 'sadly' to Naples 'upon the Mediterranean flote' (I.ii.234). Ariel does refer to Bermuda, but pointedly as the place they are not: the Italians' ship, he tells Prospero, is safe in the harbour 'where once / Thou call'dst me up at midnight to fetch dew / From the still-vex'd Bermoothes' (I.ii.227–9). The only other explicit textual connections are the two references to 'Setebos', whom Caliban identifies as 'my dam's god' (I.ii.375) and editors have identified in accounts of Magellan's voyages as a 'great devil' of the Patagonian religion. Trinculo observes that the English who 'will not give a doit to relieve a lame beggar … will lay out ten to see a dead Indian' (II.ii.31–3), but Trinculo never takes the creature hiding beneath the cloak for an Indian; it is some kind of 'monster' that 'smells like a fish'. That's it.

Some would add Gonzalo's use of the word 'plantation', its only appearance in Shakespeare, though 'plantation' is a word apparently coined for *old* world domination, to describe the English colonial project in Ireland, and even when applied to the new world is used to describe an exclusively English enclave: 'a plantation of the people of your owne English nation', as John Hooker writes to Raleigh.[11] And, of course, Gonzalo's utopian fantasy is based on a passage in Montaigne's essay on the cannibals of Brazil. But its primitivist vision has little relevance to the dreams and desires of the Italian courtiers, as is revealed by its self-contradiction, where Gonzalo's imaginings of a world with 'no sovereignty' (II.i.158) originate in its opposite, in a fantasy of power: 'Had I plantation of this isle, my lord ... And were the king on't ...' (II.i.145, 147).

In all there is very little to go on, especially to validate the now commonplace insistence that new world colonialism provides the play's 'dominant discursive con-texts'.[12] Though Prospero does locate Caliban in anthropological, social, moral, even theological discourses – 'beast', 'slave', 'demi-devil' – that sanction and support his own hierarchical superiority, we might note that Caliban is described as 'freckled' and of a 'blue-ey'd' dam (I.ii.283, 269); and though editors regularly remind us that 'blue-eyed may well refer to the dark blue of the eyelid understood as a mark of pregnancy or even be an error for "blear-eyed" ', to an English audience for whom blue eyes were not at all unusual the term must inevitably have been heard, if not necessarily intended, conventionally, as an indication of the colour of the iris. Caliban is not, therefore, easily imagined either as an indigenous American or African slave. Indeed, as long ago as 1927, E. E. Stoll would emphatically deny that the play had any relation to the new world at all. 'There is not a word in *The Tempest*', he writes, 'about America or Virginia, colonies or colonising, Indians or tomahawks, maize, mocking-birds, or tobacco. Nothing but the Bermudas, once barely mentioned as faraway places, like Tokio or Mandalay.'[13] And more recently Geoffrey Bullough stated bluntly: '*The Tempest* is not a play about colonisation.'[14]

Stoll and Bullough are, of course, too absolute, but if the play has a relation to the new world colonial activity it is not writ deep into its texture; the relation is allusive and elusive, existing primarily in the negations, like Ariel's or Trinculo's, that deny that the experience on the island is the experience of the Americas. The negations, of course, make the new world present, in a sense, but we may wonder why, if colonialism is, as Francis Barker and Peter Hulme put it, 'the articulatory principle of the play', the principle is almost completely effaced and when present is established negatively rather than by a direct engagement with the material of Virginia.[15]

Possibly this is evidence of the play's uneasy conscience about the colonial project, or possibly our hypersensitivity to it is evidence merely of our own uneasy conscience in the postcolonial world we inhabit. In any case, part of the desire to locate the play within the discourses of early colonialism, to return the play to a historical moment, is evidence of the degree to which the imagination of the past now enthralls us as once we were enthralled by the imagination of the future, and seems worthily motivated by the felt need to rescue the play from the banality of the moral claims made for it in the name of its putative timelessness and transcendence. Yet one might ask about the specific historicising gesture: why this moment, why these discourses that are arguably no less eccentric in the play than they were in the culture of Jacobean England? Certainly, it is possible to suggest other and more obvious contexts, and then perhaps to wonder about why they do not appear to us the play's 'articulatory principle', if only to suggest that the Americanisation of *The Tempest* may be itself an act of cultural imperialism.

The play is much more obviously a play about European dynastic concerns than European colonial activities, but this has largely slipped from view – or at least from critical comment. The Italian courtiers have no interest in colonising the island on which they find themselves, no desire to 'plant a nation / Where none before had stood', as Rich's *News From Virginia* (1610, sig. B2ʳ) defines the goals of the first English settlers. The Italians' journey was not to explore or settle a new world but was intended as a return home, a return from a royal wedding of Alonso's daughter Claribel to the King of Tunis. And only Trinculo and Stephano worry about sovereignty on the island: 'the King and all our company else being drowned', says Stephano, 'we will inherit *here*' (II.ii.173); Antonio and Sebastian, on the contrary, think only about crowns in Europe: 'As thou got'st Milan, / I'll come by Naples' (II.i.292–3), Sebastian eagerly declares, urging Antonio to draw his sword and murder the Neapolitan king. Even Ferdinand immediately understands and articulates his situation in the explicitly dynastic terms of the world he has come from. When he hears Miranda speak, he responds with amazement: 'My language! heavens! / I am the best of them that speak this speech' (I.ii.431–2), instantly locating his sorrow in a set of political relations: 'myself am Naples, / Who with mine eyes, never since at ebb, beheld / The King my father wrack'd' (I.ii.437–9), just as he, with the same alacrity, finds political measure for his love for Miranda: 'I'll make you / The Queen of Naples' (I.ii.451–2). And Alonso at the end, hearing that Prospero has 'lost' *his* daughter, thinks of her and his own lost son as a royal couple to provide the terms of loss for the tragic cutting off of their children's too brief lives: 'O heavens, that they were living both in Naples, / The King and Queen there' (V.i.149–50).

Indeed, the critical emphasis upon the new world not only obscures the play's more prominent discourses of dynastic politics but also blinds us to disturbances in the text that should alert us to this aspect of the play's engagement with its own historical moment. When Alonso mourns the apparent death of his son, he, perhaps predictably, identifies him not by name but by his dynastic position: 'O thou mine heir / Of Naples and Milan' (II.i.113–14). No edition of the play feels the line worthy of comment, but it seemingly poses a problem. As son of the Neapolitan King, Ferdinand is obviously heir to the crown of Naples, but why is he heir of 'Milan'? Antonio has replaced Prospero as duke – and Antonio has a son who presumably would be his successor: reporting on his experience of the tempest, Ferdinand reports his dismay at seeing Antonio 'and his brave son being twain' (I.ii.441), a line that editors usually gloss by predicating some earlier and then abandoned conception of the play in which this dynastic relation would have been developed. Thus Dover Wilson writes in his note in the New Cambridge edition (now, of course, the 'old' New Cambridge) that 'he must be one of the Alonso group in an earlier version' of the play, as if a prior, and differing, version of *The Tempest* is certain to have existed. Stephen Orgel in his Oxford edition more cautiously writes that 'possibly a parallel to Ferdinand was originally contemplated by Shakespeare, and then abandoned as the drama took shape'. And Frank Kermode, in his Arden edition, somewhat despairingly concludes that 'Shakespeare began writing with a somewhat hazy understanding of the dynastic relationships he was to deal with'.

But the 'dynastic relations' are adequately, indeed tellingly, developed here. Antonio's arrangement with Naples, in which, in return, as Prospero says, for 'homage and I know not how much tribute' (I.ii.124), Alonso has conferred 'fair Milan, / With all the honours, on my brother' (I.ii.126–7), clearly reserves Milanese sovereignty for Naples, alienating Antonio's son from the succession. Indeed, when Alonso at the end begs Prospero to 'pardon' his wrongs, it is he, not Antonio, who offers: 'Thy dukedom I resign' (V.i.118), another line that has generally escaped critical comment. The romance action is to rescue Milan from vassalage to Naples and yet still allow the merging of national interests that James's fantasy of

European peace and coherence would demand. As the truth of the strange events of the play emerges fully, leading those who will to 'rejoice / Beyond a common joy' (V.i.206–7), even the utopian Gonzalo recognises that the true source of wonder is the political miracle that has been performed: 'Was Milan thrust from Milan, that his issue / Should become Kings of Naples?' (V.i.205–6). It is this happy dynastic resolution that he would see set down 'With gold on lasting pillars' (V.i.208), invoking the imperial iconography of Charles V, which was soon adopted by other European monarchies.[16] Ariel's terms for the success of Prospero's tempest are thus homonymically apt; in the play's magical rewriting of history there is 'not so much perdition as an hair' (I.ii.30). Indeed the only thing that apparently is lost in the tempest is the usurper Antonio's disinherited son, the one 'hair' – or heir – that can be cut from the restorative action of the play.

Certainly, for the audience of *The Tempest* at Court in 1613, when the play was performed as one of fourteen plays selected for the festivities leading up to the marriage of the King's daughter, Elizabeth, to Frederick, the Elector Palatine (this was, it should be noted, the second recorded performance of the play, the first on Hallowmas night of 1611 at Whitehall before 'ye kinges Maiestie'[17]), the play's events were more likely to resonate with political issues in Europe rather than in the Americas. Alonso's sadness at having apparently lost his son and married his daughter to a foreign prince might well have seemed a virtual mirror of the situation of their King, whose son, Henry, had died the previous year, and who now was marrying his daughter, Elizabeth, to a foreign prince (and who would, exactly as Alonso feared for himself, never see his daughter again).

The marriage of the Princess Elizabeth was, like all royal weddings, politics by other means, designed primarily to serve the political interests of the nation or at least its king, rather than the emotional needs of the marrying couple. The match had long been rumoured, and negotiations for it had begun as early as 1608, though there were always other prominent candidates for Elizabeth's hand, most notably the Prince of Piedmont, heir of the Duke of Savoy, and the recently widowed King of Spain, Philip III. A contemporary discussion of 'suitable alliances' for Elizabeth interestingly comments: 'the Prince of Piedmont an unequal match for the Princess, unless the King of Spain will give him the Duchy of Milan on his marriage, which is not likely, as that King is said to want her for himself. She could not marry him without changing her religion, and such a marriage would be dangerous to the two that are between her and the Crown. A match with Sweden or the Prince Palatine suggested for her ...' (Calendar of State Papers and Documents [*CSPD*] 1611–18, p. 97).

It was the match with the Prince Palatine to which James finally agreed. In many ways the 'most suitable' (*CSPD*, 1611–18, p. 97), the choice, of course, was designed not least to satisfy the interests of the Protestant nation and more immediately to tie James to the Union of Protestant Princes in the struggle against the Austrian Habsburgs and the states of the Catholic League. Though James's original hope had been to avoid sectarian alliance – or rather, while Henry lived, to pair sectarian alliances – Henry to the Spanish Infanta; Elizabeth to the Palatine prince – in order to play his planned role as mediator of Europe's religious conflicts, with Henry's death in 1612, that particular balancing act was impossible. While the Treaty of Antwerp in 1609, reconciling Spain to the United Provinces, seemed initially to promise peace in Europe, within a few weeks a dispute over succession in the Rhine principality of Cleves–Jülich divided the Protestant and Catholic States and again pushed Europe toward full-scale religious war, 'a generall altercacion in Christendome', as Salisbury feared.[18] James had little choice then but to side with the Protestant princes – and, indeed, the marriage of Elizabeth to the Palatine Prince was finally agreed to as a result of the negotiations with the Evangelical Union for English support in their struggle against the Catholic League.[19]

England seemed now fully committed to the international Protestant cause. Dudley Carleton reported that 'all well-affected people take great pleasure and contentment in this Match, as being a firm foundation and stablishing of religion ... and the Roman Catholics malign it as much, as being the ruin of their hopes'.[20] Though, in fact, as James's almost immediate search for a Spanish match for Prince Charles reveals, the King never abandoned his fantasy of being Rex Pacificus, to play the role of mediator between the rival religious blocs to secure a lasting peace. His willingness to side with the Evangelical Union was motivated less by his commitment to international Protestantism than by the desire to counterbalance the destabilising aggressions of the Habsburg monarchy.

This all may seem to be taking us far from the island world of *The Tempest*, even farther than the new world narratives claimed as the play's source; but it may well bring us closer to the historical centre of the play – and possibly to the heart of the interpretive problem it poses – than, do the tracts of the Virginia Company. While southern Europe, including the Kingdom of Naples and the Dukedom of Milan, was largely at peace under the administration of the Spanish monarchy, the Holy Roman Empire was marked by a crisis of authority. In 1606, the Habsburg archdukes stripped administrative control from the Emperor, Rudolf II, conferring it upon his brother Matthias. In 1608, Rudolf was forced to surrender to his brother the crowns of Austria, Hungary, and Moravia, keeping only the imperial crown and the crown of Bohemia. In April 1611, Rudolf was deposed from the throne of Bohemia as his brother was proclaimed Emperor.[21]

Rudolf turned to the Evangelical Union for support, and to James. Envoys were sent to England from the Diet of Protestant Princes in November asking James to back the reinstatement of the deposed Habsburg and to agree to the marriage of Elizabeth with the Elector Palatine to secure his commitment. While James's respect for the authority of princes could perhaps alone be reasonably expected to produce support for the reinstatement – and James had dedicated his own 1609 *Apology for the Oath of Allegiance* to 'the Most Sacred and invincible Prince, Rudolf the II' – the English King certainly knew that the Emperor had brought about his own troubles by being irascible, indecisive, and increasingly unavailable. As early as 1591, Sir Henry Wotton had observed that Rudolf seems 'now rather to bear the title of Emperor for fashion sake, than authority to command by virtue of it'.[22] Gradually the Emperor withdrew from the affairs of state, shutting himself up in his palace, dedicating himself to scientific and occult study. Indeed, in 1606 the archdukes justified the reassignment of authority to Matthias by commenting that '[h]is majesty is interested only in wizards, alkymists, Kabbalists, and the like, sparing no expense to find all kinds of treasure, learn secrets, and use scandalous ways of harming his enemies' and noted his 'whole library of magic books'.[23] The responsibilities of government of little interest and increasingly beyond his control, Rudolf took refuge in his books behind the walls of his palace, uncannily like another ruler 'transported / And rapt in secret studies' (I.ii.76–7) who would be deposed by his brother for 'neglecting worldly ends' (I.ii.89).

Part two of John Barclay's popular *roman à clef, Euphormionis Lusinini Satyricon*, published in Paris in 1609 (but circulating widely in England, so much so that it is named as what any 'Young

Gentleman of the Universitie' would be reading in the character in John Earle's *MicroCosmographie*), has a readily identifiable portrait of Rudolf in the Theban ruler Aquilius who 'abandons all thoughts of public matters, foreign and domestic' (sig. K2^r; translation mine) for 'voluntary solitude' (sig. 12^r) in his 'beloved laboratory' (sig. K5^r) where he 'searches into nature's secret places' (sig. K2^r). Similarly, Jonson's *Alchemist*, performed in 1610, reveals the English knowledge of Rudolf's habits in its reference to the alchemist and medium Edward Kelly, who, along with John Dee, was, like Jonson's 'divine instructor' Subtle, 'courted' by 'the Emp'ror' (IV.i.90–2) in Prague with the extraordinary commitment to alchemy and magic.

Though Rudolf's interests and political fate would inevitably have been known to many, I certainly am not claiming that Rudolf II is the sole inspiration for Shakespeare's Duke.[24] Here I am primarily concerned with showing the relevance of an available and unquestionably urgent European courtly context for the concerns of the play, and one that accounts for more of its textual density than the colonial theme that has come to dominate our readings. This is perhaps merely the move of the old historicism, eurocentric and courtly; though James, of course, would never have approved of either Rudolf's or Prospero's interest in magic or neglect of the concerns of state. Though George Marcelline hailed James as 'The king of wonders, or the wonder of Kings' (1610, sig. H3^v), what 'wonders' James achieved and his own appeal as an object of admiration were far more predictably worldly than the arcane interests and attractions of Rudolf's court in Prague or, more modestly, in Prospero's island cell.

In his *Daemonologie*, James explicitly condemns 'diuerse Christian Princes' who allow magicians to live in their realms, and 'euen some-times delight to see them prooue some of their practicques'; these princes, he says 'sinne heavilie against their office in that poynt'.[25] And in *Basilikon Doron* he instructs his son that 'it is necessarie yee delight in reading and seeking the knowledge of all lawful things, but with these two restrictions. First, that yee choose idle houres for it, not interfering therewith the discharge of your office: and next, that yee studie not for knowledge nakedly, but that your principall ende be, to make you able thereby to vse your office.'[26] The renunciation of magic to return to the responsibilities of rule allows Prospero to redeem Rudolf's kingship – or rather allows him to escape the damning parallel with Rudolf and achieve a saving one with James himself. Prospero drowns his magic book, not, of course, the only reading matter with which Gonzalo had provided him, and returns to the teachings of the *speculum principiis*, like James's own *Basilikon Doron*, which always knows the priority of the arts of rule over the rules of magical art.

All interpretation is in a sense allegorical, offering a meaning other than the literal. But I am not suggesting here that we should substitute another allegory, not the biographical one of Prospero as Shakespeare, or the humanistic one of his magic as art, or in its recent, suspicious form as colonial domination, in order to see Prospero now as the Holy Roman Emperor; though certainly I am arguing that the world of European politics has receded too far from our view. In *The Winter's Tale*, Shakespeare, in following Greene's *Pandosto*, may well have mistakenly given Bohemia a seacoast, but the complex politics of Bohemia and the other Habsburg states were arguably more deeply connected to the hopes and anxieties of the Jacobean court than were the struggling settlements in the new world.

This shift in focus from the new world to the old is not to evade or erase the history of colonialism as it has left its traces in the play but to individualise and clarify that history – perhaps indeed to motivate it. The colonial activity of seventeenth-century Europe must itself be understood in relation to the politics of the great European powers, to recognise at once England's deep involvements in Europe (a historical dimension that has worryingly dropped out of our recent attentions to the politics of early modern England) and the differing forms of colonial activity produced by its differing impulses and circumstances in England, Spain, and the Netherlands. If our attention to early modern colonialism is to be more than reflexive it must see its practices for what they were, as various and admittedly overdetermined activities within the conflicts of seventeenth-century European absolutism rather than as examples of a unified and transhistorical imperial desire and administration.[27]

Certainly, European expansionism is evident in the play, but more, it must be insisted, in the marriage of Claribel to the King of Tunis or Alonso's support of Antonio in exchange for Milan's vassalage than in Prospero's domination of the island. Or rather, the old world examples reveal the old technologies of expansion; the action on the island is symbolic of the new. And the two were always understood to support one another. Even as Europe looked west, it was mainly as it sought to thrive at home. Thinking about the incredible riches available in the new world, Hakluyt, that quin-tessential voice of English imperialism, observes enthusiastically (and in terms that uncannily explain something of the geopolitics of *The Tempest*): 'with this great treasure, did not the emperor Charles get from the French king the kingdom of Naples, the dukedom of Milan, and all other his dominions in Italy, Lombardy, Piedmont, and Savoy.'[28]

But though I would say (and have said) that the play clearly engages the social and political concerns of seventeenth-century Europe, concerns that the insistent focus on the new world in recent criticism has largely obscured, I am not now claiming that European court politics must replace new world colonialism as the 'dominant discursive con-text' that reveals the meaning of *The Tempest*. Indeed, I am as much interested in the process by which a historical reading of a text is generated and grounded as I am in any particular reading, especially given the familiar charge of the arbitrariness of New Historicism's strategies of contextualisation (in its most expansive form, evident in Dominick LaCapra's laundry-list of disparaging epithets: 'facile associationism, juxtapo-sition or pastiche ... weak montage, or, if you prefer, cut-and-paste bricolage'[29]).

Facile or not, New Historicism has often brilliantly connected ap-parently disparate cultural moments and practices to reveal their common participation in a cultural system. In part, this has worked to erase the familiar opposition of text and context. Where the context once served as the flat backdrop against which the text's verbal display showed brilliantly in all of its artistic and intellectual complexity, now context and text are not so easily distinguished. Literary texts are no longer understood as repositories of meaning, but are seen as places where meanings are being made – places no more necessarily efficacious or valuable in this construction of social meaning than any other discursive form. It is this refusal to privilege automatically the literary over other discursive activities that has produced much of the hostility to New Historicism (and other poststructural critical modes). The literary text, however, is seen to be imbricated with a range of material and symbolic prac-tices that make its distinction, in both senses of the word, from what formerly was understood as its context no longer sustainable.

The notion of context has thus been usefully problematised, understood now not as the static ground external to the text and reflected by it, but as the set of discourses that the literary text in-

tersects and is intersected by. Texts and contexts are thus related
dynamically rather than hierarchically: the text inevitably serves as
a context for other texts, while the context is itself revealed as a
text demanding interpretation before it yields its meanings. Many
critics have therefore grown uncomfortable with the very term
'context', fearing that its use reinstates the autonomy and presump-
tive value of the literary text that has been pointedly called into
question.

Yet clearly the notion of context cannot be dispensed with.
Indeed, once the meaning of the literary work is no longer sought in
its aesthetic autonomy and formal perfection, all that is left is
context. The text as it is both written and read is necessarily
context-rich and context-dependent, and this is the source of its
meaning. The written text takes meaning from the discourses that
circulate through it; the text as read becomes meaningful through
the contexts that structure the reader's engagement. That is, the text
'means' only through the processes by which its particularities are
seen to exist in relation to something outside it. Meaning may be of
'different kinds', as Richard Palmer recognises, 'but it is always a
kind of cohesion, relationship, or binding force; it is always in a
context'.[30]

But if meaning is necessarily context-bound, the number of meaningful contexts is apparently boundless.[31] By definition they can be
neither singular nor inevitable. Certainly the frames in which one
chooses to see a text, the horizons of interpretation, to use
Gadamer's term, through which an interpreter engages it,[32] logically
are virtually infinite (a single point can be intersected by an infinite
number of lines), and they are valuable as they – and only as they –
serve the interests and needs of the interpreter.

Once this is granted, however, it must be worth asking more
about the contexts that appear to us to be relevant. *The Tempest*
can profitably be viewed in relation to various historical and non-
historical (e.g., ethical, psychological, theological, even, may I say
it, aesthetic) contexts, and no one is inevitable and determining. If,
however, one's interpretive desire is to reinsert the play into its own
historical moment, into the space of its own diegetic setting as well
as the performative space of its own earliest productions (and this is
a thoroughly reasonable and productive desire, though hardly the
only useful interpretive desire we might have), it seems to me that
we should look more closely at the old world than the new, at the
wedding of Elizabeth and Frederick rather than of Pocahontas and

John Rolfe, at James's own writings rather than the writings from Jamestown. This seems to me so both because old world history marks the play (context as discourse) more insistently than does the history of the new world that has dominated recent criticism – a history which, in fact, the play conspicuously avoids – and because the European history allows a reader to make sense of more in the text (context as frame) that would otherwise seem arbitrary or inexplicable. If, however, one's interpretive desire is to locate the play in *our* historical moment – also a reasonable and productive desire – then the colonial reading has more purchase; plays absorb history as much as they are marked by it at their inception.[33]

In either case, the critical attention to the new world is not, of course, merely wilful; the play does find its source in the narrative accounts of a shipwreck of would-be colonists bound for Jamestown. But Shakespeare's relocation of the narrative from the new world to the old is not the unconscious displacement of this imperial theme as much as it is its deliberate erasure. In *The Tempest*, Shakespeare actively chooses *not* to tell the new world story that was before him. And if a later history has insisted that we restore the tale of colonial adventurism to the play, it is at least as much because we know we can use Shakespeare's cultural authority to claim a hearing for our political interests as because Shakespeare's political interests demand it from us. Certainly, such readings tell us something important, but arguably more about our world than about Shakespeare's. But if the shift in focus from Bermuda to Bohemia, from Harriot to Habsburg, removes the play from the colonial encounter of Europe with the Americas, it is not to evade or dull its political edges. Indeed, arguably it is to sharpen them, but it is to find them less in the conquest of the new world than in the killing religious conflicts and territorial ambitions of the old, where tragically they can still be found.[34]

The Tempest effectively stages and manages these anxieties about European politics and England's role within them, harmonising and securing absolutist desire through the marriage of Miranda and Ferdinand. The play drives purposefully to fulfil Gonzalo's prayer: 'look down, you gods, / And on this couple drop a blessed crown' (V.i.201–2). But this utopian solution to the problem of political conflict – a solution that by temperament, ideology, and financial limitation appealed to James and led him to conduct his foreign policy through marriage negotiation – is vulnerable, if only to irony. If the crown is 'blessed', we should remember that the impending marriage will accomplish precisely what the 'inveterate' (I.ii.122) hatred of Alonso for Prospero attempted: the dissolution of Milanese sovereignty into Neapolitan dynastic rule. However, in the reparative fantasy of the *The Tempest*, nothing – nothing, that is, except the brave son of Antonio, who has no place in its ambitious political relations – is finally lost.

From David Scott Kastan, *Shakespeare After Theory* (London, 1999), pp. 183–97.

NOTES

[David Scott Kastan's is, to date, the most cogent critical voice to contest the virtual monopoly which colonial readings have exercised over recent criticism of *The Tempest*, by arguing for the need to restore the play to its European political milieu (see 'Further Reading', Skura [1989], Wilson [1997], Brotton [1999]). In his view, the presumption that colonial activities in the Americas constitute the play's 'dominant discursive con-text' is more indicative of the concerns of 'our anxious postcolonial moment' than those of the play itself, in which Shakespeare 'actively chooses *not* to tell the new world story that was before him'. Dramatic events in *The Tempest*, he concludes, resonate far more strongly with the dynastic concerns, religious conflicts and territorial ambitions of the old world which directly impinged on the Jacobean court in a way that 'the struggling settlements in the new world' did not. Ed.]

1. *The Comedy of Errors*, III.ii.133–5. It is worth noting that 'America', perhaps inevitably for a play written in the early 1590s, is here associated with a Spanish colonial interest rather than an English one.

2. Edmond Malone, *An account of the incidents from which the title and part of the story of Shakespeare's 'Tempest' were derived and its true date determined* (London, 1808).

3. *The Tempest*, ed. Morton Luce (London, 1901), pp. xii, xlii.

4. John Gillies, *Shakespeare and the Geography of Difference* (Cambridge, 1994), p. 149. On Shakespeare's relations with the Virginia Company, see Charles Mills Gayley, *Shakespeare and the Founders of Liberty in America* (New York, 1917).

5. The phrase, now a staple of *Tempest* criticism, derives from Antonio de Nebrija's justification to Queen Isabella for his Spanish grammar: 'language is the perfect instrument of empire' (quoted from Louis Hanke, *Aristotle and the American Indians* [Bloomington, IN, 1959], p. 8). Nebrija (or, more properly, Lebrija) was, however, a bit less

explicit about the instrumental relation of language and empire; 'siempre la lengua fue compañera del imperio' (sig. a2ʳ) is what he wrote in his *Grammatica Castellana* (1492). For the play's 'implication' in the English colonial project, see, for example, Paul Brown, ' "This thing of darkness I acknowledge mine": *The Tempest* and the Discourse of Colonialism', in *Political Shakespeare: New Essays in Cultural Materialism*, ed. Jonathan Dollimore and Alan Sinfield (Ithaca, NY, 1985), esp. pp. 56 and 64.

6. Geoffrey Bullough, *Narrative and Dramatic Sources of Shakespeare* (London, 1975), vol. 8, p. 245.

7. *Coleridge on Shakespeare: The Text of the Lectures of 1811–1812*, ed. R. A. Foakes (Charlottesville, VA, 1971), p. 106.

8. Stephen Greenblatt, *Shakespearean Negotiations: The Circulation of Social Energy in Renaissance England* (Berkeley and Los Angeles, 1988), p. 156; and Peter Hulme, 'Hurricanes in the Caribbees: The Constitution of the Discourse of English Colonialism', in *1642: Literature and Power in the Seventeenth Century*, ed. Francis Barker et al. (Colchester, 1981), p. 74.

9. Ralph Berry, *On Directing Shakespeare: Interviews with Contemporary Directors* (London, 1977), p. 34.

10. Leslie A. Fiedler, *The Stranger in Shakespeare* (New York, 1972), p. 238.

11. Epistle Dedicatory to *The Second Volume of Chronicles* in *The First and Second Volumes of Chronicles*, ed. Raphael Holinshed et al. (London, 1586), sig. A3ᵛ.

12. Francis Barker and Peter Hulme, ' "Nymphs and reapers heavily vanish": The Discursive Con-texts of *The Tempest*', in *Alternative Shakespeares*, ed. John Drakakis (London, 1985), p. 198. Richard Halpern similarly says that 'colonialism has established itself as a dominant, if not the dominant code for interpreting *The Tempest*', in his ' "The Picture of Nobody": White Cannibalism in *The Tempest*', in *The Production of English Renaissance Culture*, ed. David Lee Miller, Sharon O'Dair, and Harold Weber (Ithaca, NY, 1994), p. 265.

13. E. E. Stoll, 'Certain Fallacies and Irrelevancies in the Literary Scholarship of the Day', *Studies in Philology*, 24 (1927), 484.

14. Bullough, *Narrative and Dramatic Sources of Shakespeare*, vol. 8, p. 241.

15. Barker and Hulme, 'Nymphs', p. 204. Greenblatt, while basing his account of *The Tempest* upon its relation to the Virginia Company narratives, does see the play's 'swerve away from these materials', though he sees this swerve as evidence 'of the process by which the Bermuda material is made negotiable'; that is, even as the play trans-

forms the source material, for Greenblatt, it remains centrally grounded in the new world and 'colonial discourse' (*Shakespearean Negotiations*, pp. 154–5).

16. Dennis Kay identifies the allusion here to the pillars of Hercules, adopted as an imperial emblem first by Charles V and then by other European rulers, including Elizabeth. See his 'Gonzalo's "Lasting Pillars". *The Tempest*, V.i.208', *Shakespeare Quarterly*, 35 (1984), 322–4.

17. See E. K. Chambers, *William Shakespeare: A Study of Facts and Problems* (Oxford, 1930), vol. 2, p. 342.

18. *Parliamentary Debates in 1610*, ed. S. R. Gardiner (London, 1861), p. 53.

19. See Roger Lockyer, *The Early Stuarts: A Political History of England* (London and New York 1989), esp. p. 15. It is perhaps of interest here that Pembroke and Southampton, to both of whom Shakespeare had connections, were proponents of an aggressive pro-Protestant foreign policy. See Thomas Cogswell, *The Blessed Revolution: English Politics and the Coming of War, 1621–1624* (Cambridge, 1989), esp. pp. 12–50.

20. John Nichols, *Progresses of King James the First* (1828; rpt. New York: AMS Press, n.d.), vol. 2, pp. 601–2.

21. Henry Wotton wrote in May 1611 of how Rudolf was forced 'to make Matthias King of the Romans'. Commenting on the treatment of Rudolf by the supporters of Matthias, Wotton notes, 'having first spoiled him of obedience and reverence, next of his estates and titles, they have now reduced him to so low a case, that he is no longer patron of his voice'. See *Life and Letters of Sir Henry Wotton*, ed. Logan Pearsall Smith (Oxford, 1907), vol. 1, p. 507.

22. *Life and Letters of Sir Henry Wotton*, vol. 1, p. 268.

23. Quoted in R. J. W. Evans, *Rudolph II and his World* (Oxford, 1973), p. 196. See also Hugh Trevor-Roper, *Princes and Artists: Patronage and Ideology at Four Habsburg Courts 1517–1633* (London, 1976), esp. pp. 122–3.

24. Michael Srigley's *Images of Regeneration: A Study of Shakespeare's 'The Tempest' and its Cultural Background* (Uppsala, 1985) does make an argument for such topical allegory, though, of course, we should remember that as early as *Love's Labor's Lost* Shakespeare had begun thinking about rulers who preferred the study to the affairs of state.

25. *Daemonologie (1597) and News From Scotland*, ed. G.B. Harrison (London, 1924), pp. 24–5.

26. *The Political Works of James I*, ed. Charles Howard McIlwain (Cambridge, MA, 1918), p. 38.

27. Even Marc Ferro's ambitious synthesis, *Colonization: A Global History* (London and New York, 1997), admits that 'it is true that one colonisation was different from another' (p. viii).

28. *The Original Writings and Correspondence of the Two Richard Hakluyts*, ed. Eva G. R. Taylor (London, 1935), p. 243. See Jeffrey Knapp's fine *An Empire Nowhere: England, America, and Literature from 'Utopia' to the 'The Tempest'* (Berkeley, CA, 1992), esp. pp. 231–4.

29. Dominick LaCapra, *Soundings in Critical Theory* (Ithaca, NY, 1989), p. 193.

30. Richard E. Palmer, *Hermeneutics* (Evanston, IL, 1969), p. 120.

31. The terms here are familiar. Jonathan Culler writes, 'meaning is context-bound, but context is boundless' in his *On Deconstruction: Theory and Criticism after Structuralism* (Ithaca, NY, 1982), p. 123. But, for example, Susan Horton invokes the same wordplay ('although meaning itself may be "context bound" … context itself is boundless') in her *Interpreting Interpreting: Interpreting Dickens's 'Dombey'* (Baltimore, MD, 1979), p. x.

32. Hans-Georg Gadamer, *Truth and Method*, trans. Garrett Barden and John Cumming (London, 1975), p. 269.

33. It is in the work of George Lamming, Roberto Fernández Retamar, Aimé Césaire, and others writing from within the anticolonial struggles of the mid-twentieth century that *The Tempest* suffers its sea-change and becomes the paradigmatic drama of colonialism.

34. Howard Felperin has recently argued similarly that 'the colonialism of the New World' has been overemphasised. Its traces in the play, he argues, have been 'overread', mistaking 'the part for the whole'. Felperin, however, wants finally to see the 'whole' not as a larger historical picture but 'as a projection of nothing less than a historical totality' itself, or, as he says, 'a vision of history as a cycle of repetition'. This, however, seems to me to return the play to the very idealism that historical criticism has tried to counter. See his 'Political Criticism at the Crossroads: The Utopian Historicism of *The Tempest*', in *The Tempest*, ed. Nigel Wood (Buckingham and Philadelphia, 1995), esp. pp. 47–55. For a different relocation of *The Tempest* in relation to new world colonial activity, see Meredith Anne Skura's 'Discourse and the Individual: The Case of Colonialism in *The Tempest*', *Shakespeare Quarterly*, 40 (1989), 42–69 and reprinted in *Critical Essays on Shakespeare's 'The Tempest'*, ed. Alden and Virginia Vaughan (New York, 1998).

Further Reading

The books and articles listed below represent a highly selective sample of the voluminous criticism published on the 'romances', especially *The Tempest*, since 1980. Owing to the pressures on space, no mention is made here of works already cited in my introduction, and readers are advised to consult the endnotes to the introduction for further bibliographical references. In terms of critical practice, the majority of items listed draw upon one or more of the various strains of poststructuralist theory (feminism, pyschoanalysis, new historicism, cultural materialism, etc.) that have helped determine the direction of literary studies over this period. However, I have also chosen to include several pieces exemplifying more traditional approaches (marked by an asterisk) where they have made a significant contribution to the critical debate regarding the 'romances'. Two recent collections of essays provide an excellent introduction to the issues and concerns currently shaping that debate: Kiernan Ryan (ed.), *Shakespeare: The Last Plays* (London and New York: Longman, 1999), and Jennifer Richards and James Knowles (eds), *Shakespeare's Late Plays: New Readings* (Edinburgh: Edinburgh University Press, 1999).

GENERAL STUDIES

Catherine Belsey, *Shakespeare and the Loss of Eden: The Construction of Family Values in Early Modern Culture* (Basingstoke: Macmillan — now Palgrave Macmillan, 1999) – includes chapters on *Cymbeline* and The *Winter's Tale*.

John D. Cox, 'Ruling Taste and the Late Plays', in *Shakespeare and the Dramaturgy of Power* (New York: Princeton University Press, 1989), pp. 194–65.

Lawrence Danson, 'The Catastrophe is a Nuptial: The Space of Masculine Desire in *Othello*, *Cymbeline* and *The Winter's Tale*', *Shakespeare Survey*, 46 (1994), 69–79.

Charles Frey, '"O sacred, shadowy, cold, and constant queen": Shakespeare's Imperiled and Chastening Daughters of Romance', in Carolyn Ruth Swift Lenz et al. (eds), *The Woman's Part: Feminist Criticism of Shakespeare* (Urbana and Chicago: University of Illinois Press, 1980), pp. 295–313.

Helen Hackett, '"Gracious be the Issue": Maternity and Narrative in Shakespeare's Late Plays', in Richards and Knowles (eds), *Shakespeare's Late Plays*, pp. 25–39.

Maurice Hunt, '"Stir" and Work in Shakespeare's Last Plays', *Studies in English Literature*, 21 (1982), 285–304.

Maurice Hunt, *Shakespeare's Romance of the Word* (Lewisburg: Bucknell University Press, 1990).

Marianne Novy, 'Transformed Images of Manhood in the Romances', in *Love's Argument: Gender Relations in Shakespeare* (Chapel Hill and London: University of N. Carolina Press, 1984), pp. 164–87.

Kay Stockholder, *Dream Works: Lovers and Families in Shakespeare's Plays* (Toronto: University of Toronto Press, 1987) -- includes chapters on all four 'romances'.

Roger Warren, *Staging Shakespeare's Late Plays* (Oxford: Clarendon Press, 1990).*

Richard Wilson, 'Observations on English bodies: licensing maternity in Shakespeare's late plays', in *Will Power: Essays on Shakespearean Authority* (Hemel Hempstead: Harvester Wheatsheaf, 1993), pp. 158–83.

PERICLES

Stephen Dickey, 'Language and Role in *Pericles*', *English Literary Renaissance*, 16 (1986), 550–66.*

Lorraine Helms, 'The Saint in the Brothel – Or, Eloquence Rewarded', *Shakespeare Quarterly*, 41 (1990), 319–32.

Richard Hillman, 'Shakespeare's Gower and Gower's Shakespeare: The Larger Debt of *Pericles*', *Shakespeare Quarterly*, 36 (1985), 427–37.*

Constance Jordan, '"Eating the Mother": Property and Propriety in *Pericles*', in David Quint et al. (eds), *Creative Imitation: New Essays on Renaissance Literature in Honor of Thomas M. Greene* (Binghamton, NY: Medieval and Renaissance Texts and Studies, 1992), pp. 331–53.

Stuart Kurland, '"The care ... of subjects' good": *Pericles*, James I, and the Neglect of Government', *Comparative Drama*, 30 (1996), 220–44.

Anthony J. Lewis, '"I Feed on Mother's Flesh": Incest and Eating in *Pericles*', *Essays in Literature*, 15: 2 (1988), 147–63.

Steven Mullaney, '"All That Monarchs Do": The Obscured Stages of Authority in *Pericles*', in *The Place of the Stage: License, Play, and Power in Renaissance England* (Chicago and London: Chicago University Press, 1988), pp. 135–51.

Claire Preston, 'The Emblematic Structure of *Pericles*', *Word and Image*, 8:1 (1992), 21–38.*

CYMBELINE

David Bergeron, '*Cymbeline*: Shakespeare's Last Roman Play', *Shakespeare Quarterly*, 31 (1980), 31–41.

Ronald J. Boling, 'Anglo-Welsh Relations in *Cymbeline*', *Shakespeare Quarterly*, 51 (2000), 33–66.

John E. Curran, Jr, 'Royalty Unlearned, Honor Untaught: British Savages and Historiographical Change in *Cymbeline*', *Comparative Drama*, 31 (1997), 277–303.

Coppélia Kahn, 'Postscript: *Cymbeline*: Paying Tribute to Rome', in *Roman Shakespeare: Warriors, Wounds, and Women* (New York and London: Routledge, 1997), pp. 160–70.

Willy Maley, '"Postcolonial Shakespeare: British Identity Formation and *Cymbeline*', in Richards and Knowles (eds), *Shakespeare's Late Plays*, pp. 145–57.

Robert S. Miola, '*Cymbeline*: Shakespeare's Valediction to Rome', in Annabel Patterson (ed.), *Roman Images: Selected Papers from the English Institute, 1982* (Baltimore: Johns Hopkins University Press, 1984), pp. 51–62.*

Patricia Parker, 'Romance and Empire: Anachronistic Cymbeline', in George M. Logan and Gordon Teskey (eds), *Unfolded Tales: Essays on Renaissance Romance* (Ithaca and London: Cornell University Press, 1989), pp. 189–207.

Murray M. Schwartz, 'Between Fantasy and Imagination: A Psychological Exploration of *Cymbeline*', in F. C. Crews (ed.), *Psychoanalysis and Literary Process* (Cambridge, MA: Winthrop, 1970), pp. 219–83.

Erica Sheen, '"The Agent for his Master": Political Service and Professional Liberty in *Cymbeline*', in Gordon McMullan and Jonathan Hope (eds), *The Politics of Tragicomedy: Shakespeare and After* (London and New York: Routledge, 1992), pp. 55–76.

Meredith Skura, 'Interpreting Posthumus' Dream from Above and Below: Families, Psychoanalysts and Literary Critics', in Murray Schwartz and Coppélia Kahn (eds), *Representing Shakespeare: New Psychoanalytic Essays* (Baltimore: Johns Hopkins University Press, 1980), pp. 203–16.

THE WINTER'S TALE

Leonard Barkan, '"Living Sculptures": Ovid, Michelangelo and *The Winter's Tale*', *English Literary History*, 48 (1981), 639–67.*

Michael D. Bristol, '*In Search of the Bear: Spatiotemporal Form and the Heterogeneity of Economies in* The Winter's Tale', *Shakespeare Quarterly, 42 (1991)*, 145–67.

Stanley Cavell, 'Recounting Gains, Showing Losses: Reading *The Winter's Tale*', in *Disowning Knowledge in Six Plays of Shakespeare* (Cambridge: Cambridge University Press, 1987), pp. 193–222.

Lynn Enterline, '"You speak a language that I understand not": The Rhetoric of Animation in *The Winter's Tale*', *Shakespeare Quarterly*, 48 (1997), 17–44.

Peter Erickson, 'The Limitations of Reformed Masculinity in *The Winter's Tale*', in *Patriarchal Structures in Shakespeare's Drama* (Berkeley: University of California Press, 1985), pp. 148–72.

Howard Felperin, '"Tongue-tied our queen?": the deconstruction of presence in *The Winter's Tale*', in Patricia Parker and Geoffrey Hartman (eds), *Shakespeare and the Question of Theory* (New York and London: Methuen, 1985), pp. 3–18.

Charles Frey, *Shakespeare's Vast Romance: A Study of 'The Winter's Tale'* (Columbia: University of Missouri Press, 1980).*

Donna B. Hamilton, '*The Winter's Tale* and the Language of Union, 1604–10', *Shakespeare Studies*, 22 (1993), 228–50.

Barbara A. Mowat, 'Rogues, Shepherds, and the Counterfeit Distressed: Texts and Infracontexts of *The Winter's Tale*, 4.3', *Shakespeare Studies*, 22 (1994), 58–76.

Stephen Orgel, 'The Poetics of Incomprehensibility', *Shakespeare Quarterly*, 42 (1991), 431–7.

B. J. Sokol, *Art and Illusion in 'The Winter's Tale'* (Manchester: Manchester University Press, 1994).*

Susan Snyder, 'Mamillius and Gender Polarization in *The Winter's Tale*', *Shakespeare Quarterly*, 50 (1999), 1–8.

THE TEMPEST

Jerry Brotton, '"This Tunis, sir, was Carthage": contesting colonialism in The Tempest', in Ania Loomba and Martin Orkin (eds), *Post-Colonial Shakespeares* (London and New York: Routledge, 1998), pp. 23–42.

Thomas Cartelli, 'Prospero in Africa: The Tempest as colonialist text and pretext', in Jean Howard and Marion O'Connor (eds), *Shakespeare Reproduced: The Text in History and Ideology* (New York and London: Methuen, 1987), pp. 99–115.

Peter Childs (ed.), *Post-colonial Theory and English Literature* (Edinburgh: Edinburgh University Press, 1999) — reprints important essays by Trevor Griffiths, Rob Nixon and Sylvia Wynter on postcolonial appropriations of the play.

Barbara Fuchs, 'Conquering Islands: Contextualising *The Tempest*', *Shakespeare Quarterly*, 48 (1997), 45–62.

Stephen Greenblatt, 'Learning to Curse: Aspects of Linguistic Colonialism in the 16th Century', in *Learning to Curse: Essays in Early Modern Culture* (New York and London: Routledge, 1990), pp.16–39.

Peter Hulme, 'Prospero and Caliban', in *Colonial Encounters: Europe and the Native Carribean, 1492–1797* (London and New York: Methuen, 1986), pp. 89–134.

Alvin Kernan: 'The King and the Poet: *The Tempest*, Whitehall, Winter 1613', in *Shakespeare, the King's Playwright: Theater in the Stuart Court 1603–1613* (New Haven and London: Yale University Press, 1995), pp. 150–69.

Lorie Jerrell Leininger, 'The Miranda Trap: Sexism and Racism in Shakespeare's *Tempest*', in Lenz et al. (eds), *The Woman's Part*, pp. 285–94.

Ania Loomba, 'Seizing the book', in *Gender, Race, Renaissance Drama* (Manchester: Manchester University Press, 1989), pp. 142–58.

Meredith Ann Skura, 'Discourse and the Individual: The Case of Colonialism in *The Tempest*', *Shakespeare Quarterly*, 40 (1989), 42–69.

Alden T. Vaughan and Virginia Mason Vaughan, *Shakespeare's Caliban: A Cultural History* (Cambridge: Cambridge University Press, 1991).*

Virginia Mason Vaughan and Alden T. Vaughan (eds), *Critical Essays on Shakespeare's 'The Tempest'* (New York: G.K. Hall, 1998) — a wide-ranging, methodologically diverse collection of recent criticism on the play.

R. S. White (ed.), *The Tempest*, New Casebook series (Basingstoke: Macmillan — now Palgrave Macmillan, 1999) — an anthology of recent theoretical readings of the play.

Deborah Willis, 'Shakespeare's *The Tempest* and the Discourse of Colonialism', *Studies in English Literature*, 29 (1989), 277–89.

Richard Wilson, 'Voyage to Tunis: New History and the Old World of *The Tempest*', *English Literary History*, 64 (1997), 333–57.

Notes on Contributors

Janet Adelman is Professor and Department Chair at the University of California, Berkeley. She is the author of *The Common Liar: An Essay on 'Antony and Cleopatra'* (Yale University Press, 1973), and *Suffocating Mothers: Fantasies of Maternal Origin in Shakespeare, 'Hamlet' to 'The Tempest'* (Routledge, 1992). She has also edited *Twentieth-Century Interpretations of 'King Lear'* (Prentice-Hall, 1978) and has published numerous articles on Shakespeare and other Renaissance writers.

James Ellison is Research Fellow at the University of Strathclyde. He has taught at the Universities of Oxford and Strathclyde and is the author of *George Sandys: Humanism, Travel, and Toleration* (forthcoming from Boydell Press), as well as a series of articles on religion and politics in Shakespeare. He is currently engaged on a book about representations of the Earl of Essex in Elizabethan drama.

Margaret Healy is a Lecturer in English at the University of Sussex. She has published a study of Shakespeare's *Richard II* (Northcote House in association with the British Council, 1998). She is also the author of *Fictions of Disease in Early Modern England: Bodies, Plagues and Politics* (Palgrave – now Palgrave Macmillan, 2001), and has published many essays on literature, art and medicine 1500–1700.

David Scott Kastan is the Old Dominion Professor in the Humanities at Columbia University. Among his many publications are *Shakespeare and the Shapes of Time* (Macmillan – now Palgrave Macmillan, 1982), *Shakespeare after Theory* (Routledge, 1999) and *Shakespeare and the Book* (Cambridge University Press, 2001). He has also co-edited (with Peter Stallybrass) *Staging the Renaissance: Reinterpretations of Elizabethan and Stuart Drama* (Routledge, 1991), and edited *A Companion to Shakespeare* (Blackwell, 1999). He is a General Editor of the Arden Shakespeare.

Jodi Mikalachki is Associate Professor of English at Wellesley College in Massachusetts. Her essays on Shakespeare, Milton, female vagrants, and Renaissance drama have appeared in such journals as *Shakespeare Quarterly* and *Renaissance Drama*, and she is the author of *The Legacy of Boadicea: Gender and Nation in Early Modern England* (Routledge,

1998). She is currently working on a study of the intersections of social, aesthetic and theological grace in Renaissance English literature.

Ruth Nevo was born in South Africa and in 1950 settled in Israel, where she taught at the Hebrew University until retirement. She has published *The Dial of Virtue* (1963), *Tragic Form in Shakespeare* (1972), *Comic Transformations in Shakespeare* (1980), *Shakespeare's Other Language* (1987), and translations of Hebrew poetry. Since retirement she has taken up an old preoccupation and has become a full-time painter. She is a member of the Israel Association of Painters and Sculptors and of the Israel Academy of Sciences and Humanities.

Constance C. Relihan is Hargis Associate Professor of English at Auburn University. She is the author of *Fashioning Authority: The Development of Elizabethan Novelistic Discourse* (Kent State University Press, 1994) and editor of *Framing Elizabethan Fictions: Contemporary Approaches to Early Modern Narrative Prose* (Kent State University Press, 1996), and has also published essays on Shakespeare, Sidney, Greene and Nashe. She is currently completing a book-length study of the role of ethnographic discourse in the construction of Elizabethan fiction and co-editing (with Goran Stanivukovic) a collection of essays on the representation of sexuality within early modern prose fiction.

Kiernan Ryan is Professor of English at Royal Holloway, University of London, and a Fellow of New Hall, University of Cambridge. He is the author of *Shakespeare* (third edition, Palgrave – now Palgrave Macmillan, 2001) and the editor of *King Lear: Contemporary Critical Essays* (Macmillan – now Palgrave Macmillan, 1993), *New Historicism and Cultural Materialism: A Reader* (Arnold, 1996), *Shakespeare: The Last Plays* (Longman, 1999), and *Shakespeare: Texts and Contexts* (Macmillan – now Palgrave Macmillan, 2000).

Jyotsna G. Singh is Associate Professor of English at Michigan State University. She is the author of *Colonial Narratives/ Cultural Dialogues: 'Discoveries' of India in the Language of Colonialism* (Routledge, 1996), co-author of *The Weyward Sisters: Shakespeare and Feminist Politics* (Blackwell, 1995), and co-editor (with Ivo Kamps) of *Travel Knowledge: European 'Discoveries' in the Early Modern Period* (Palgrave – now Palgrave Macmillan, 2000). She is currently working on a book, tentatively entitled *Locating Caliban's Island: Geographical Representations in Early Modern Literature and Culture 1533–1625*.

Index